Medieval tailor's assistant

Tailor, 1320-1330, English

He is fashionably dressed in a loose surcote with peaked sleeves and fitchets (side slits) which give access to the belt and purse beneath. His fitted cote sleeves emerge at the wrists. He wears well-fitted hose and plain shoes; a loose hood with a long point is thrown back round his shoulders. He appears to be cutting out and shaping a cote, using a large pair of shears (probably exaggerated), and appropriating a remnant at the same time.

Hours of the Blessed Virgin Mary, British Library MS Harley 6563, f. 65

The Medieval Tailor's Assistant

making common garments 1200 - 1500

SARAH THURSFIELD

RUTH BEAN
Carlton, Bedford

First published 2001 in the United Kingdom by
Ruth Bean Publishers
Victoria Farmhouse, Carlton, Bedford MK43 7LP

First published 2001 in the USA by
Costume & Fashion Press
an imprint of
Quite Specific Media Group Ltd
7373 Pyramid Place, Hollywood, CA 90046

ISBN-10: 0-903585-32-4
ISBN-13: 978-0-903585-32-3
A catalogue record for this book is available from the British Library

Design Alan Bultitude
Photo styling Caryl Mossop
Photography Mark Scudder & Les Goodey
Digital artwork Personabilia Design & Print, Higham Ferrers, Northants
Printed in Hong Kong

Cover
Modern version of the chaperon, mid 15th century
The classic chaperon, seen here in black broadcloth, is made up of three parts – the
liripipe and shoulder cape (gorget), which are sewn to a padded roll. The roll
sometimes appears quite solid and may have been felted. The chaperon is often seen
slung over the shoulder where it would stay in place with a long enough liripipe.

Contents

5

List of plates

Acknowledgements

I would like to thank the many people who have contributed to this book in different ways.

I am grateful to the late Janet Arnold, Dr Jane Bridgeman, Henry Cobb, Zillah Halls and Frances Pritchard for specialist advice, information and critical comments.

Many kind friends and customers have allowed me to test ideas and patterns, patiently acted as models, and provided stimulating discussion. They include Barbara and Len Allen, Jill Burton, Amanda Clark, Wayne and Emma Cooper, Carol Evison, Paul Harston, Jen Heard, the late Joy Hilbert, Paul Mason, Carrie-May Mealor, Matthew Nettle, Lindy Pickard, Elizabeth Reed, Penny and Kevin Roberts, Dave Rushworth, Matthew Sutton, Elaine Tasker, and Andrea Wright. I am indebted to them all; also to the Shropshire County Library who obtained help and information from far and wide; to my sister Ruth Gilbert (Beth the weaver), a ready source of advice; and to Mark Scudder and Les Goodey for their fine photographic work.

Without the unfailing support of my husband Nick, or his patient help together with my son Sam on the computer, this project could not have been launched. Without the experience and major contribution of Ruth and Nigel Bean, who brought it to its final form, it would not have been realized.

Photograph credits

Bibliothèque nationale de France, Paris, *Pl 11*; Bibliothèque Royale Albert 1er, Bruxelles, *Pls 9, 15*; Bodleian Library, University of Oxford, *cover* (USA edition); the British Library, London, frontispiece, *Pls 5, 17, 18*; Stedlijke Musea, Brugge, *Pl 16*; Cambridge University Library, Photography Department, *cover* (UK edition), *Pls 1-4, 6-8, 10, 12-14, 19*.

Introduction

During the years I have been making historical garments I have been especially drawn to the dress of the later middle ages. We can see in the contemporary images of dress, now our main source of information, the features which give the period such appeal – bright colours, flowing fabrics, the contrasting styles of simple working dress and the elaborate, sumptuous clothes of the nobility. But the images tell us little about how the clothes were made: evidence is limited compared with later periods, from which more garments and documents have been preserved.

So the challenge for the dressmaker today is how to recreate the 'look' of the period. I have tried to achieve this firstly by using visual sources like effigies and brasses, wall hangings, paintings, and illuminated manuscripts as models. Then, by applying experience of traditional sewing techniques and modern tailoring – and of course much experiment – I have prepared working patterns for a range of garments. I have aimed to achieve the look and fit of the time, in a way that is practicable for the modern sewer. As for the method, it is my own interpretation of the evidence I have seen. Others may interpret their sources differently, and further research may in time increase our limited knowledge. But many people have asked me for patterns and I believe this practical guide to the cut and construction of common garments will fill a need and perhaps stimulate enquiry.

The book is intended for anyone wishing to reproduce historical dress, for re-enactment, displays, drama or personal use. It is assumed that the reader has a basic knowledge of dressmaking. The instructions throughout aim at the high standard of hand finishing appropriate for 'living history', but the reader may equally use modern techniques. The garments are presented, with brief notes on their historical background, in three main layers: underwear, main garments, and outer garments, for men, women and children. Head-wear and accessories are covered separately. Examples of the basic forms are included for each garment, and most are followed by their later or more elaborate styles. Initial guidance is given in *How to use the book*, and detailed instructions on techniques, planning and materials are provided and referred to throughout. Garments are drawn mainly from English and West European sources, though the selection could include only some of the many variations in style that existed.

Several types of illustration are used for each garment. They include drawings from historical sources, with modern style drawings to model the period look. Patterns, cutting layouts, and enlarged details then allow personal working patterns to be planned, cut and made up. Photographs show several finished garments and details of techniques.

Readers new to historical dressmaking and re-enactment will find that the conditions and practice of tailoring were very different then from today. Clothes, like other possessions, were fewer and valuable. They would be painstakingly made, often by craftsmen, well maintained, and expected to last and be passed on. They were also important in reflecting the wearer's status. The different idea of 'fit' and the different tailoring and sewing techniques, which were all part of the period look, are covered in the introductory chapters. Take time if you can to explore the period and its dress. This will add to your enjoyment as you make the garments and will help you to qualify as a medieval tailor's assistant!

How to use the book

The instructions are intended for readers with basic dressmaking skills. Beginners are advised to use a modern dressmaking manual or, better still, work with an experienced sewer or a teacher.

1. Choosing your garment or outfit

Read the *Preparation* section, choose your garment, and consider what is to be worn with it, and in what context.

2. For your chosen garment

Find the section for your garment and see what you will need in practice. Read the historical background, methods of planning, cutting and making up, materials, etc. For each main garment the opening page illustrates a complete outfit to go with it.

3. Simpler garments

For simpler garments based on rectangles and triangles of cloth, such as shirts, smocks, cotes and surcotes, follow the instructions for the garment. Sketch the pattern pieces to scale using your personal measurements. Make a toile or full paper pattern before cutting. Always try to cut the straight lines of the pattern on the grain of the fabric.

4. Fitted garments

For fitted garments you first need to prepare a personal pattern or Block. Read the *Blocks* section: measure the wearer (Figs 1-3) then model the toile and prepare the Block (Figs 4-21). The Block is essential to achieving the 'look' of the period: it offers a close fit for both layers of garments made from it while allowing freedom of movement.

Blocks shown in the *Blocks* section are based on the measurements of four individuals. The Blocks and patterns for fitted garments illustrated throughout the book were custom made to fit two individuals: a size 42 man and a size 14 woman.

Don't worry if your Block looks different! Since the Block provides a close *personal* fit, the Blocks shown are intended *only as a guide* – not as patterns to enlarge and copy. The patterns for head-wear, however, can be scaled up and adjusted on the wearer.

Once your Block is prepared, it can be used to plan any fitted garment you choose.

5. Adapting the Block

To adapt your Block for a particular pattern see *Blocks* again, starting at 'From Block to pattern'. Then go to the chosen garment and follow the instructions.

6. Reading the patterns

Patterns are shown with a scale. Fitted garments are shown on a grid scale: the original Block appears in fine outline with the adapted pattern sections on top in heavier outline. Fine straight lines are used for construction lines. Heavy broken lines indicate alternative shapes. The Straight Grain is shown by arrows.

Letters indicate joining or measuring points, and short marks on seam lines show balance points. ⌐ Fold ⌐ outside the edge of a grid indicates the fold of the fabric. ⌐ Fold ⌐ inside the edge of a pattern piece indicates that the edge should be placed on folded fabric and cut in one piece.

Abbreviations

CB – Centre Back	UP – Underarm Point
CF – Centre Front	FO – Front opening
BP – Back Point	FL – Front line
SP – Shoulder Point	FP – Front Point
NP – Neck Point	AL – Arm length

Measurements – Metric units: metres (m), centimetres (cm) and millimetres (mm) are used throughout. To convert to inches see the scale below, or use a tape measure marked with both scales. Use 1 in = 2.5 cm as a rule of thumb.

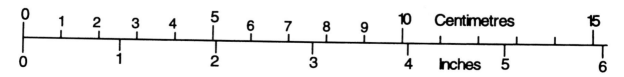

Conversion scale: centimetres to inches

7. Planning your working pattern

Follow the instructions for the garment, where key sections are highlighted by a tint. Remember that the increases and other alterations to Blocks shown were made for the two models used throughout. Use smaller adjustments for children and larger ones for larger adults. Women with over 110 cm (43 in) bust and men over 120 cm (47 in) chest require proportionately greater alterations: it would be wiser to avoid tightly fitted styles for these larger sizes.

For garments with skirts check that the side seams are of equal length and at the same angle to the construction line on Back and Front. Add balance points where shown.

Seam allowances – These are included in the dimensions for simpler garments made without a Block.

Pattern diagrams planned from a Block are shown throughout *without seam allowances*. You can *either* draw seam allowances round each pattern piece or leave the patterns net and mark the seam allowances onto the material before cutting. The standard allowance is 1.5 cm, but allow extra if you are unsure of the fit. Edges with openings and fastenings may need more, and hems should have 5 cm allowance. Note on each piece whether seam allowances are included.

8. Materials

Read the *Materials* section before buying fabrics, fastenings and trimmings. For patterned fabrics allow enough length for repeats, and for matching the design of left and right halves and sleeves.

9. Cutting

Garments made from the Block are usually cut from four separate panels, even if illustrated on the fabric fold. The four seams will help achieve a proper fit.

Napped fabrics – ensure the nap runs in the same direction on both halves of Front and Back.

Patterned fabrics – match the design for left and right halves, and if possible for the sleeves. Match the Straight Grain (SG) of the pattern to the SG of the fabric.

Lining – cut the lining on the same grain as the outer fabric.

10. Making up

Identify each pattern piece on the back. Transfer balance points and other marks. Secure longer bias edges on a stay band. A summary of the order of working is given in *Methods*, p. 46. Specific directions are included with garment patterns.

Preparation

Our knowledge of dress and its construction in the medieval period is scarce since there are so few surviving garments. Attempts at reconstruction have to rely on interpreting visual sources that can be studied at first hand, or in reproduction, and on scholarly books about the period. Readers can enhance their knowledge and understanding of the subject, and often have fun in doing so, by looking closely at the sources they can find for themselves.

Sources of information

Good visual sources include illuminated manuscripts, paintings, memorial brasses and effigies. Some may be dated fairly accurately, but there are also pitfalls to consider.

Many of the manuscripts and paintings of the period in British collections are from other European countries. Historical characters shown in manuscripts might be clothed in garments of the illustrator's times rather than their own. Also, medieval painters often put religious figures into 'antique' dress, which might include turbans and other exotic head-wear, or long, flowing sleeves emerging from short tight ones; while the minor figures – soldiers, peasants and onlookers – were usually dressed in current styles, as were the 'donors' who paid for the painting, sometimes seen kneeling in the foreground.

Memorial brasses and effigies offer useful and accessible records of British dress, but may be stylised and misleading in date. Lack of colour and detail, particularly on brasses, can make it difficult to distinguish between layers of clothing.

Paintings, manuscripts and monuments may not always be readily accessible without prior arrangement, but many can be seen in publications. The most helpful books on costume history will indicate their sources, including countries of origin. The Bibliography lists titles I have found helpful.

Art gallery and library collections are increasingly accessible for study on the internet.

Collecting information

Besides the more obvious items such as a postcards, slides and guidebooks, which you can gather during visits to country houses, churches, museums and galleries, you may find it useful to draw objects of particular interest. Drawing will make you look more closely and may reveal significant detail such as a seam line.

Establishing the period for your outfit

This is a key decision. Don't be tempted to wear something out of period just because you like it or it is more convenient! It is safer to go for an earlier style: garments for best would probably be worn by at least two generations and even working clothes might be passed on. There was a lively trade in used clothing.

Some basic garments were virtually unchanged over the three centuries covered in this book: others, especially head-dresses and outer garments, changed more frequently; but who wore what depended on status. Styles for working dress changed slowly, so they should be possible to date within about fifty years. More fashionable styles may be more closely dated.

The garments and the period

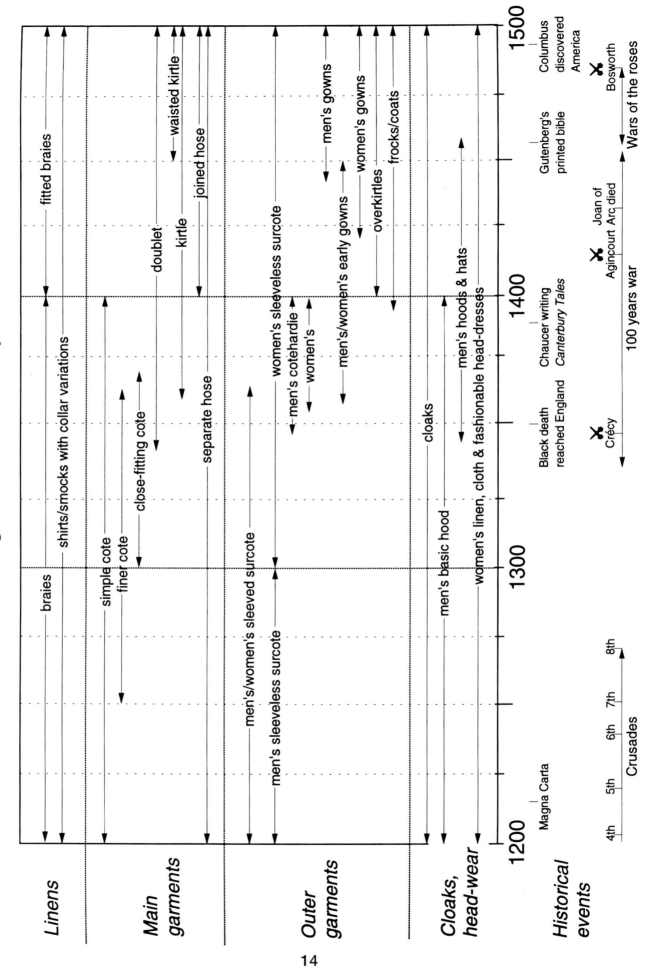

Linens

braies

fitted braies

shirts/smocks with collar variations

Main garments

simple cote

finer cote

close-fitting cote

doublet

kirtle

waisted kirtle

separate hose

joined hose

Outer garments

men's/women's sleeved surcote

men's sleeveless surcote

women's sleeveless surcote

men's cotehardie

women's

men's/women's early gowns

men's gowns

women's gowns

overkirtles

frocks/coats

Cloaks, head-wear

men's basic hood

cloaks

men's hoods & hats

women's linen, cloth & fashionable head-dresses

Historical events

Magna Carta

Crusades

4th 5th 6th 7th 8th

Black death reached England

Crécy

Agincourt

Joan of Arc died

100 years war

Chaucer writing *Canterbury Tales*

Gutenberg's printed bible

Bosworth

Wars of the roses

Columbus discovered America

1200   1300   1400   1500

14

Defining the wearer

Two main factors need to be taken into account in deciding what dress is appropriate.

Wealth and status – Dress was an important indicator of income and status. The dress of the wealthy demonstrated that they were not subject to the hardships of normal work, and had the leisure and servants required to dress them.

Visual sources show that male manual workers wore their clothes around knee length for convenience and might strip off their outer clothes in hot weather, while professionals such as lawyers and doctors wore sober calf-length garments of finer quality, and full-length robes were worn by senior clergy, noblemen and royalty. Women's clothes were long, but working women might tuck up their skirts above their ankles, while grander ladies wore them trailing over their feet.

A rural worker would usually be limited to the cloth available in his local market and the skills of the person making (or remaking) his garment. Town-dwellers had a wider choice but their clothes would still be made to last, so they tended to be plain and substantial. The nobility and gentry would use finer fabrics with richer adornments, reserving their finest and most elaborate for ceremonial occasions. They had access to a range of luxury imports and to innovative craftsmen.

Age – Young men wore short outer garments, but older men wore them calf-length or longer. Unmarried women could wear their hair loose and their necklines low; married women were expected to cover their hair and be more modest, while widows often dressed plainly and in earlier styles.

Selecting your garments

You will need to select garments from the categories below to match your chosen period and wearer. Each category is described in detail in its own section later in the book.

Many people wore three layers of clothing: linens, main garment and outer garment, but some garments such as the cote and kirtle may be used in both the main and outer layers. If your sewing experience or your budget is limited start off with simple styles.

Body linens

This is medieval underclothing, a layer of washable linen between the body and the outer clothes. Even if it can't be seen, the shirt or smock helps the other garments to hang well and will save on dry-cleaning bills. Medieval women wore nothing under the smock, but modern women must decide for themselves, bearing in mind that a bra will affect the line of the outer garment. Men should wear the appropriate style of braies, unless their outer clothing is long enough to keep everything covered even during active movement.

1. Body linens

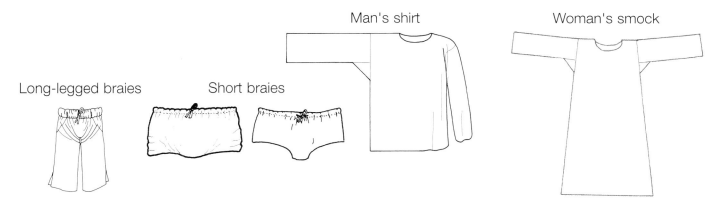

Long-legged braies   Short braies   Man's shirt   Woman's smock

Main garments

This second layer is worn over the linens. Both men and women wore a cote of some kind from well before 1200 until about the mid 14th century, and it persisted even into the 15th century. About 1340 men started wearing the doublet, and by 1400 it was generally worn: the hose (see below) were fastened to it. The length of the doublet was related to the style of hose. By about 1370 women were wearing the kirtle, and it was widely adopted by the early 15th century. When working, men occasionally showed their doublets, but the kirtle was usually hidden.

2. Main garments – cotes or tunics

Man's basic cote, 1200 onwards

Woman's finer cote, mid 13th to early 14th century (Pl. 6)

3. Main garments – kirtles

Basic kirtle, later 14th century onwards

Flat-fronted kirtle, mid 15th century onwards

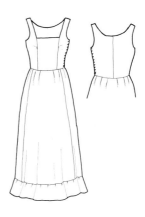

4. Main garments – doublets

Basic doublet, mid 14th century onwards

Fashionable doublet, mid to late 15th century (Pls 7&8)

Hose

Men's hose developed from short stockings to waist-high 'tights' (joined hose), while women's hose remained separate and much the same throughout the period. Joined hose were tied to a short doublet, but many men went on wearing separate hose and a long doublet right through the 15th century.

5. Hose

Separate hose, 1200-1500, *left & centre* for men, *right* for women.

Joined hose, 15th century

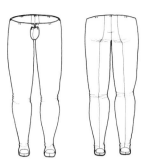

Outer garments

This is the third layer of the outfit and, together with the head-wear, the defining feature. Several different styles were in use at a time, and all but the very poorest people would have clothes for both 'working' and 'best'. Manual workers might remove the outer garment when working, but normally it would be kept on in public, or hitched up, or arranged to reveal the inner clothing.

6. Outer garments – surcotes

Simple sleeved surcote, 13th and early 14th century

Woman's fashionable sleeved surcote, mid 14th century

Woman's sleeveless surcote, first half of 14th century (Pl 10)

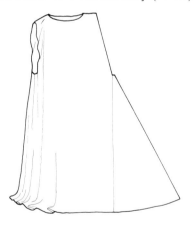

Sleeveless surcotes, 13th to mid 14th century, *left* man's, *right* woman's

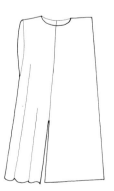

Women's open surcotes, mid 14th century on, *left* simple, *right* ceremonial

7. Outer garments – cotehardies

Men's cotehardies, second half of 14th century

Woman's cotehardie, later 14th century

8. Outer garments – early gowns for men and woman

Early buttoned gown, later 14th and early 15th century

Men's short gowns, late 14th and early 15th century

Fashionable gown, end of 14th and early 15th century

9. Outer garments – men's gowns

Pleated gown, middle 15th century (Pls 12&13)

10. Outer garments – women's gowns

Flared gown, early to mid 15th century

Late medieval fitted gown, later 15th century

11. Outer garments – working dress

In the 15th century women wore a second, fuller kirtle over the first. The skirts were usually tucked up revealing the kirtle beneath.

Men wore an outer garment either loose and belted, or closer-fitting and buttoned. Patterns for these are not included as the cut is based on the gown or cotehardie.

Overkirtle, 15th century

Belted frock and buttoned cote, 15th century

Cloaks

Cloaks were worn throughout the period but are not essential for your outfit.

12. Cloaks

Cloaks were circular in shape with different shoulder styles and fastenings.

Cloak necklines and fastenings

Children's wear

Children's clothes would normally reflect the status of their family unless supplied by an employer.

13. Children's wear

Cote   Boy's gown, 15th century   Girls' kirtle and V-fronted gown

Head-wear

Men wore a hood or a hat, or sometimes both. Most women just wore a kerchief, sometimes with a veil or hood over it, but head-dresses for the wealthy became increasingly complex from the mid 14th century.

14. Head-wear – men's hats and caps
A selection from the 14th and 15th centuries.
a. Felt hat
b. Fur hat
c. Knitted cap
d. Straw hat
e. Coif

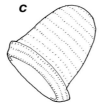
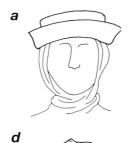

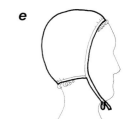

15. Head-wear – men's hoods
a. Basic hood, 13th and 14th century
b. Hood worn as a hat, mid 14th to mid 15th century
c. Chaperon, mid 15th century (Pl 19)

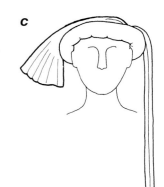

16. Head-wear – women's linen head-dresses
a. Wrapped kerchief, 1200 onwards
b. Knotted kerchief, 15th century
c. Kerchief with shaped and pinched wimple, 15th century

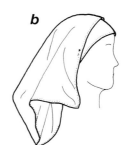
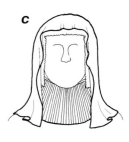

17. Head-wear – women's cloth head-dresses and hoods
a. Open hood, mid 14th century onwards
b. Black head-dress, late 15th century

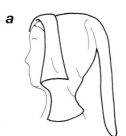
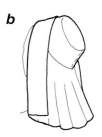

18. Head-wear – women's fashionable head-dresses

A selection from the elaborate head-dresses and their components worn by women of status.

a. Plaits, 14th and early 15th century
b. Hair nets, mid 13th to mid 15th century
c. Barbette and fillet, 13th and early 14th century
d. Frilled veil, second half of 14th century
e. Templers, early 15th century
f. Separate horns, mid 15th century
g. Padded roll, early to later 15th century

a
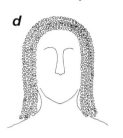

b

c
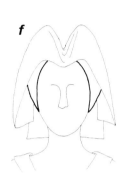

d
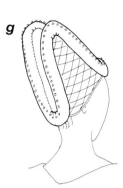

e
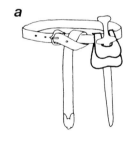

f

g

Accessories

A belt and a pair of shoes are vital for every outfit. Notes on shoes are included under Hose, but making them is not covered in this book. Belts, purses and other items such as aprons and mittens indicate status and will enhance your finished outfit.

19. Accessories

a. Man's belt with purse and knife
b. Woman's drawstring purse
c. Split mitten
d. Woman's apron
e. Basket

a
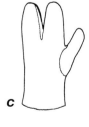

b

c
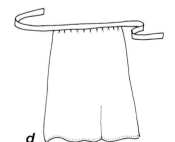

d

e

Wearing your outfit

Get used to putting on your outfit layer by layer. Practise pinning the kerchief and draping the hood, as well as movements like lifting objects and climbing steps. Women need to know just where to hitch up the skirts for free movement, and 'ladies' need to practise walking *without* hitching them up. Try the following exercise: with arms loose at your sides grab the outer skirt in each hand and lift it forward until the front is clear of your feet. Kick forward as you walk to keep the bulk moving, but remember not to stride – ladies don't have to hurry!

Your clothes only become fully 'yours' by using them. Learning how to move in them and how to keep your head-dress in place will enhance your confidence and enjoyment. For each historic role you will need to assume a different comportment to match the clothes, for example a consciousness of rank which makes you deferential, or superior, in a way that is unknown today.

Care and storage

Re-enactors and frequent users should repair any damage promptly and as neatly as possible. You can renovate old garments, or cut them down for children, as would have been customary.

Wash all body linens regularly. If you are a purist you will use pure soap or ecological detergent, without modern synthetic fragrances. If you can, air-dry linens on a line so they don't need ironing.

Your other clothing should rarely need washing or cleaning if it is well dried and aired. Brush off dried mud, and clean off grease. Wear an apron for cooking or dirty work.

Store heavy garments laid flat, or folded: if left on a coat hanger they may droop out of shape. If they aren't used regularly put them in a plastic bag, or wrap them in an old sheet or muslin, to keep out moths. Medieval pest controls such as rue, lavender or rosemary smell better than camphor mothballs, but are less effective. You should take clothes out regularly to give them a shake and check for moth grubs.

The personal pattern Block

This chapter shows how to make garments to fit an individual wearer. Two very different techniques are used for cutting body garments, but the measurements you must take will serve as the basis for either:

a. Planning directly from personal measurements This method is used for the simple shapes of linen undergarments, cotes and surcotes, and is explained in detail in the appropriate chapters. It consists of planning the pattern pieces from a set of personal measurements. The pieces are cut in paper or spare fabric first, though experienced workers may prefer to work directly on the cloth.

b. Using a personal Block The Block is a personal bodice pattern, giving an exact fit from neck to waist or hip, combined with a set-in sleeve. The doublet and kirtle (main garments) are based closely on the Block, and the outer garments are developed from it.

The personal Block is the main subject of this chapter. It is prepared in the following stages: measuring – modelling the toile – making and adjusting an intermediate pattern – making the Block.

Note on fitted garments

A medieval fitted garment had to touch everywhere – waist, chest, shoulders, armpits – yet leave the wearer free to move. To the medieval tailor 'fit' meant something very different from today. As most modern clothing is mass-produced and looser, most people's clothes do not fit them so precisely, particularly around the armholes and shoulders, and a modern pattern cannot produce a convincing medieval garment. This offers a technical challenge, but with individually tailored garments the right level of fit is perfectly feasible.

A cutter today will notice major differences between a modern block and the blocks shown here. A very small amount of ease is allowed round the body, just enough for muscle movement. The armhole is high under the arm and the shoulder very narrow, so the ball-joint of the shoulder is inside the sleeve. Dropped armholes and wide shoulders were unknown. The sleeve is made with the main seam at the back of the arm and with much more length to the underarm than a modern sleeve. Women's garments do not have darts nor, for the most part, waist seams: the shaping is achieved in the lengthways seams.

Hose are made by fitting on the body and have a chapter to themselves.

Measurements, Figs 1-3

The individual being fitted must be measured by someone else to ensure accuracy. Not all the measurements listed are needed for every garment, but it is useful to have a full set for reference. The measuring process will also help you absorb the wearer's physical characteristics. Once you have the list you can either go to the chapters covering garments planned directly (see above), or continue here through the various stages of producing a personal Block.

Modelling a bodice toile

The toile is the fabric template used for making a personal Block. 'Modelling' describes the process of fitting fabric round the body to produce a toile. Since the Block provides the basis of every fitted garment made for an individual it is well worth taking the time and trouble to get it right. As it is impractical to model a bodice on oneself, someone else must do the fitting and the instructions below are directed at that person. The wearer is referred to as the model. It may help to study first the finished Blocks in Figs 16-19, observing how they fit around the body, before starting. Do remember, however, that the Blocks illustrated were made for particular individuals, so don't be surprised if yours looks different!

The modelling fabric for the toile must be woven, not knitted: light calico or sheeting is best, and used material will do. You need a tape measure, plenty of pins, a good pair of scissors, a ruler and a fine pen to mark the fabric.

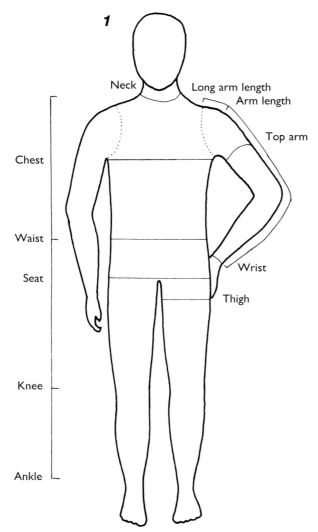

1

1. Measurements for men

Copy the list, right, and enter the measurements against each dimension. Measure the vertical distances on the side of the body, except the Back length which is measured down the spine.

The Body rise measurement is needed only for fitted braies; take it while the subject is seated on a hard flat surface.

The dotted lines show the positions of the armholes on a Block. The upper end, above the ball joint of the shoulder, is the starting point for measuring the Long arm length for the Block sleeve. For sleeves of garments not planned from a Block, measure the Arm length from the tip of the shoulder.

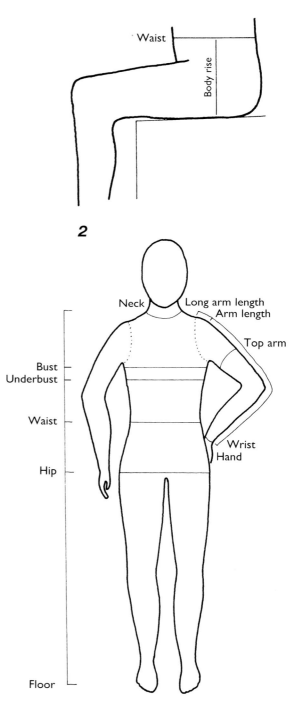

2

2. Measurements for women

Copy the list below and enter the measurements against each dimension. Measure the vertical distances on the side of the body, except the Back length which is measured down the spine.

The second bust measurement is taken under the breasts, and used for more fitted kirtles.

The dotted lines show the positions of the armholes on a Block. The upper end, above the ball joint of the shoulder, is the starting point for measuring the Long arm length for the Block sleeve. For sleeves of garments not planned from a Block, measure the Arm length from the tip of the shoulder.

Bust (round the breasts)
Bust (under the breasts)
Waist
Hips
Back length (from nape to waist)
Waist to hip
Waist to floor
Base of neck
Long arm length (over shoulder joint)
Arm length (from tip of shoulder)
Top arm
Wrist
Hand (smallest loop that will slip over)

24

Chest (with lungs filled)
Waist
Seat
Back length (nape to waist)
Waist to knee
Waist to ankle
Thigh (at widest point)
Base of neck
Long arm length (over shoulder joint)
Arm length (from tip of shoulder)
Top arm
Wrist
Hand (smallest loop that will slip over)
Body rise (for fitted braies)

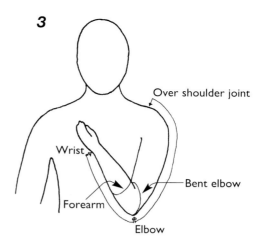

3. Measurements for tight sleeves

These may be needed for men's or women's garments.

Shoulder to elbow (over shoulder joint)
Elbow to wrist
Round bent elbow joint
Round forearm

How to proceed

Cut two rectangles of fabric on the straight grain, 10 to 20 cm longer than the model's shoulder to hip measurement, and 10 to 20 cm wider than half the largest body girth – for men this is usually the chest size; for women either the bust or hip measurement. Draw a Centre line on the straight grain of the material down the middle of each piece. These pieces will form the Back and Front of the toile.

The model should wear a medieval shirt or smock, or a T-shirt. Women should not wear a bra, since one will not be worn with the finished clothes. They should try to stand in a normal relaxed posture while you work. Ask the model to rotate his/her arms at the shoulder. You can then feel the bone structure and position the armhole so that all joint movement occurs in the sleeve. The front armhole should follow the hollow under the collarbone.

Work gradually and evenly during the fitting process, placing pins on both sides of the body as you proceed. Keep the balance between the two sides, centre front and centre back. Snip into the edge when the material drags, and trim away the spare a little at a time to avoid taking off too much. Work by smoothing the material from the middle of each panel towards the edges, until the toile fits snugly round the body without wrinkles, but with enough ease to move freely. At each stage ask the model to move a bit, breathe deeply and otherwise test the fit.

Modelling a toile for a man, Figs 4-9

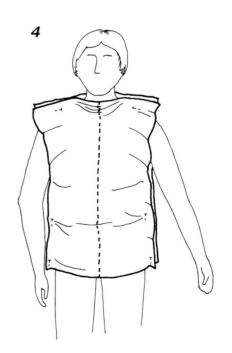

4. Modelling a toile for a man

Pin the Back and Front loosely together over the model's shoulders, making sure the Centre Lines lie down the centre at the front (broken line) and back of the body. Pin them together again near the edges, at waist and hip level.

5

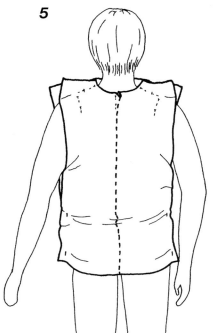

5. Back

On each side in turn, smooth the toile horizontally from the Centre line over the shoulder blade towards the position of the armhole, then smooth gently upwards to the top of the shoulder. Re-pin the Back to the Front over the shoulder.

Mark the shape of each armhole with pins, from the shoulder to the broadest part of the back.

On each side in turn, smooth the toile up the shoulder towards the base of the neck, pinning it to the Front in two or three places. If the toile is dragging at the front, snip into the edge under the chin to free it. Trim away the material at the back of the neck to form a shallow curve. There should be a little excess width here: pinch it on the Centre Back line and pin a short vertical dart.

6. Front

On each side in turn, as for the Back, smooth the material horizontally across the upper chest towards the position of the armhole and up to the shoulder. Re-pin the Front to the Back, working up the shoulder to the base of the neck.

6

Mark the line of each armhole with pins, from the shoulder to the hollow in front of the arm. Trim away the material to form the front neck curve, which is deeper than the back neck curve. There should be excess material here: pinch it on the Centre Front line and pin a vertical dart, which will be longer and deeper than the Centre Back dart.

7

7. Side seams and main vertical darts

At waist level, move in the pins slightly at the sides to pull the toile in closer. Still at waist level, pinch the surplus material on the Centre Back line and pin, then do the same on the Centre Front line.

Work up from the waist, pinning the two side seams and the two vertical darts on the Centre Front and Centre Back lines. Stop forming the side seams when the material starts to drag under the arms.

Below the waist, pin the side seams and darts over the hips, down to the lower edge of the toile. Re-pin more tightly at waist level, so that the material drags into horizontal wrinkles.

The Centre Back dart will normally reach from the middle of the back to the buttocks. The Centre Front dart may reach from the chest to below the waist on a young man; on an older man it will start from a low waist level (below the belly) and reach to the edge of the toile.

8. Waist darts

At waist level, form and pin the spare material into horizontal darts. One continuous dart may form across the Back, tapering to nothing at the side seams, or two separate darts may form on the two halves. Two darts will form on the Front. They may be horizontal, or they may slope down towards the centre on a mature model. These darts are quite narrow.

9. Armholes, toile removal

Go back to the top of the side seams. With the model's arms raised, fit and pin the two sides right up into the armpits, trimming away spare material as necessary. At the top of each side seam, on Back and Front, start cutting horizontally to form the armhole, then curve the cut up to the shoulder following the line of pins.

Check the fit once more, and check the length: the toile should reach to the tops of the legs. Draw onto the toile the outlines of the two vertical Centre Front darts – remember to draw both sides. Now take the pins out of the two darts and cut carefully up the Centre Front line to remove the toile from the model.

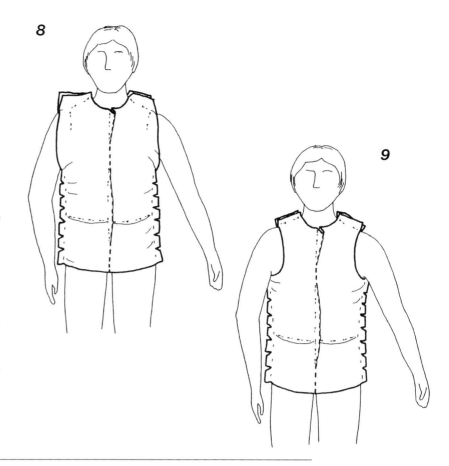

Modelling a toile for a woman, Figs 10-14

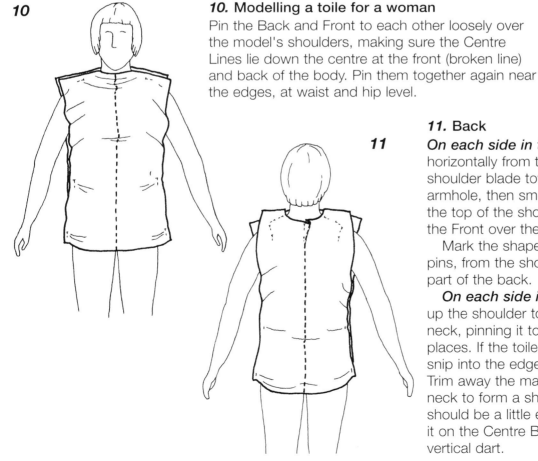

10. Modelling a toile for a woman

Pin the Back and Front to each other loosely over the model's shoulders, making sure the Centre Lines lie down the centre at the front (broken line) and back of the body. Pin them together again near the edges, at waist and hip level.

11. Back

On each side in turn, smooth the toile horizontally from the Centre line over the shoulder blade towards the position of the armhole, then smooth gently upwards to the top of the shoulder. Re-pin the Back to the Front over the shoulder.

Mark the shape of each armhole with pins, from the shoulder to the broadest part of the back.

On each side in turn, smooth the toile up the shoulder towards the base of the neck, pinning it to the Front in two or three places. If the toile is dragging at the front, snip into the edge under the chin to free it. Trim away the material at the back of the neck to form a shallow curve. There should be a little excess width here: pinch it on the Centre Back line and pin a short vertical dart.

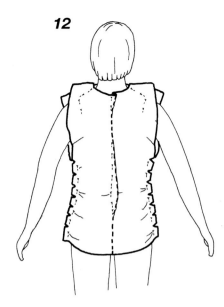

12. Side seams and main vertical darts

Aim to get a close fit round the hips and ribcage, while letting the toile skim the waist. If horizontal wrinkles form round the waist the toile has been pulled too tight.

At waist level, move in the pins slightly at the sides. Still at waist level, pinch the surplus material on the Centre Back line and pin it, then do the same on the Centre Front line. Work down from the waist, pinning the two side seams and the two vertical darts on the Centre Front and Centre Back lines to fit over the hips. Both darts will usually taper to nothing over the hips.

Now work up from the waist, again pinning the side seams and Centre Front and Centre Back darts. The side seams should fit closely round the lower ribcage: stop pinning when you reach bust level.

The length of the vertical darts will depend on the model's figure. If she has a larger bust than hip size, both darts will taper to nothing below the level of the bust. For a model with small breasts, the Centre Front dart may continue right up the chest to the neck. For a full bottom the Centre Back dart may continue right up to the neck, engulfing the small dart already formed. In this case you will have to adjust the back shoulders, neckline and armhole markings.

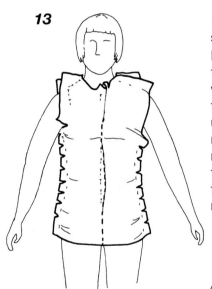

13. Front – shoulders and bust shaping

During pinning of the side seams, two horizontal folds of spare material will have formed on the Front across the bust. Smooth this spare material upwards and, with the model's arms raised, pin the tops of the side seams right up into the armpits, snipping out the base of the armholes and trimming away the excess as needed.

Continue to smooth the spare material upwards and inwards on each side, re-pinning the Front to the Back when you reach the shoulders. The Front should fit smoothly and all the surplus material will come together to form a vertical dart at the Centre Front neck. If the Centre Front dart from the waist reaches over the bust, continue it into the neckline.

Trim away the top of the toile to form the Front neck curve, which is deeper than the Back neck curve. Mark the line of each armhole with pins, from the shoulder to the hollow in front of the arm.

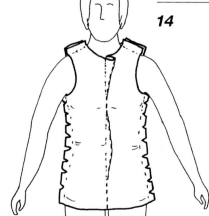

14. Armholes, toile removal

Cut out the armholes on each side, starting horizontally from the side seams and curving up to meet the pins marking the upper shape, to the shoulder.

Check the fit once more, and check the length of the toile: it should cover the fullest part of the hips and reach the tops of the legs. Draw onto the toile the outlines of the two vertical Centre Front darts – remember to draw both sides. Now take the pins out of the two darts and cut carefully up the Centre Front line to remove the toile from the model.

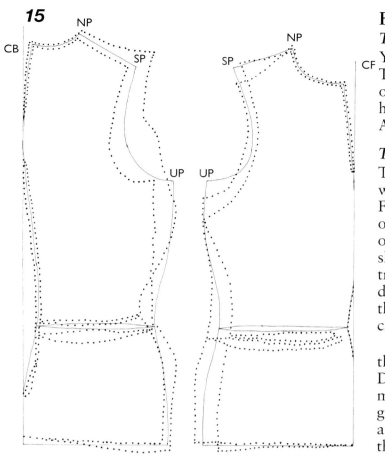

15

NP

CB

SP

NP

SP

CF

UP   UP

From toile to Block, Fig 15
Transferring the toile to paper
You will need large sheets of pattern paper. This is firm and semi-transparent, either plain or marked with a grid, and can be found at a haberdasher, though brown paper can be used. A long ruler and set-square are also useful.

The intermediate pattern
Trace the trial outline of Back and Front (for women), or Back and Front, and Back and Front hip sections (for men), onto a fresh sheet of pattern paper. Add seam allowances and cut out the pieces in a new piece of calico or sheeting. Tack or machine these together and try it on the model, pinning it firmly closed down the Centre Front. If you prefer to cut out the paper pieces without seam allowances, you can add them on the fabric before cutting.

Look carefully at the fit. Is it smooth over the whole torso, with no significant wrinkles? Do the armholes follow the shape of the moving shoulder joint, without sagging or gaping, and do they come right under the armpit, without dragging under the arm? Does the neckline follow the base of the neck? Make any necessary adjustments.

15. From toile to Block

The dotted lines are the fitting lines of the two halves of the toile, as it came off the figure. The fine vertical lines are the Centre Front and Centre Back lines, as marked on the toile. The solid line is the trial outline for the intermediate pattern, drawn from the toile but taking account of the model's measurements. Note how much higher the final armhole is than on the toile.

Marking fitting lines – After removing the toile from the model, lay it on a flat surface. With a fine marker or soft pencil, draw all the fitting lines on the toile by following the lines of pins. Make balance (alignment) marks on the side seams at waist level. Check you have marked both sides of every fitting line before taking out the pins. At this point the toile, with the Front and Back folded vertically, may be irregular like the dotted outlines.

Transferring fitting lines onto paper – If the toile material is light enough, mark through it with a fine pen or sharp pencil. Otherwise cut along the fitting lines and draw round the edges. Remember to label each piece of the toile, e.g. 'Left Front', 'Right Back', etc. Draw lines in pencil to allow for corrections.

Back – Rule a vertical line longer than the toile on a sheet of pattern paper, close to the left edge, and mark this 'CB' (Centre Back). Centre the Back of the open toile on this line and transfer the fitting lines of the right half onto the paper. Turn the toile over and re-centre the Back on the line. Transfer the fitting lines from the left half of the Back on top of the Right Back.

Front – Rule another vertical line, for the Centre Front, on the right of the paper, leaving enough space to transfer both Fronts to the left of this line. Transfer as for the Back.

Checking measurements – Compare the dimensions of the toile, now on paper, with the model's listed chest/bust, waist and hip measurements. The toile sizes should be about 5 cm larger (up to 10 cm on very large sizes) to allow for ease; a woman's waist should have 8 to 10 cm ease.

Trial outline – Draw a trial outline from the two dotted versions, smoothing out the irregularities. Check that the shoulder lines are the same length on Back and Front. Make the Underarm Point (UP) higher rather than lower, as it is hard to cut it high enough on the model. On women's patterns (Fig 18) it is often useful to move some of the hip shaping on the Back from the side seam to the Centre Back, beyond the Centre Back line.

16

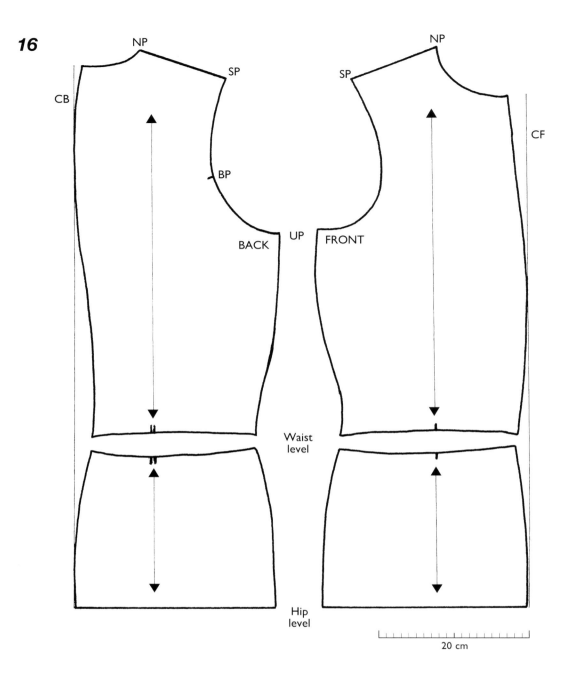

CB · NP · SP · BP · BACK · UP · FRONT · CF · NP · SP · Waist level · Hip level

20 cm

From intermediate pattern to Block

Mark adjustments from the fitting onto your trial outline drawing (Fig 15). For major alterations, repeat the previous stage and make another trial fitting. When you are satisfied with the fit, draft a sleeve pattern to match (see below). Check the fit again with the sleeves set into the bodice (see below).

Make a clean copy on paper of the final pattern, marking the main balance points (add BP on the Back armhole after making the sleeve Block). Add a list of measurements beside it for reference. This is your personal bodice Block: keep the original and trace it off for each new garment pattern. For frequent use, it's worth drawing it on a sheet of mounting board.

16. Young man's Block

The final version of the Block used for male garments throughout the book. Chest 105 cm; waist 87 cm; seat 102 cm; modern size about 42. The following abbreviations are used throughout.

CB = Centre Back
CF = Centre Front
UP = Underarm Point
NP = Neck Point, at the top of the shoulder seam.
SP = Shoulder Point, at the outer end of the shoulder seam and the top of the sleeve head.
BP = Back Point, where the sleeve seam joins the armhole, fixed from finished sleeve Block. Arrows indicate the Straight Grain.

30

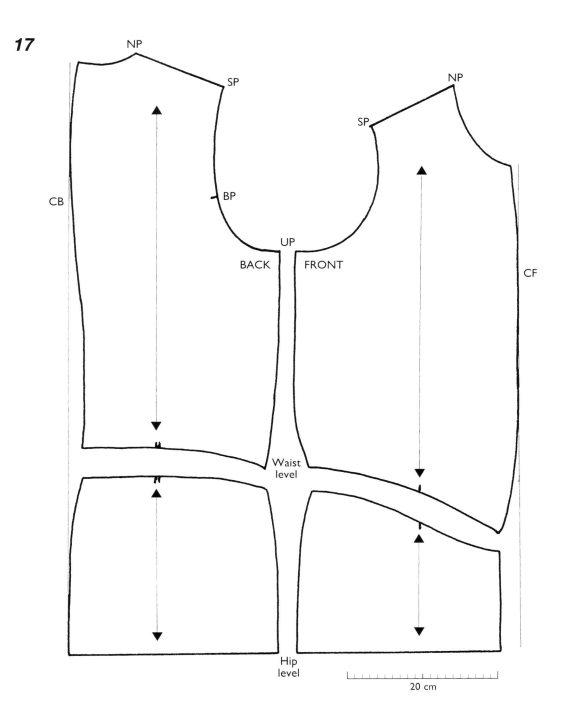

17 NP SP BP UP BACK FRONT CB CF Waist level Hip level

20 cm

17. Mature man's Block – an example

Chest 108 cm; waist 94 cm; seat 102 cm; modern size about 44.

Although the measurements are not very different from Fig 16, the slightly corpulent figure produces quite a different shape where the waist dips under the belly.

18

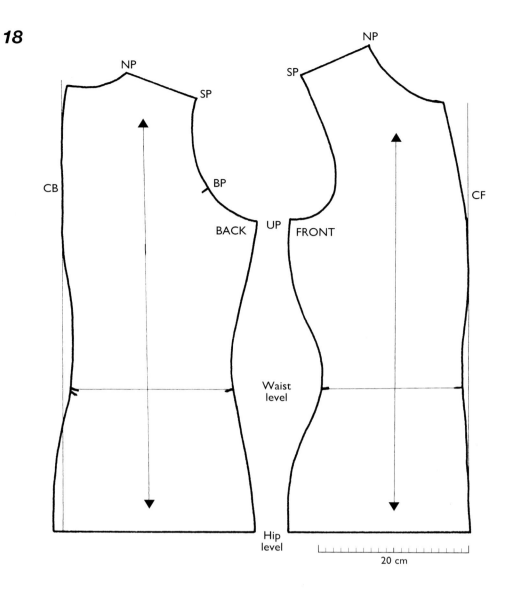

18. Young woman's Block

The final version of the Block used for female garments throughout the book. Bust 94 cm; waist 72 cm; hips 97 cm; modern size about 14.
The following abbreviations are used throughout.

CB = Centre Back

CF = Centre Front

UP = Underarm Point

NP = Neck Point, at the top of the shoulder seam.

SP = Shoulder Point, at the outer end of the shoulder seam and the top of the sleeve head.

BP = Back Point, where the sleeve seam joins the armhole, fixed from finished sleeve Block. Arrows indicate the Straight Grain.

As described in the text, some of the hip shaping for the Back has been moved from the side seam to the Centre Back: the vertical line marks the original Centre Back. Unlike the male Block there is no seam or dart at the waist. 8 cm ease has been added to the total waist, and 4 cm to the bust. Waist level is marked on the Block for reference.

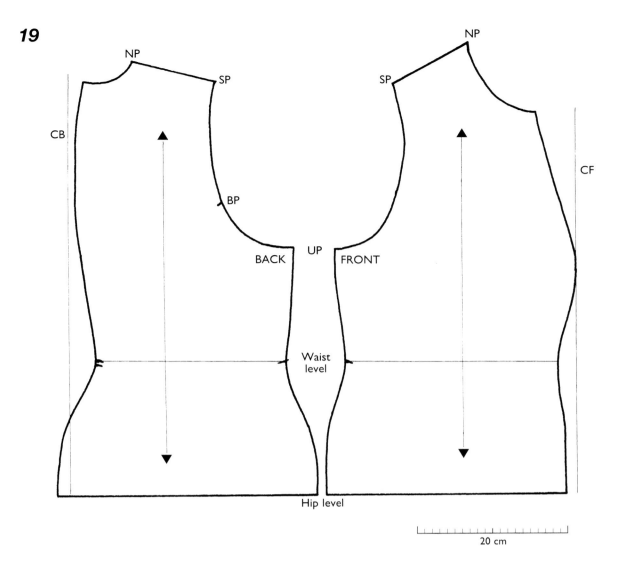

NP

SP

CB

NP

SP

CF

BP

UP

BACK

FRONT

Waist
level

Hip level

20 cm

19. Larger woman's Block – an example

Bust 113 cm; waist 97 cm; hips 127 cm; modern size about 22.

As the model is larger, with a fuller bottom, the centre back dart is continuous from the neck to below the waist (note the position of the CB line).

Also, some extra width has been transferred from the side seam to the Centre Back. There is slightly more ease all round than on the previous Block.

The sleeve Block, Figs 20, 21

The medieval set-in sleeve was quite different from the modern one: the seam was normally at the back of the arm, and the sleeve fitted high under the arm to match the high armhole.

Drafting the sleeve on paper is more reliable than trying to model it on the figure. It is initially drawn (Fig 20) as if the sleeve is made up, with a fold down the Front line and the seam down the back. It is then 'opened up' by tracing it off down the Front line to give the complete pattern (Fig 21). It is next tried out in calico together with the bodice Block for any final adjustment.

20a

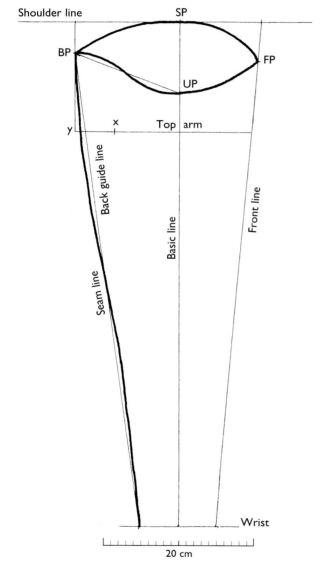

a. **Distance *x-y* is about 5 cm.** In this case, measure down from the Shoulder line, using the distances in Table 1, to mark FP, BP and UP. Rule a guide line from UP to BP.

20. Drafting the sleeve

The method applies for men and women. This sleeve was drafted for the young man's Block (Fig 16) and is based on his measurements: Long arm length 69 cm; Armhole 53 cm; Sleeve head 54 cm; Top arm 32 cm; Wrist 19 cm.

You will require your Long arm, Wrist and Top arm measurements; also the Armhole measurement from your bodice Block, which is needed to find the sleeve head length. You can then draft the Basic line, the Wrist line, the Shoulder line and the Front line. The Back Point (BP) position and the Back Seam line will be fixed later.

Finding the sleeve head measurement

Carefully measure the total back and front armholes on the Block, using a tape measure on edge. Round up the total by from 0.5 cm to 1.4 cm to give a whole number: e.g. 46.2 cm rounds up to 47 cm; 62.6 cm rounds up to 64 cm. This is the sleeve head measurement.

Drawing the sleeve structure

On a large sheet of paper rule the Basic line, equal to your Long arm length. Rule shorter lines at top and bottom at right angles; these are the Shoulder line and Wrist line.

On the Wrist line, mark *half* your Wrist size, plus 0.5-1 cm ease, and centre it on the Basic line. This gives a close-fitting sleeve needing a wrist opening: for a slip-on sleeve use half your Hand measurement instead of half the Wrist.

From SP mark a fifth of the sleeve head measurement to the right along the Shoulder line. Join this point to the right end of the Wrist to give the Front line.

To the left of SP mark a fifth of the sleeve head measurement plus 3 cm. Draw a vertical guide line 15 cm long (20 cm for sleeve heads over 60 cm) down from here. Draw a line parallel to the Shoulder line from here to the Front line.

From the Front line, measure in half the Top arm size plus 2 cm. Mark *x* and measure the remaining distance to *y*. The distance *x-y* is normally 3-5 cm, but variations in *x-y* affect the sleeve head shape, as illustrated in *b.* and *c.*

34

20b

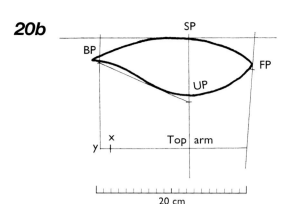

20 cm

b. Distance *x-y* is about 1.5 cm, reflecting a larger Top arm. Sleeve head is 43 cm, Top arm 31 cm. BP has been moved out, and UP up, to compensate, using Table 1.

20c

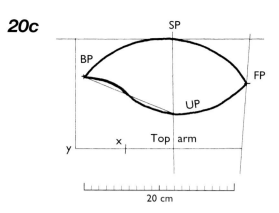

20 cm

c. Distance *x-y* is 6 cm, reflecting a smaller Top arm. Sleeve head is 50 cm, Top arm 27 cm. BP has been moved in to compensate. In this case Table 2 was used to fix the FP, BP, and UP positions.

Table 1
When x-y is up to 5 cm

	Distance from Shoulder line (cm)
Mark FP on the Front line	1/10 of sleeve head
Mark BP on the Back guide line	1/10 of sleeve head – 1 cm
Mark UP on the Basic line	1/5 of sleeve head – 1 cm

Table 2
When x-y is over 5 cm

	Distance from Shoulder line (cm)
Mark FP on the Front line	1/10 of sleeve head + 1 cm
Mark BP on the Back guide line	1/10 of sleeve head
Mark UP on the Basic line	1/5 of sleeve head

Drawing the sleeve head curves

The upper and lower curves together equal the sleeve head measurement. Their final shape will require some adjustment, so draw them lightly at first.

Starting at FP, draw the upper curve to the Shoulder Point (SP), follow the Shoulder line for 2-3 cm, and curve down to the Back Point (BP).

Draw the lower curve from FP through UP (its lowest point) to BP. Draw the curve between UP and BP in the shape of a very shallow S, as shown.

Using a tape measure on edge measure the upper and lower curves, which should be roughly

equal. Adjust the curves until together they equal the sleeve head measurement. Flatten or swell the curves to make slight adjustments to the sleeve head; for greater adjustments move BP or UP in to reduce it, or out to enlarge it.

The seam line

Draw a guide line from BP down to the left Wrist point, and draw the Seam line over it, checking that it passes outside x. Its final shape will depend on the model: on a short plump arm it may follow the guide line almost exactly; on a thin arm it will curve in from the sleeve head. Leave it wide rather than narrow: it is easy to adjust the seam shape later.

21

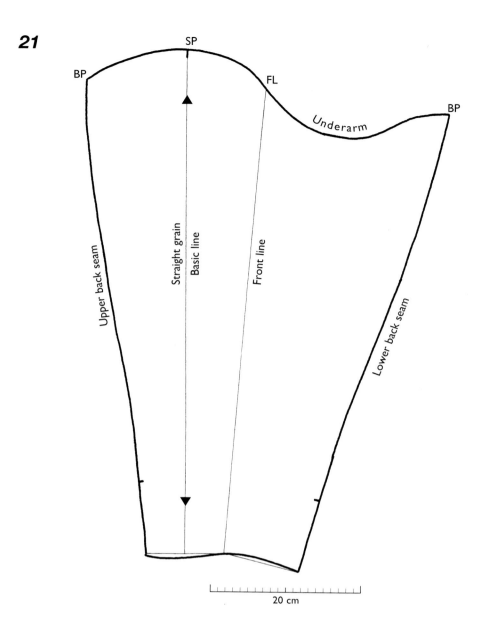

SP

BP

FL

BP

Underarm

Upper back seam

Straight grain
Basic line

Front line

Lower back seam

20 cm

21. Finished sleeve draft

Trace the draft (Fig 20), turn it over along the Front line, then trace the Wrist, the Seam line and the lower sleeve head curve to see the full sleeve pattern. Check that the sleeve head forms a continuous curve. Draw a slightly curved wrist shape to eliminate the angle on the Front line. The shaping has been exaggerated a little here. Mark both the Front line and Basic line on the finished Block for reference. The Straight Grain normally falls on the Basic line. Mark the wrist opening 10 cm up each seam line.

On the sleeve head, measure the distance from SP to BP. Transfer this length less 0.5 cm down the back armhole of the bodice Block, starting from the shoulder (SP). Label the lower point BP. This provides the basic reference point for setting in sleeves.

36

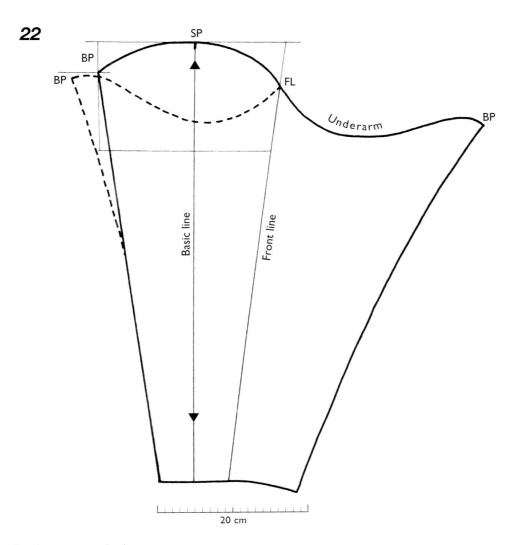

22

SP

BP

BP

FL

BP

Underarm

Basic line

Front line

20 cm

22. Sleeve for larger armhole

This method of adapting the sleeve Block from Fig 20 applies for both men and women. Here it is used for the larger woman's Block (Fig 19) and is based on the following measurements: Long arm length 60 cm; Sleeve head 58 cm; Top arm 37 cm; Wrist 16 cm. It should always be used where the sleeve head is over 60 cm.

The broken lines show the extra sleeve width applied to the underarm curve, extending BP outside its original position. Use the method of Fig 20, but limit the length of the upper curve to 30 cm, and put the additional length into the lower curve. This extends the lower curve beyond the construction line, requiring a new back seam line. Trace off the extended draft to obtain the complete sleeve Block.

Trying out the sleeve with the bodice Block

Trace off the sleeve pattern and cut out a pair of sleeves in calico or sheeting. Mark the Shoulder Point on the sleeve heads. Seam allowances should be added to the pattern, or drawn onto the fabric before cutting. Stitch the back seams, leaving a 10 cm wrist opening, and set the sleeves into your trial bodice: match the Shoulder Point of the sleeve to the shoulder seam of the bodice, and the sleeve seam to the Back Point, easing the fullness of the sleeve head into the armhole.

With the bodice fastened round the model the sleeves should allow free arm movement: try lifting a basket, or the movement of drawing a longbow! If the bodice is straining across the back it may need more width. The high fit under the arms will feel unfamiliar at first. If it is cutting into you it is too high: lower the armhole on the Back and Front and try again.

Make a clean copy of the final pattern on paper, with a list of measurements beside it for reference. This pattern is the sleeve Block. It is used as a basis for different sleeves.

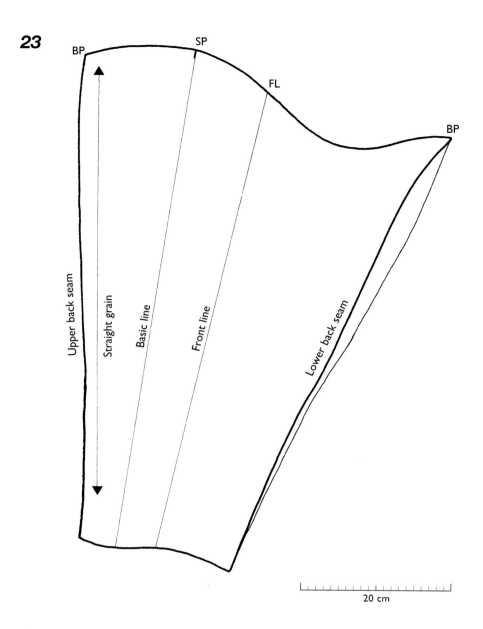

23

BP SP FL BP

Upper back seam

Straight grain

Basic line

Front line

Lower back seam

20 cm

23. Adapting the sleeve Block for a closer fit

To make a closer-fitting sleeve, trace the sleeve Block so that the Straight Grain runs parallel with the upper Back seam and draw a new lower Back seam as shown. The more shaped seam line can be based on the tight sleeve measurements (Fig 3) or fitted on the wearer. At least 2 cm ease is needed round the upper arm, but the wrist can be very close-fitting.

Cutting the sleeve

When cutting a sleeve the Basic line will normally lie along the Straight Grain of the fabric, indicated by arrows in Fig 21, but in some cases the Straight Grain can lie parallel to the Back Seam (Fig 23): this puts the under part of the sleeve somewhat on the bias, which can improve the fit.

Blocks for children, Fig 24

Children's garments are normally less fitted than those for adults, and they can be based on a simple block which allows for growth. Following the method described above, make a loose-fitting block without waist darts or Centre Front and Centre Back shaping. Make the sleeve wide enough to slip over the hand without wrist fastenings.

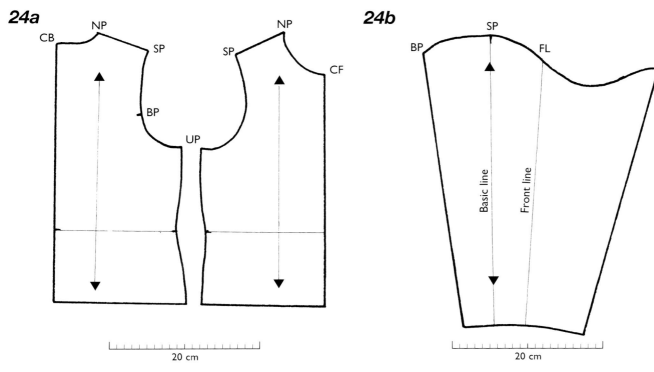

24a | **24b**

20 cm | 20 cm

24. Small child's Block
Height 110 cm; Chest 59 cm; Waist 56 cm;
Seat 62 cm.
a. This is much simpler than the fitted adult Block.
It has no shaping on CF and CB lines, so you only

need to fit the shoulders, neck and armholes and
make some slight shaping on the sides. Make a
looser-fitting armhole than for adults.
b. Plan a simple slip-on sleeve.

From Block to working pattern

Once you have a finished Block for your bodice
and sleeve, it is best to plan your doublet or kirtle
and then proceed to an appropriate outer garment.

Patterns in the book are examples based on two
individuals whose Blocks are shown in Figs 16 &
18, and are given as a guide to making your own.
They are shown at a scale of 1:5 throughout. Block
outlines are shown with a fine line, and patterns
adapted from them with a heavy one. Instructions
assume the usual range of adult sizes, but smaller
increases may be needed for children, and greater
ones for unusually large figures.

To adapt your Block follow the guidelines
outlined below and in Figs 25-27. Start with the
Front and Back body, including hip sections or
skirts; then the neckline or collar, followed by
sleeves and any other parts. Some may require
simple geometric calculations to find the
circumference from a radius, or vice versa. Use the
formulas:

Circumference = 2π x R, or

R = Circumference ÷ 2π

R is the radius and π = 3.14 (or 3 approximately).

Seam allowances

Pattern diagrams are shown throughout *without
seam allowances*. You can either draw seam
allowances round each pattern piece or leave the
patterns net and mark the seam allowances onto
the material before cutting. The standard
allowance is 1.5 cm, but allow extra if you are
unsure of the fit. Edges with openings and
fastenings may need more, and hems should have
5 cm allowance.

Enlarging the Block for outer garments, Fig 25

25a

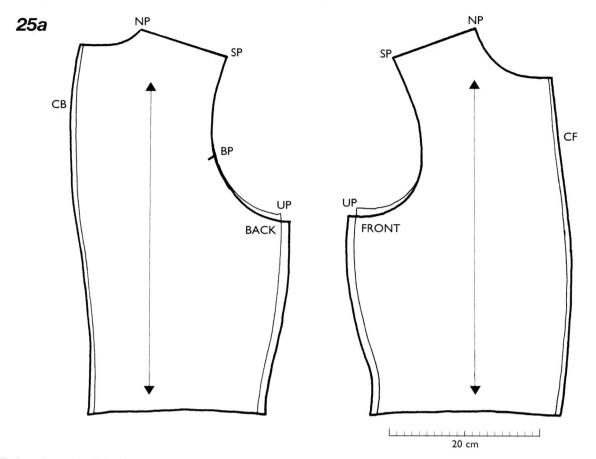

NP · SP · CB · BP · UP · BACK · NP · SP · CF · UP · FRONT

20 cm

25. Enlarging the Block for outer garments
This example illustrates the method of enlarging the Block. Amounts to be added for different garments are indicated in their captions.

a. Enlarging the bodice. Trace off your personal Block. Add 0.5 cm to CF and CB, and 1 cm to each side seam; lower the underarm (UP) by 1 cm. Redraw the outlines. This has added 3 cm to the Block width, and therefore 6 cm to the whole bodice – enough for a close-fitting outer garment such as a cotehardie.

Adapting the Block to add length, width or fullness, Fig 26

26. Adapting the Block to add length, width or fullness
There are three ways of doing this, which can be used in combination.
a. Extending the Block This is the normal way of adding skirts, also of making patterns slightly wider.
b. Slashing and spreading This is mainly used in this book for sleeves. Cut the pattern into pieces and space them out.

c. Slashing and flaring. Slash the pattern from one edge almost to the other. Open the cut at one edge, so the other edge retains its original length. This method is used for one gown (Gowns, Fig 18, Pls 12 & 13) and for making pattern pieces such as cuffs. Make a rectangle as long as the wrist end, and as wide as the proposed cuff. Slash it into equal sections and fan them out evenly, then retrace the long edges as smooth curves.

b. Enlarging the sleeve. Measure the new armhole and note the increase. Trace off your sleeve Block and cut it out with a margin all round. Slash the Block down the Front line to the wrist. Open the slash at the sleeve head by half the armhole increase, and paste down onto paper. Add a quarter of the increase to each seam line on either side of the sleeve at BP. Redraw the sleeve head curve and new seam lines.

The tapering gap will maintain the narrow wrist. For a wider wrist open the slash equally along its whole length, or flare it (Fig 26b).

When adapting the sleeve Block, the SG normally remains along the Basic line. Provided enlargement and fullness are divided fairly evenly – half on FL and a quarter on each Back seam edge – the balance of the sleeve will be maintained.

The Back Point on the bodice remains at the same position, so the SP on an enlarged sleeve will move backwards a little, as shown. Check the length SP-BP on the back bodice, add 0.5 cm and mark the new SP on the sleeve.

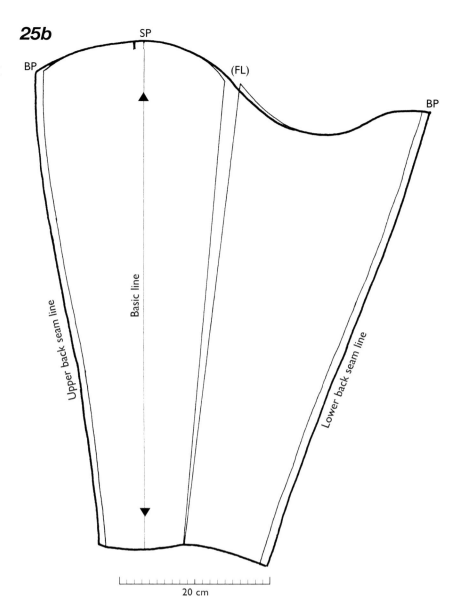

25b

20 cm

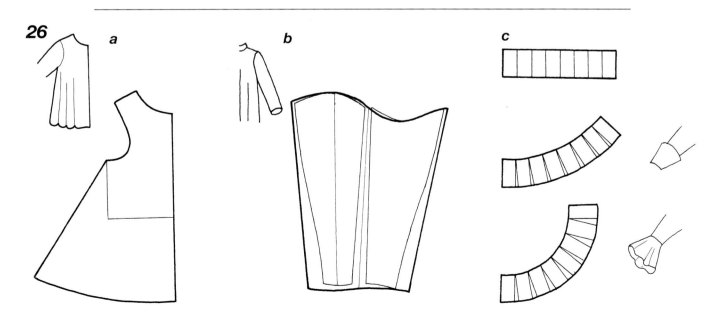

26　a　b　c

41

Adapting the Block for long skirts, Fig 27

27

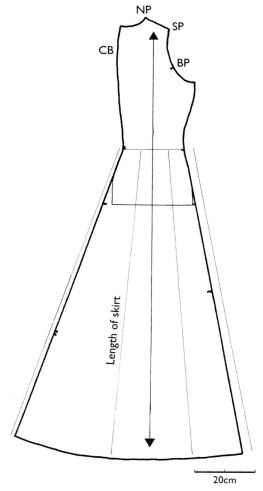

Length of skirt

NP

SP

CB

BP

20cm

27. Adapting the Block for long skirts

Many garments for both men and women have long skirts. Ensure you have enough room and pattern paper!

Mark waist level on the bodice pattern, and check the required length of the garment from waist to hem. Mark the centre of the waist line on Front and Back and rule a construction line (on SG) through this point, extending it to the required garment length.

At hem level measure and mark the hem width of the pattern piece. This may be centered on the construction line, or placed off centre to move fullness from CF to side or, as here, from side to CB. Back and Front side seams should be planned the same distance from the construction line, so they flare at the same angle. Using a tape measure, mark the skirt length at regular intervals to form a curved hem line.

Hem widths for different garments are covered in their captions. The side seams may reach to the waist, or may join the curve of the hips. Add balance marks at waist and hip level, and on skirt seam lines.

This method for planning skirts is used for the woman's cotehardie, kirtle, overkirtle and late medieval gown.

To make the working pattern for a garment

Identify the garment and style required (e.g. Doublets, Figs 4, 6), and read the instructions. Trace off your Block onto clean paper leaving plenty of space around. Draw in the required alterations lightly at first. Check that the seams match each other: two edges to be sewn together are normally the same length, though a sleeve head should always be slightly larger than the armhole. Where a seam meets an edge, both sides of the seam should meet the edge at right angles.

Mark the start of any seam openings, e.g. for a sleeve or the front of a kirtle. Add reference points, such as waist level and balance marks, as an aid to matching seams. Mark BP on the back armhole, and SP on the sleeve head, ensuring that SP is correctly positioned if the sleeve Block has been altered (Fig 25). Mark the Straight Grain on every piece.

Always label each pattern piece with its name, the number to cut out, and whether seam allowances are included. Keep pattern pieces in a transparent pocket with a sketch of the design; they can be stored in a ring binder.

You may prefer to try the pattern in a cheaper fabric before cutting a more expensive material.

Linings

No separate patterns are given for linings: they are almost always the same as the outer pattern pieces and are cut on the same grain. Where parts of a garment have been cut without a paper pattern, use these to cut the lining. It doesn't matter if the lining is pieced to fit (see below).

Fabric quantities, pattern layout and piecing, Fig 28

For average-sized men, a doublet will come out of 1.5 m of 150 cm wide fabric. For gowns and long dresses allow at least twice the length of the finished garment, and for large sizes or very full styles allow the length of the sleeves as well; most of these garments are shown laid out on the fabric, which will help you estimate how much you need.

28. Piecing patterns

These examples show the proper use of piecing. The Straight Grain of the piecing must be the same as in the main pattern and seam allowances must be added to both edges.
For the hose pattern only one of the three piecings should be used at a time.

'Wheel piece' for skirts on narrow cloth.
Left Cut the 'missing' triangle as shown, and reverse it to complete the skirt.
Right 'Wheel piece' in position, shown on the wrong side.

To plan a cutting layout always start with the biggest or most awkward pieces. For the medieval tailor the fabric was by far the most expensive part of the exercise, so material was saved by 'piecing' – adding a small bit to the edge of a pattern piece to allow it to be cut economically. Careful piecing can save a surprising amount of material.

Piecing should be discreet as well as careful. Remember that both edges will need a small seam allowance, and that the piece added must be on the same grain. Sew on the piece before starting to make up the garment.

28

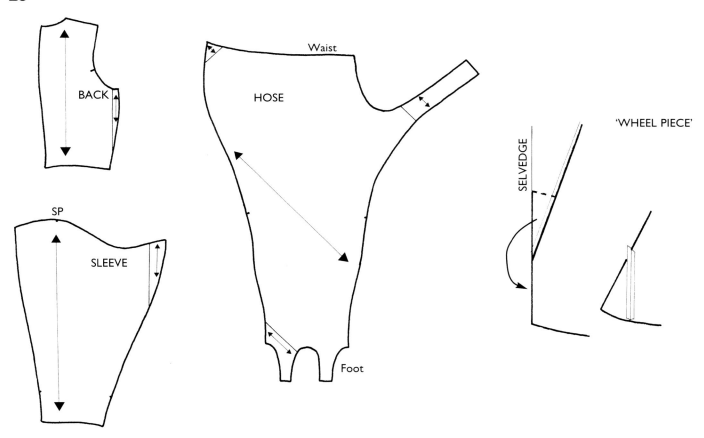

Methods

The working methods you choose will depend on the degree of authenticity you want in your clothing. The basic tools – scissors, needles and thread, pins – are unchanged since the Middle Ages but the modern sewer has many new aids, from iron-on interfacing to overlockers (sergers). Some of these are useful time-savers, but other tasks can still only be done by hand. This chapter concentrates on hand methods which are not covered in detail in modern sewing manuals.

Hand or machine stitching?

Hand stitching and garment construction have evolved over thousands of years, with the sewing sometimes worked from the right side. The sewing machine has altered the way garments are put together, with more of the work being done from the wrong side.

Sewing stitches

1

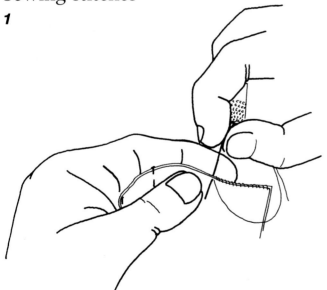

You should consider how much hand sewing you will use as it will affect the construction of your garment. For instance, a hand-sewn shirt (Fig 7) would be made with two-stage seams and the sleeves set in after the side seams are sewn, with felled hems (Fig 2) round the neck, sleeve ends and lower edge. A machine-sewn shirt (Fig 8) would be more efficiently made with overlocked seams, the sleeves sewn on flat, and the side seams and sleeve seams sewn in one, with the folded edges of the neck, sleeve ends and lower edge held down by a row of straight machine stitching.

2a

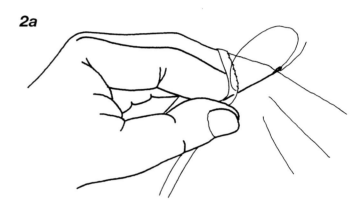

2b

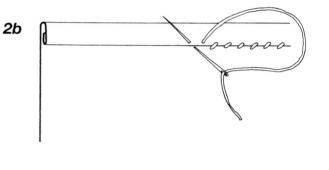

1. Oversewing (top-sewing, seaming)
For joining selvedges or folded edges on all kinds of material. If worked neatly and near the edge it will open out flat without the need for pressing.

For each stitch, push the needle through only one or two threads away from the edge. Keep the stitches close together. When the seam is complete, flatten the stitches with your thumb or index finger nail.

Oversewing should not be confused with overcasting, which is worked wide and loose over a raw edge to prevent it fraying.

2. Hemming (felling)
For holding down a folded edge.

a. Used for finishing off edges; also in two-stage seams for unlined garments (Fig 6).

Keep the folded edge narrow: six threads' depth for the first fold and twelve for the second. Hemming should be close and firm, with the stitches forming an even zigzag.

b. Insert the needle at 45° to the folded edge, pick up a couple of threads of the fabric immediately under the fold, then pass through the edge of the fold. Keep the stitches short and closely spaced.

From a distance it makes little difference whether details such as buttonholes, edge-stitching holding the lining in place round the neck, or even bands of embroidery, are worked by hand or machine. Hand work only becomes important for Living History, when clothes are presented as examples of medieval dress: these should not have visible machine stitching.

Like many basic skills, hand sewing can be learned quickly but is perfected through regular practice. Working threads should not be longer than 40 cm. Work slowly at first, paying attention to each stitch. You should find that your hands become practised and the work speeds up naturally. A thimble can save wear and tear on your fingers. For permanent hand stitching start by securing the thread with a few back stitches: this is neater and more secure than a knot. Finish by threading the end back through the last few stitches.

The instructions are drawn for right-handed people: if you are left-handed, look at the diagrams in a mirror.

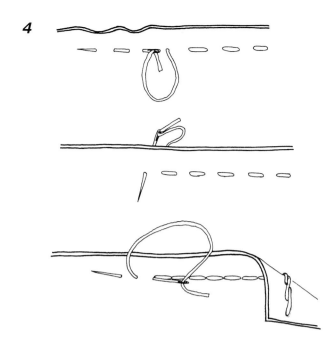

4

4. Running stitch, stab stitch, and backstitch

a. **Running stitch** is rarely used for construction as it is weak and sloppy on all but thin materials, though it can be reinforced with a backstitch every few stitches. Work horizontally making several stitches at a time.

b. **Stab stitch** is good for holding together multiple layers, such as the folded edges of lined garments. Work at right angles to the material and pull the thread through after each insertion, making one stitch at a time.

c. **Backstitch** can be used as an alternative to straight machine stitching, especially on visible edges. Work horizontally, backwards then forwards as shown.

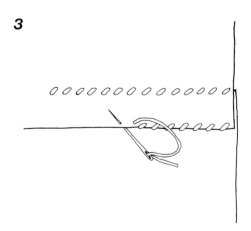

3

3. Lapping a seam

An application of hemming stitch, worked on raw edges laid flat and overlapping by 1 to 2 cm. Mainly for coarse, fraying wools. Can be decorative when worked with coloured yarn. Tack the overlapped edges together and work one row of hemming on each side.

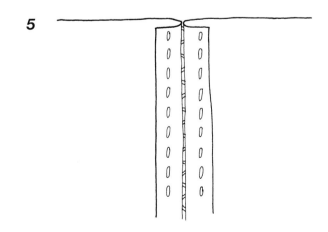

5

5. Triple-run seams

Three rows of running stitch (or backstitch for the join) are used to make a flat seam. It is commonly used for the main leg seams of hose.

6. Two-stage seams

These give a flat, fully-enclosed finish for linens and lightweight wools. They are worked in two stages.

6a

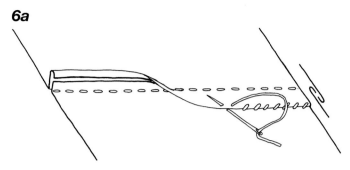

a. Run-and-fell seam, worked on the wrong side of the garment. Work machine stitching or running stitch along the fitting line. Trim one seam allowance as shown, fold the other one over it and hem it down.

b. & c. Seam-and-fell seam, worked on the right and the wrong side. This classic linen seam is slower to work, but stronger than run-and-fell. For *b*, fold the seam allowances as shown and oversew the folded edges on the right side. For c, open out the fabric and flatten the oversewing. Turn over the fabric and hem down the other folded seam allowance on the wrong side.

b

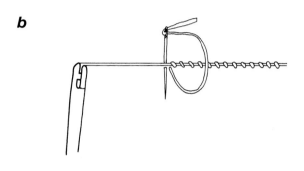

c

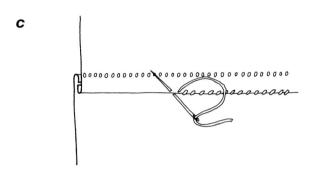

Making up, Figs 7-15

Details about making up will be found in the text and captions for many individual garments, in particular for those earlier ones planned without a Block.

> For fitted garments made from a personal Block, you will normally follow this assembly sequence:
> • Identify the cut pieces, marking them on the wrong side with chalk
> • Attach any interlining to the parts
> • Make up the body by sewing the shoulder, side, centre front and back seams (leaving an opening for putting the garment on where necessary)
> • Make up and attach the collar (if any)
> • Make up and set in the sleeves
> • Finish with lining, hem and fastenings

Waist seams – The hip sections of doublets are sewn onto the body sections before the body is made up, whereas the skirts of kirtles with waist seams are made up and sewn to the completed body.

Setting in sleeves – Figs 7 & 8 show the setting in of simple sleeves with the seam at the underarm.

Most set in sleeves in this book are made from the sleeve Block and have the seam at the back. First pin the seam to the Back Point on the armhole, and to any other balance point (Shoulder Point). Starting from the Back Point pin the lower armhole curves, then up over the shoulder, easing in the sleeve. Remember to match fitting lines, not edges. Adjust if necessary before tacking and stitching.

Setting in simple sleeves

7. Sleeves with gussets – making up and setting in by hand

All stitching is shown from the inside.

a. Sew one edge, A, of the gusset to one long edge of the sleeve (at the shoulder end for a shaped sleeve). Use one of the two-stage seams above, folding the seam allowances towards the sleeve. End the stitching slightly before the edge of the gusset and snip into the sleeve seam allowance as shown.

b. Pin and stitch the sleeve seam, catching in the gusset edge B. Fold the seam allowance towards the gusset. Try not to pucker the join with seam A.

c. The finished sleeve with gusset.

d. Set the finished sleeve into the armhole with the two-stage seam, folding the seam allowances towards the body of the garment and making a neat corner at the bottom of the gusset.

7a

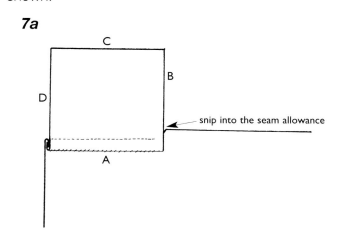

snip into the seam allowance

c

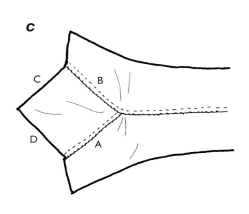

b

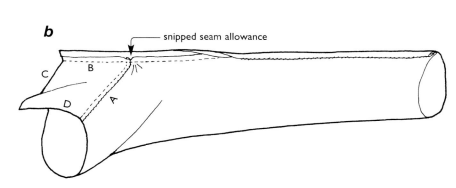

snipped seam allowance

d

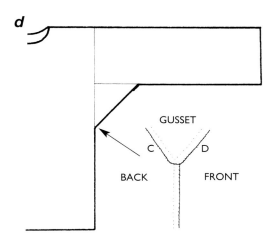

GUSSET

BACK   FRONT

8. Sleeves with gussets – making up and setting in by machine

Stitch one side of the gusset to the sleeve, and stitch the flat sleeve to the body. Match the garment shoulder line to the sleeve Centre line, indicated by a fine broken line. Tack the seams, carefully matching the gusset to the underarm. Stitch the side seams and sleeve seams in one, pivoting the work round the machine needle at the corners.

8

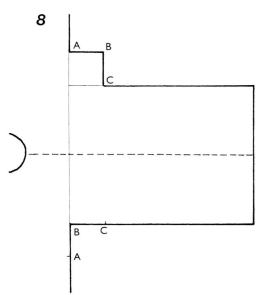

Finishing raw edges

9

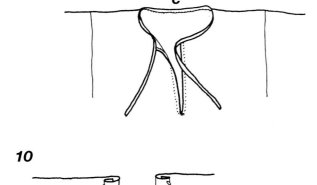

9. Binding

Used for finishing, including slit openings, head-wear, etc. by enclosing raw edges (single or multi-layered) with a strip of fabric, ribbon or braid.

a. Straight strip of fabric, with raw edges turned in and stitched; here eased round the end of a slit.

b. Ribbon pleated to fit a curved edge.

c. Binding used as a neck finish and fastening on a shirt, with the fabric extended to form ties. Hem the narrow binding over the neck edge and oversew the extensions.

10

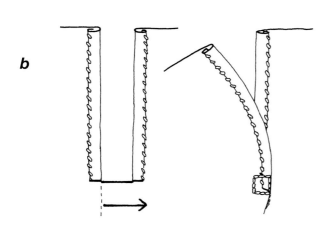

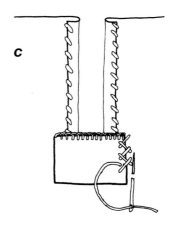

10. Finishes for slit openings

Methods to avoid tearing of slit openings on unlined garments.

a. For linen or lightweight cloth. Hem the sides of the plain slit, taper the hems to nothing at the base and reinforce it with blanket stitch (shown in progress).

b. For almost any material. Cut the slit in at the base on each side. Hem the sides and fold the base across to form a pleat. Stab-stitch this in place through all layers.

c. For heavier cloths. Hem down the raw edges and sew a patch at the base with blanket or herringbone stitch (shown in progress).

Slits for fitchets, slashes for sleeves,
These slits (*Surcotes*, Fig 5; *Gowns*, Fig 18) are
worked on the finished garment. Put the garment
on the wearer and mark the planned position of
the slit with pins, if possible on the straight grain
of the fabric.

Take off the garment and check the length and
position of the slits match on both sides, and that
all layers of fabric are lying correctly. Tack round
the position of each slit – like a giant buttonhole
– stitching through all layers. Cut the slit inside
the tacking. Oversew or blanket stitch the raw
edges, or turn in narrow edges and stitch. For
finishing lined edges see Pl. 1. On sleeves the slash
can be bound (Fig 9) or edged with fur, p.53.

Plate 1. Lined edge finished in stab stitch
Lined garments are normally finished by turning in the raw edges together and
hand-stitching close to the folded edge. This gives a flat, firm edge on necklines,
cuffs, hems and head-wear as well as on slit openings.

Interlining

Interlining (interfacing), Fig 11

Both terms are used for extra layers of material, added through all or part of a garment, to increase weight or stiffness. For good quality doublets use canvas or calico throughout, with extra layers for high collars. For a tight-fitting kirtle bodice use heavy canvas, and soft wool to add weight and bulk to a large gown.

Always cut the interlining on the same grain as the outer material. It is best if both layers are caught together with regular rows of pad-stitching or large herringbone stitches before making up. After stitching the seams, trim the interlining close to the stitching to reduce bulk; and on edges trim the interlining to the fitting line before finishing.

Interlining flat pieces, Fig 13

Parts of dress such as cuffs, collars, some head-wear and accessories are often interlined to stiffen them and also lined. Depending on its purpose, the interlining can be anything from linen canvas to heavy buckram: if it is too heavy to tack through easily, hold the covering materials in place with clothes pegs or spring clips. If the outer material is to be decorated with embroidery or braiding, work this before you make up the shape, if necessary through the interlining.

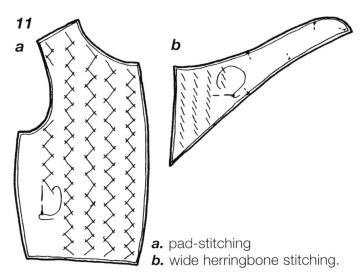

a. pad-stitching
b. wide herringbone stitching.

11. Interlining
For large pattern pieces the interlining should be permanently attached by regular rows of stitches so the two layers of material will work as one. Use tiny stitches, which will not show on the right side.

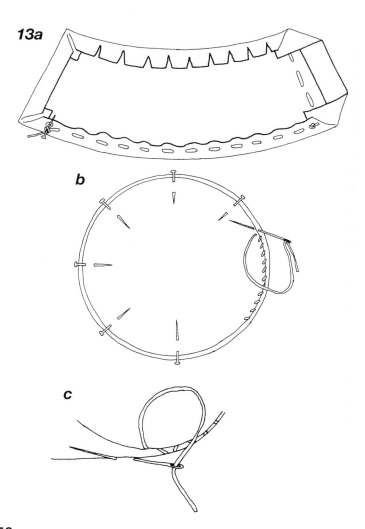

13. Interlining, lining and joining flat pieces
Cut three layers: the outer material, with seam allowances; the stiff interlining of buckram or canvas, without seam allowances or very slightly undersized; and a lightweight lining, again with seam allowances.
a. Interlining a (curved) shape. Tack the interlining to the outer material as shown. Turn the seam allowances over the interlining, snipping or gathering the edges as needed. Tack again through the seam allowances to secure them, then pin the lining in place.
b. Lining a (round) shape, already interlined.
Smooth out the lining so that all three layers lie flat on the same grain. Start by pinning the halves and quarters along the straight grain, then place further pins between them. Hem the lining onto the seam allowances of the outer fabric, just inside the folded edge.
c. Joining completed parts. If they are too stiff to pin, use bulldog clips or clothes pegs to hold the parts in position. Use slip stitch to draw them together as shown.

Lining

Lining, Fig 12, Pl 1

The lining is normally cut to the same shape as the outer layer of the garment. If you don't use a complete pattern for the garment cut the outer material and use this as a pattern for the lining.

Make up the lining separately. Put it inside the garment with the wrong sides together, smoothing the layers and pinning them along the seams (Fig 12, Pl 1). Turn in the seam allowances round the edges, tack the two layers together and stitch them from the right side. This method will avoid the bag-like effect, especially for large hems, that can be produced by machining in the lining from the wrong side.

For doublets with eyelets round the lower edge, cut extra seam allowances on the outer material and fold this to the inside for 2-3 cm. Make the lining correspondingly shorter (Fig 12).

For long garments with wide hems it is best to pin or tack the lining in as described, leaving them on a hanger or dress-stand overnight to let the skirts drop. Stitch the lining into the neck and armholes, and sleeves; lay the garment flat and smooth the two layers together, matching the seams and pinning if necessary for their whole length. Trim both layers level, leaving 3-5 cm seam allowance, and turn in the two edges before stitching them together. If you prefer, fold the lining slightly shorter than the outer fabric and hem it down. Despite the length it is still worth finishing the hem by hand: if the lining eventually starts to sag and show round the edge it is easier to unpick.

Lining close-fitting sleeves

An alternative lining method for close-fitting set-in sleeves, as on a doublet (Doublets, Fig 9), is to make up each sleeve with its lining, finish off the wrist edge and the shoulder puff (if included), and set the completed sleeves into the armholes.

Make up the lining of the body and pin it into the outer layer; turn in the seam allowances round the armholes, and hem the lining into place. This is a good alternative with any set-in sleeve.

Facings

Facings are used to neaten edges on the inside of unlined garments. The medieval tailor used narrow facing strips, cut on the straight grain, since shaped ones were unknown. Being narrow they could be eased round curved edges without much difficulty.

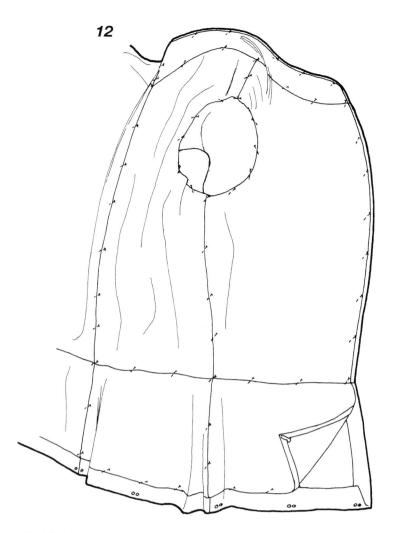

12

12. Lining

The inside of a doublet with the lining pinned in place. Pin, tack, and stitch the lining to the garment round the collar, waist seam and armholes before hemming or top-stitching the edges. Shorten the lining at the lower edge so that the eyelets (to attach hose) can be worked through the unlined folded edge.

Use narrow strips of linen or plain silk, perhaps 3 cm wide (with narrow seam allowances), but allow enough width for any buttonholes. Join the strip to the garment edge at the fitting line on the right side of the fabric, turn it to the inside and hem down the folded edge. Fig 21 shows a faced edge with buttonholes.

Collars and cuffs, Fig 14

Guide to the construction of collars on tailored garments, mainly doublets and gowns. Those for linens are included with the garment.

A tailored collar consists of three layers: under collar, interlining and upper collar (facing). Collars are either standing or lie flat.

- The **under collar** is attached to or is a continuation of the garment's outer fabric, and is normally cut from the same fabric. The under collar is visible on a standing collar.
- The **interlining** is sewn to the wrong side of the under collar before making up, and may be in more than one layer.

- The **facing** (upper collar) completes the collar. It may match the garment's outer fabric or lining, or be in a contrasting fabric. It is the visible part of a flat collar, but is the inside on a standing collar.

The **neck edge** is sewn to the neck of the garment. The **outer** or **top edge** is the free edge of the collar.

Tack the interlining to the under collar pieces and make up the under collar. Sew the under collar to the neck edge of the garment; trim off the seam allowances from the interlining up to the seam lines.

Make up the facing and pin it in place,

14. Making up collars

a. 2-piece collars (*Doublets,* Fig 4; *Gowns,* Fig 4; *Children,* Fig 7). See also *Gowns,* Fig 13)

Round collars – Sew the bodice CB and shoulder seams. Sew together the interlined under-collar pieces at CB. Attach the under-collar to the garment matching CB, CF and any balance marks. Tack and stitch the collar to the neckline, taking care to ease the curves. Complete with the facing

14a

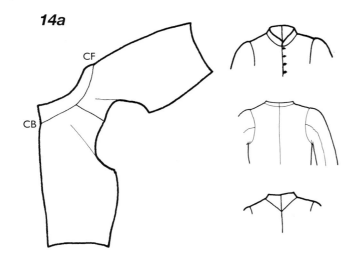

b

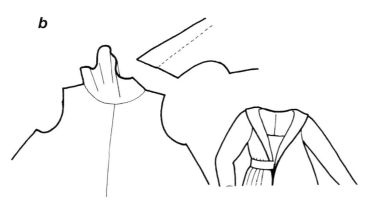

Collars with a V-back – It is easier to start by joining the garment backs and fronts at their shoulder edges, then sew each interlined collar half to the bodice neck edges before sewing the collar CB seam. Take care to match the seams, then add the lining.

b. 3-piece collars (*Gowns,* Figs 24, 28). For Fig 24, where the front under collars are part of the gown Front, first sew the bodice CB seam, then sew the back under collar to the back neck edge. Join the Backs and Fronts at the shoulders, including the back and front collar ends. If the lining fabric is used for facing, make it up as for the outer fabric. When inserting the lining, tack round the neck and finish the CF edges and collar in one.

Gowns, Fig 28 is a different 3-piece collar. Make it up as described in its caption.

c. 4-piece collars (*Doublets*, Fig 6; *Gowns,* Fig 12). If these have a V-back, set them on like a 2-piece collar. Join the shoulder seams of the garment, and the side seams of the under collar. Sew each half under collar to the garment neck edge before sewing the CB seam of bodice and collar in one. For high collars needing extra interlining, add this before attaching the facing.

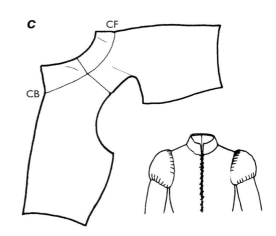

carefully matching all seams. Turn in and tack the raw outer edges, then topstitch or slipstitch the facing to the under collar. Tack the facing round the neck edge to hold it in place before putting in the garment lining.

For a facing of fur, put the garment lining in first.

Cuffs – The cuffs on later women's gowns (Gowns, Fig 28) are made up like collars. The *under cuff* is visible when the cuff is worn down over the hand, and the *facing* is visible when the cuff is drawn back over the sleeve. These may be extensions of the sleeve and its lining, or separate pieces.

Stomachers, Fig 15

These were worn by women, and sometimes men, in the middle and later 15th century. They consisted of a visible piece of material, usually brightly coloured or patterned, lined and interlined as described above. The shape is based on the pattern of the gown or doublet it is worn with (*Gowns,* Fig 24; *Children,* Fig 10).

15. Stomacher

Stomacher for a woman's low-necked gown, second half of 15th century. The shape will depend on the opening in the garment worn with it. The (embroidered) outer fabric is made up over a fabric interlining and backed with a lining (as shown), see Fig 13.

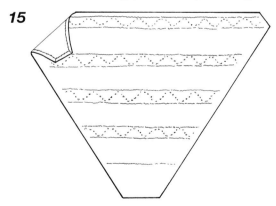

15

Working with fur

There are different techniques for real fur and fur fabric, which is made on a knitted backing. Both are made up with the pile running down the garment, and on collars and cuffs the fur is cut in wedge-shaped sections to keep the direction of the pile consistent.

The fur lining should extend beyond the edge of the garment so it can be turned to enclose the edge on sleeve ends and hems. For slashed openings on sleeves add a band of fur to bind the edge.

On both fur and fur fabric, mark and cut the pattern shapes on the wrong side. Lift the scissors slightly to keep the lower blade close to the backing and avoid cutting the pile more than you can help. Cut fur fabric with normal seam allowances and stitch the seams as for other fabrics. Pick the pile out of the stitching and trim it off the seam allowances to reduce the bulk. Cut real fur with little or no seam allowances and oversew the edges together on the wrong side. You don't need a leather needle: if the skin is so thick it is too heavy for lining.

Fastenings, Figs 16-21

Many early garments had no fastenings, but were controlled by a belt. They might be held at the neck with a brooch clasp. In the late 13th century tight-fitting fashionable sleeves would be fastened by sewing round the forearm. Sewing was also used to fasten tight-fitting cotes round the body.

For sewn fastenings hem the edges of the opening and stitch them together with a strong thread each time the garment is put on.

Lacing and eyelets, Figs 16-18

As 14th century clothing became increasingly fitted, lacing tended to replace sewing as a fastening. It was discreet and purely functional. As a practical fastening, lacing is a good way to close a fitted garment and works best under tension. It is used on fitted cotes, doublets and kirtles more often than on outer garments.

Lacing on doublets was normally at the centre front; on cotes it seems to have been at the side or centre back. On kirtles the position of the lacing depended on the style, but back lacing seems to have been unusual. It is possible to fasten side-lacing on yourself if you thread it from the top down.

The riveted metal eyelet is a modern invention: the medieval tailor worked eyelets by hand. The lace or cord can be a leather thong, a narrow tape, or a handmade cord (see below). A round braided boot lace will do, or for good quality clothing buy 3-ply rayon cord from a haberdasher and split it into separate strands. Anything other than leather will need aglets – tag ends which prevent fraying and ease threading. These can be made from short lengths of fine brass tubing, obtainable from model shops. Work the end of the lace to a point with a little beeswax, or all-purpose glue, to insert it into the tube. File the cut ends smooth and crimp the aglet firmly onto your lace or cord. If you buy your aglets, ensure they are of plain bronze and will fit through the eyelets.

Lacing and eyelets

16

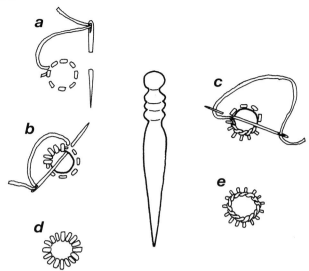

16. Working eyelets

Trim down the seam allowances and hem or top stitch the garment edges, to reduce bulk. Mark the eyelet positions with pins, not more than 3 cm apart and within 15 mm of the garment edge. Use a heavy top-stitching or buttonhole thread.

a. Outline the eyelet with a ring of stab-stitching and force the weave apart with a stiletto, centre. If you can't find one, a neatly sharpened stick will do. Push steadily, from either side in turn, until the hole almost reaches the stitching at the edge.

b. & c. Use oversewing *(b)* or blanket stitch *(c)* to reinforce the opening. Lay the stitches so they just touch round the hole. Bring up the thread just outside the ring of stab-stitch. Pull each stitch tight.

d. & e. Completed eyelets; oversewn *(d)* and blanket stitched *(e)*. They should form a small, tight ring; finish off the thread with a few small stitches on the back.

Eyelets are also used on mantles, for cords or metal ornaments to pass through, and for the buckle pins on fabric belts. The latter are generally made on a firm foundation, so for this you need to make a hole with a leather punch before stitching round it.

17. Methods of lacing

Tie one end of the lace into the lowest eyelet and pass the other end through each eyelet on alternate sides, as shown. At the top thread back through one eyelet and tie a knot. The edges of the garment are shown open for clarity, but should meet in wear.

a. The usual method, with the lace passed through each side in turn.

b. The lace passes through two eyelets on each side in turn, to form a 'ladder'.

c. Concealed lacing. This came with the fitted gowns of the late 15th century: tiny brass rings were sewn inside the front opening of the gown and the lace passed through them in a 'ladder' as in *b*. The smallest brass curtain rings can be used for this.

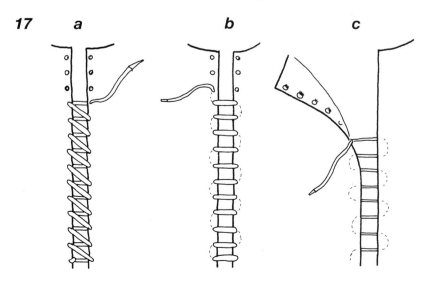

18. Latchet fastening and garters

Latchet fastening was used on men's doublets, especially for tying on hose. The short laces for latchet fastening are known as 'points'.

On the front of a doublet work pairs of eyelets on each edge at regular intervals, not more than 10 cm apart. Work nine pairs round the hip edge of the doublet and the top of joined hose. Add more to close the hose front opening and secure the codpiece. Use the materials specified under Lacing and eyelets, 20-25 cm long and with aglets on both ends.

Garters were worn by women to hold up short hose, and sometimes by men to pull in loose hose, or just for show.

a. Shaped point, cut from hide, for heavy-duty wear.

b. Loop for heavy points which will not slip undone.

c. Half bow for finer cords (with aglets), here looped through single eyelets.

d. Tied garter of worsted braid, and buckled garter with embroidered motto.

18a

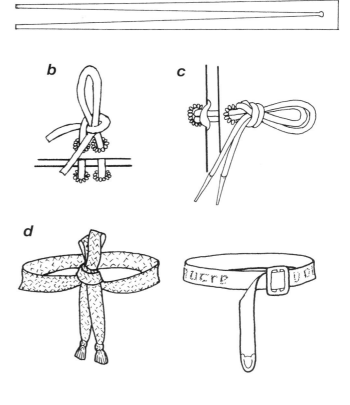

Garters, Fig 18d

These were worn just below the knee and over the calf muscle to support short hose, by women and sometimes by men. Simple garters were strips of soft braid or fabric tied in place. More elaborate garters were made like miniature belts, with buckles, tag ends, and straps of silk braid or embroidery.

Buttons & buttonholes, Figs 19-21, Pls 2, 3

Buttons replaced sewing up as a wrist fastening for fitted sleeves in the 14th century, when a dozen per sleeve was quite normal for the clothes of the wealthy. In the 15th century this decreased to just one or two buttons at the wrist.

The first garment to be closed by buttons was the cotehardie, where they were set very close together, followed by the early gown. After 1400 buttons appeared on the workman's frock or coat. He often had just five, a number easy to position between neck and waist by folding.

The medieval button seems to have been round, with a loop or shank to sew it on, so modern pierced buttons are inappropriate. Buttons were sewn to the very edge of the garment and the buttonholes worked close to the other edge (Pls 2 & 3). The buttonholes were almost always on the wearer's left, for both sexes.

Buttons were often of cloth, or of cast metal. Some modern buttons make convincing substitutes, but they should be small and at least *look* like metal; or cast reproduction buttons can be obtained from traders. Instead of sewing on metal buttons, you could work eyelets in the garment, pass the button shanks through them and hold them in place behind with a cord threaded through the shanks.

Hooks and eyes

Hooks and eyes have existed since prehistoric times: in the 15th century they provided hidden fastenings on gowns. As they are hidden, ordinary large hooks and eyes are suitable for most uses. To avoid the garment slipping open sew hooks and eyes alternately, 5 to 10 cm apart, to each edge.

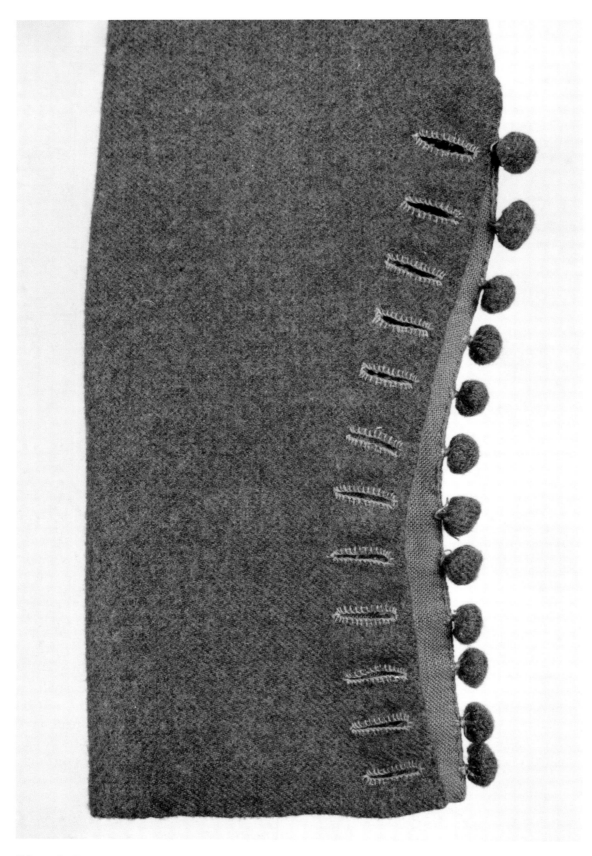

Plate 2. Fastening for a mitten sleeve

A mitten sleeve, shown unbuttoned. It was worn more by women (*Kirtles,* Fig 2), but also seen on men. The buttonholes are very close to the garment edge: their ends are whipped, not barred. Note how the buttons are sewn on the very edge.

Plate 3. **Partly buttoned mitten sleeve**
In wear the buttons would pull to the ends of the buttonholes, standing prominently
down the outside of the arm. More than a dozen might be worn, sometimes set so
closely that they touched.

Buttons and buttonholes

19

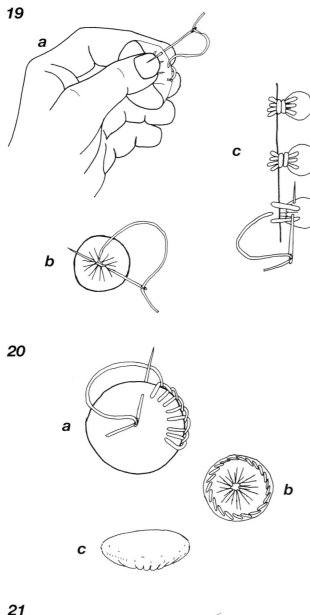

20

21

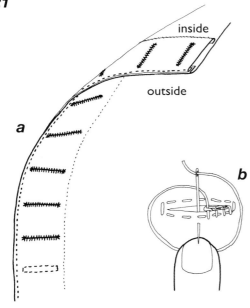

19. Ball buttons of cloth

The finished button may be from 6 to 15 mm in diameter; anything larger needs too big a buttonhole. Work a few samples first. Use the garment fabric. Most wools are suitable, but for heavy or bulky cloth make flat buttons (Fig 20). Light fabric or silk may need padding with a pellet of cotton wool.

Make each button from a circle of cloth, 2.5 to 6 cm in diameter, using one circle as a pattern to ensure they are all the same size. Use a strong topstitching or buttonhole thread and sew each button on as you complete it.

a. Turn in the edge of the circle, a little at a time, working long stitches (8 to 10 in all) through the folded edge, drawing them up a little as you go. Pull them up tightly, pushing the raw edges to the inside and working the button between your fingers to form it.

b. Make a few tight stitches through the back to secure the gathered edge.

c. Sew the button to the edge of the garment, whipping round the stitches to make a shank.

20. Flat buttons of cloth

Use one of these for large buttons on cloaks, or as an alternative to ball buttons.

a. Blanket stitch together two or three circles of thick cloth.

b. For fine linen or silk, gather the folded edge of a circle and draw it up tightly. Flatten it out and backstitch round the edge to stiffen it (back view).

c. Gather and draw up a circle of cloth round a disc of wood or a plastic button. Useful for strong cloak buttons, also suitable for 15th-century doublet sleeves if made of linen over a small button.

21. Buttonholes

These were worked very close to the edge and at right angles to it.

a. Buttonholes on a narrow facing stitched to the inside of the garment, or they can be worked through a lined edge. Trim the seam allowances well to reduce the bulk. Space the buttonholes from 1 to 3 cm (maximum) apart. You can reinforce the edge by sewing on a tiny braid.

b. Working the buttonhole. Outline it in stab stitch before cutting the slit. Work the sides in buttonhole stitch, as shown, and oversew a few stitches round each end.

58

Decorations

Embroidery, Figs 22, 23

Even the simplest garments were often decorated, while spectacular embroideries were added on royal and noble dress. Less expensively, but still for the wealthy, a garment could be 'powdered' all over with a repeated motif or finished with deep embroidered borders, which were worked separately and applied to the garment. For the less wealthy there was still scope for embellishment, with fancy stitching round the neck and sleeves, or bands of ribbon or contrasting cloth applied to edges and hems.

Work simple stitches (Fig 22) in a contrasting colour. Use embroidery wool (crewel or tapestry) for any woollen cloth, coton perlé or stranded silk on finer fabrics. Bands of more elaborate embroidery can be worked by hand or machine directly onto the garment or, more conveniently, onto strips of material to be applied later. For suitable designs look at contemporary sculptures and book illuminations, as well as needlework; the scrolling stem design is a common feature (Fig 23).

Cable stitch is a useful machine embroidery technique. Wind a thick thread such as coton perlé onto the bobbin (the bottom thread) and work the design from the wrong side with a normal sewing thread in the needle. On the right side this looks like hand couching.

For strips of embroidery to be applied later, trace the design onto light iron-on interlining and apply it to the back of the material. This will give you the design to follow and support the material when sewn onto the garment.

Programmable sewing machines offer the possibility of repeated spot patterns or more elaborate borders. Really elaborate embroidery, whether by hand or machine, is a specialist skill. It needs to be done well to look convincing.

22. Simple stitch decoration

Use an embroidery stitch you know, or one of these:

a. Stem stitch.

b. Two rows of stem stitch with French knots.

c. Chain stitch: very effective in thick yarn.

d. Zigzag stitch, a form of back stitch producing a double line on the other side.

22

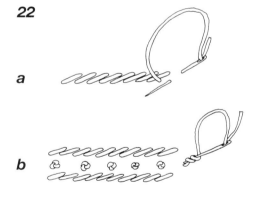

a

b

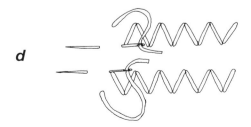

c

d

23. Band and border patterns

Examples like these can be scaled up or down and worked by hand or machine.

23

59

24

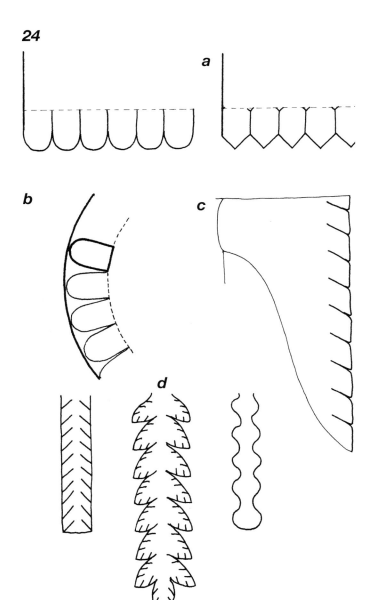

Dagging, Fig 24, Pl 4

Dagging appeared about the middle of the 14th century and continued into the early 15th (*Cotehardies*, Fig 2; *Gowns*, Fig 8). It was first seen round the capes of hoods, then on the hems of short cotehardies and sometimes on cloaks. It was more common on men's dress. The huge open sleeves seen on some gowns were often edged with round or square shapes.

24. Dagging

On hoods and some hems dagging would normally be left raw. Any lining can end before the dagging (at the broken lines), or the lining and outer fabric can be tacked and cut as one, and the edges overcast. On gowns with wide open sleeves and dagged hems the dagging would be edged with fancy stitching or narrow braid, or with the fur lining turned out to edge the shapes.

 Decide the depth of the cut, 5-10 cm. At this depth measure the length to be dagged and mark regular divisions, 5-8 cm apart. Cut a template and draw round it on the cloth with tailor's chalk, checking the spacing before you cut.

a. Simple shapes for hems and edges. Pl 4 shows a more elaborate shape, suitable only for non-fraying cloth.

b. Curved edges, such as the cape of a hood. The template is positioned on a guideline.

c. Open sleeves of gowns generally have the dagging slanted downwards.

d. Streamers for hanging from head wear or gown armholes. The central (leaf) pattern has additional cuts made into each shape.

Plate 4. Dagged edge of chaperon in Pl 19
An elaborate shape made in black broadcloth, which will not fray easily.

60

Small-wares & other techniques, Figs 25-27

This summarises techniques for making trims, fastenings and accessories. Many modern commercial products are structurally identical to medieval forms, so making these yourself is by no means essential. Specialist books on the techniques are listed in the Bibliography.

Small-wares

Narrow looms for weaving ribbons and tapes did exist and were occasionally illustrated. Tapes were woven in linen, and ribbon in silk or worsted, but modern cotton tape can be used. Narrow silk ribbons are available; otherwise look for rayon as it is not as stiff and shiny as polyester.

Cords and laces, Figs 25, 26

Mainly used for lacing, purse-strings and sewing to garment edges as trimming. They include round and flat versions. The round braids are comparable to Japanese Kumihimo braiding, or the wider forms of finger-looping. The lucet, or chain fork, was used to produce round cords similar to French knitting.

Tablet weaving

An ancient and widely-used technique for making bands, often with elaborate patterns. Worsted, linen or silk tablet-woven bands were used for belts, for fillets (headbands), for purse strings and for sewing onto clothing.

Netting

This is an ancient technique, and nets were used for hunting, storage and cooking, as well as in dress. Hair nets of silk thread were widely worn in the 14th and 15th centuries.

Netting was worked with a shuttle, and a mesh gauge which regulated the size of the stitches. Tools and information may now be hard to find.

Knitting

Our knowledge of medieval knitting is limited. Knitting of caps was established in the 14th century and widespread in the 15th. Caps were knitted in the round on four or more needles, then fulled (felted) and brushed to give them a napped finish. Other items such as leggings, mittens and socks may also have been knitted.

25. Finger-looped cords

The drawings are opened out here to show the structure, but both should be pulled up tightly when working. The two-stranded method will make a square cord. Both should be worked under tension, with the starting end attached to a fixed point.

a. One stranded

b. Two stranded, using two colours. Knot the two strands together, then form a loop from strand 1, insert a loop from strand 2 into it, and pull strand 1 tight. Insert a loop from strand 1 and tighten strand 2 round it. Continue forming alternate loops and tightening them. You can insert the loops either from above or from beneath, but be consistent. Practise to achieve an even finish.

26. Plaiting

This is a basic method. Knot the starting ends together, attaching them to a fixed point to keep the work under tension. For the 3-stranded plait shown, lay the left and right strands alternately to the centre.

The method can be worked with four or five strands to make a flat band.

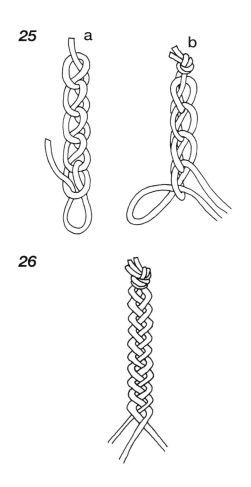

25   a   b

26

Tassels, Fig 27

Simple tassels like the one shown appear in threes on the lower edges of purse-bags. More elaborate ones for the ends of mantle laces (*Cloaks,* Fig 2) can be found in soft furnishing shops.

Mending, Figs 28, 29

This was important at a time when clothes were too valuable to replace if worn or damaged. Patching seems to have been the usual method, and it would have been more important to match the weight of the material than the colour. Careful mending looks far more 'authentic' than tattered clothes.

The commonest job is repairing split hose: don't just pull the edges together and oversew them, as this puts them under further strain and they will split again.

28. Patching

Patches from heavy fabric can be cut without seam allowances. For all fabrics make the patch square on the grain, and match this to the grain of the garment.

a. On lighter fabrics turn in the allowances before pinning.

b. Pin and hem the patch down on the right side.

c. Turn over to the wrong side. Trim away the ragged edges, snip into the corners, turn them in slightly and hem them to the patch.

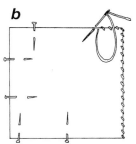
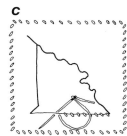

29. Mending hose

a. Hose normally tear along the grain, so match the patch to the grain.

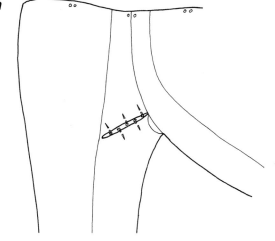

27. Making a tassel

You can use more than one colour, to match a braid for example.

a. Wind the thread round a cardboard template, enclosing the tying-off thread.

b. Slide the tassel off the template, using the thread to tie it tightly. Bind another thread round the tassel and tie it to form a 'neck'.

c. Finished tassel with the loops cut and trimmed.

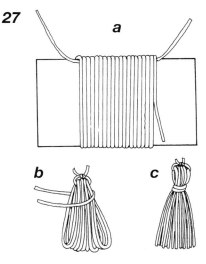

b. Pin then tack it in place before darning down the torn edges. Work the darning unevenly, as shown: if the rows end in a neat line the hose may tear again along that. Trim the patch to just outside the darning, leaving the edges raw.

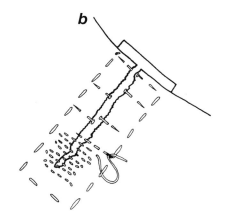

Materials

Most textiles in the Middle Ages were made by specialised craftsmen, so the quality was generally good. Even cheaper cloths were evenly spun and densely woven; more expensive ones were distinguished by finer spinning and brighter colours.

Wool and linen were the mainstay of most people's wardrobes, with silk becoming commoner in the late middle ages. Methods of production were changing throughout the period so different types of material were available at different times: what follows is a brief summary of these changes, and of what to look for today.

Wool

Woollen textiles have been produced from prehistoric times, and worn as outer clothing. Until the 14th century the fleece was generally combed before spinning, which laid the fibres parallel to spin a fairly smooth yarn, often highly twisted. Much of this yarn was woven into twill (Fig 1) or more elaborate weaves.

By the end of the 13th century, cloth production in England had dropped off and cloth was being imported from the Low Countries. This was the new 'broadcloth', woven using thread which was carded instead of combed, then spun on a wheel to give a soft, fluffy thread. When the cloth was fulled the fibres felted themselves together to give a firm, even surface. The surface was often made still smoother by raising a nap and shearing, and it was this 'finishing' which distinguished broadcloth. Broadloom weaving itself was introduced to England during the 1330s, replacing the older upright looms.

Combed yarns continued to be used to weave the fine, smooth fabrics called worsteds, and plain weave cloths remained in production for cheaper clothing. These might be woven from ready-dyed yarns to produce stripes or checks, while broadcloth was usually dyed after weaving. The most expensive dyes were only used on the finest cloths and many cheaper materials were used undyed.

Choosing your material

A wide range of pure wool fabrics is still made, but wool and polyester blends are often cheaper and can look just as good, though cloth for hose should be pure wool as it has more stretch. Wools and wool blends are almost always woven to the traditional broadcloth width of 140-160 cm.

1. Weave structures

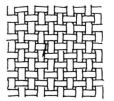

a. Tabby or plain weave

b. 2/2 twill

c. 3/1 twill

d. Satin

There are three main types.

Woollen cloth – Any woollen cloth or blend with a visible weave, tabby or twill (Fig 1) and a more or less hairy surface. The threads should be well packed together, though cloth intended for lining can be flimsier. A density of 6-15 threads per cm is typical for a working garment: a higher density is for finer garments. Use the coarser cloth for cotes and surcotes, for cheaper garments of any period, and for linings. Fine quality twill cloth is best for hose, and thick, hairy cloth makes warm cloaks.

Broadcloth – This is likely to be pure wool, and more expensive. Here the weave structure is not visible and the surface is either smooth and felt-like (Melton type), or with a fine velvety pile (faced cloth). Use broadcloth for good quality outer garments of the 14th and 15th centuries, and especially for 15th-century gowns. Heavy Melton makes excellent cloaks.

Worsted – A lighter, smoother fabric made with combed yarn, often blended with polyester. Worsteds may come in tabby or twill weave or even with a satin finish (Fig 1): use them for better quality cotes, doublets and kirtles, and lightweight gowns for warm weather.

Colours

Woollen cloth can be found undyed in the natural cream, brown or grey of the fleece: this is ideal for peasant clothing. Otherwise almost any colour can be used except bright pinks and mauves. For ordinary clothing blues, greens of any shade, yellow, orange and pink as well as drab colours are suitable. Black and red were expensive to dye so should only be used for better quality clothing. Look out for striped cloth, which is rare now but was fashionable in the mid 14th century.

Linen, canvas and cotton

The use of vegetable fibres for textiles is even more ancient than the use of wool. Linen is made from the stem fibres of the flax plant, and canvas from those of hemp. Both produce smooth fabrics which absorb water freely without shrinking, so are washable. Neither takes dye as readily as wool or silk, so they were most often used undyed and often unbleached.

Canvas could not be spun as fine or bleached as white as linen so it was used by poorer people for clothes, and for tents, sails and packaging. Linen and canvas were likely to be woven in narrow widths (50-100 cm). Fine linens for kerchiefs and veils could be woven with frilled selvedges: these could be seen from about 1300 and were particularly popular in the later 14th century. Both fabrics were used for body linens (shirts, smocks and braies) depending on the status of the wearer, and finer linens were used for women's head-dresses. Heavier linens and canvas were used for lining, interlining and stiffening in tailored garments. None of these materials seem to have been used for visible outer garments such as surcotes or gowns, but were probably used for some kirtles and doublets. Both linen and canvas were made in England during the Middle Ages, but the best linen was produced in the Low Countries.

Contemporary references to 'cotton' probably mean a lightweight woollen cloth with a fluffy finish which was used for linings. Real cotton had to be imported and was not common and the only cotton fabric in general use was fustian, a twill with a fine silky nap. By the later 15th century fustian from Naples was cheap enough for workmen's doublets.

These fabrics were most often used undyed, either unbleached or white. Blue linen was sometimes used for peasants' shirts in the 14th century and black buckram (a fairly heavy linen) and fustian are known from the 15th. Other colours were produced, but apparently not in quantity.

Choosing your material

Although linen and canvas are specified, cotton fabrics look perfectly good and are easier to get. Whichever you buy, closely-packed threads will wear better than loosely-woven fabrics. Polyester-cotton blends are not satisfactory as they are too shiny and don't crease enough, but blends of linen and viscose can look and feel like pure linen. For body linens and head-dresses a firm cotton sheeting or bleached calico will do very well, or a cotton lawn for best. All these fabrics may be found in widths from 90 cm (especially the finer ones) to 150 cm, or even more if they are woven for sheeting. See *A note about selvedges* below.

Linen tailoring canvas is still made in various weights, but at a price: for interlining unbleached calico is much cheaper. Heavy cotton canvas is useful for stiffening collars, and the bodices of later kirtles. No modern equivalent of fustian exists, but a soft twill cotton or linen fabric can be used instead for doublets.

Colours

White or unbleached fabric is usual for body linens and head-dresses. Note that both unbleached linen and hemp are brown or fawn-grey, not the yellowish colour of unbleached cotton. Avoid brightly-coloured linens: use white or unbleached, or perhaps blue, grey or black.

Silk

Silks were already reaching the British Isles in small quantities during the Dark Ages. Although the quantities later increased, silk remained a luxury which even the wealthiest people kept for best. Plain silks in tabby, twill or satin weave (Fig 1) were used for linings and facings on good quality garments. Patterned silks were elaborate and varied. Examples from the 13th and 14th centuries include circles or geometric shapes enclosing birds, beasts or castles; large scenes of angels, hunters with hounds, or animals; and all-over scrolling leaf designs. Silk takes dye readily, so the colours were varied and bright.

By the late 13th century Italian weavers had developed the technique of silk velvet weaving. The first record of velvet in Britain appeared in the royal accounts in the 1330s, but it was unusual for clothing and was used more as a furnishing fabric. During the 14th century Italian silk weaving continued to progress and by the 15th an assortment of sumptuous fabrics was available. These included damask, a single-coloured fabric with a subtle pattern in the weave; brocades, usually woven in two colours but sometimes more; velvet upon velvet, with the pattern in cut and uncut pile; and cloth-of-gold with the pattern worked in a looped pile of metal thread, sometimes combined with other techniques.

The designs themselves could be very large, with meandering stems and stylised leaves. The finest of these fabrics were extremely expensive and were worn for ceremonial occasions by nobility and royalty. Damasks and simpler patterned silks were a little more common, though more likely to be seen as a doublet or kirtle under a plain gown, than as the gown itself. Silk was used more widely for trimmings and accessories.

Velvet gowns remained rare in the 15th century, but velvet was used for hoods, frontlets and purses by the wealthy. Plain and patterned silks were used for more elaborate head-dresses, and for lining. Silk was also used to make braid and ribbon, hair nets, tablet-woven belts, and purse-tassels, and silk thread was used for embroidery.

Choosing your silk

Plain silks are generally easy to find and relatively cheap, so do use real silk rather than imitations – but avoid lumpy doupions. Use any firm, plain-coloured taffeta, habotai or fuji for linings and facings on better quality garments, and use the off-cuts for purse bags or head-dress components. Use satin, especially black, for richer doublets of the later 15th century. Use white silk organza for fine veils on 15th-century head-dresses.

All silk and half-silk velvet are still made: use these for richer ladies' hoods, for purses, frontlets, collars and cuffs. Good synthetic dress velvet may also do for these but avoid furnishing and crushed velvets.

Patterned silk, especially in a furnishing fabric, is not often suitable, but look for small patterns with a single repeated motif or all-over lattice, or a simple spot motif. Indian silk saris can be suitable, and often have splendid borders which can be made into belts, but avoid 'pine-cone' designs. For patterned or imitation silk: if in doubt, don't use it!

Buying fabrics

Be prepared to spend time and money finding good materials, especially if the clothes are to be in regular use. Look beyond your drapery store. Remnant and factory shops often have lengths of fabric which may be flawed, but are still usable. Specialist mail order suppliers are more reliable, though also more expensive. Charity shops often sell old sheets, useful for making toiles and trying out patterns, and blankets suitable for interlining; you may even find a linen sheet or a piece of new cloth there.

Materials to avoid – Any knitted (T-shirt) fabric – anything with big lumps in the spinning – anything more hole than thread – shiny synthetics in place of silk – poly/cotton and poly/viscose – printed textiles – lurex metallic fabrics – furnishing textiles.

A note about selvedges

On a traditional loom the weft thread is continuous. Where it returns round the outer edge of the warp threads it forms a firm 'self-edge', sometimes called the 'list'. This selvedge plays an important part in constructing simple garments, so it is worth looking for wools, and especially linens and cottons, with true selvedges. Unfortunately many modern fabrics of all kinds are woven on the industrial jet-loom, where each weft thread ends in a fringe caught together with a row of stitching along the edges of the piece. It needn't stop you buying an otherwise suitable material, but it may affect how you make it up.

Fur

Fur was commonly used as a warm lining for outer garments such as surcotes, gowns, cloaks and head-wear. The furs used included squirrel and weasel for finer garments, with rabbit, lamb and cat for plainer clothes. Some garments were only edged with fur and ladies' gowns of the mid 15th century could have a fur collar and cuffs.

Choosing your fur

The use of real fur is now widely condemned and is expensive, though a furrier will sell you sheets of fur ready to cut, or make up a lining for you. A cheaper option is to buy second-hand fur coats from charity shops, or ask among your older relatives. Modern coats are often from larger animals with less flexible skins, which can make the garment very stiff; but rabbit and musquash are suitable.

Lining a full-length garment will require several coats. To get the same effect, interline the garment with heavy blanket to give it bulk and put the fur round the edges. To check whether a coat is of real or imitation fur, blow gently on it. The pile of real fur will fan out into a circle, unless it is heavy beaver lamb.

Realistic acrylic fur fabrics are available as well. Coat quality fabric can be bought by the metre, or reclaimed from second-hand garments. Avoid cheaper fur fabrics intended for stuffed toys.

Threads

The thread used by a medieval tailor depended on the task. Plain woollen cloths could be sewn with wool yarn, but stronger linen thread was needed for stitching broadcloth. Linen thread was generally undyed: it was used for hidden seams while a silk thread matching the fabric was used where it was visible. The linen seamstress used linen thread, which could be spun very fine. Embroidery was worked in wool, silk or gilt metal thread.

Choosing threads

Hand sewing – For early garments in plain woollens you may be able to use a thread frayed out of the cloth, but first test its breaking strength. If this is inadequate, or you want a contrasting effect, use a fine crewel wool. For linens, quilting cotton (Gutermann or Mettler) is better than machine thread. For very fine work, or if you want to use real linen thread, lace-making suppliers sell fine cotton and linen. Linen thread is difficult to use: it frays easily and needs smoothing through a block of beeswax before use. For the visible hand finishing on outer garments you can use the same thread as for machining, or Gutermann sewing silk in a matching colour.

Machine sewing – Use any all-purpose machine thread. If it won't be seen the thread needn't match. For finishing visible areas, silk thread may look better.

Handmade buttonholes and eyelets – A heavier thread is best. Use Gutermann polyester 'topstitch' or any buttonhole twist. Gutermann also make a heavy linen thread which is ideal for plainer garments. For really high quality work, find an embroidery shop which supplies Zwicky buttonhole silk: this is both beautiful to sew with and historically accurate.

Tools for demonstrating sewing

Living History participants who demonstrate sewing, braid making etc. to the public will look for convincing replicas of period tools. Tools were precious in medieval times and would be kept together in a box or basket. Many can be obtained from re-enactment traders.

Spring shears of iron or bronze date back to the Iron Age, but hinged scissors (see *Frontispiece*) are rare before the 14th century. Pins were generally of brass or bronze and modern brass lace-making pins are suitable. Contrary to popular belief iron or bronze needles were commonly available in a variety of sizes: store them in a needle case. A stiletto for making eyelets (*Methods*, Fig 16) was usually of hardwood or bone. Thimbles were cap-shaped or open-ended. Chalk and charcoal for marking, and thread wound on a non-plastic spool, were also necessary equipment for a tailor or seamstress.

Making cords, braids or nets requires various small implements made of wood, bone or horn. Fine threads and yarns should be used for these, not thick, lumpy ones: the spinners were highly skilled too.

Body linens – braies, shirts & smocks

Body linens were regarded as a different kind of clothing from the garments made by tailors. It was the quality and cleanliness of the linen which set the rich apart from the poor. Its function differed somewhat from modern underwear and it was often quite visible.

Dyed wools and tailored clothes could not be washed, so the layer of linen formed a barrier protecting not only the body from the clothes, but also the clothes from the body. Unlike wool, linen washes without shrinking and even improves with washing. This, combined with its smooth surface and great absorbency, made it ideal for the purpose.

The main linen items were the shirt and braies (breeches, drawers) for men, and the smock (shift, chemise) for women. In addition there were many uses for plain hemmed squares and rectangles of all sizes, known collectively as 'kerchiefs', and head covering was their commonest use (see *Head-wear*). There was also the hand-kerchief, said to have been introduced by Richard II to discourage his courtiers from blowing their noses on their sleeves, and the breast-kerchief, which was worn by men in the 15th century, tucked down the front of the doublet to protect the high collar or to fill in the cut-away front. Women very often wore a long kerchief tucked inside the neck of the kirtle or gown, with the centre pinned at the back of the neck and the two ends drawn forward. This and the breast-kerchief would be of the finest linen the wearer could afford, and were intended to be seen.

1. c.1250, French
Thresher wearing a loose breech clout, wrapped round a waist cord, one leg tied up to a hose-string. Coif on head. (Maciekowski Bible, Pierpoint Morgan Library, New York, MS 638, f.12v).

The simplest form of body linen was the 'clout', an item of hygiene rather than dress, often made of a patterned weave with extra threads for greater absorbency. When pinned round the baby's bottom it was known as a tail-clout.

Making and laundering
Body linens remained simple in shape throughout the period. They were made economically, with the seamstress working to the width of the linen, rather than the shape of the wearer. Her main concern would be to make the seams flat, so they were comfortable in wear, and durable to withstand repeated washing. Medieval laundry methods are not well-recorded, but every town had its laundresses and linens were re-bleached by spreading them out in the sun.

Materials
The word 'linen' is used throughout, though the medieval seamstress would often have used hemp canvas and you may well be using cotton. Linen and hemp were both spun and woven in a wide range of weights and qualities: the finer the spinning, the more expensive the fabric.

The coarser grades were used unbleached in their natural brown or greyish colour, which became paler with repeated washing and exposure to the sun. Fine linens were bleached white. Body linens were usually undyed although some 14th century peasants are shown in blue shirts, probably dyed with woad. This may have been preferred to unbleached linen by men who couldn't afford the bleached quality.

1

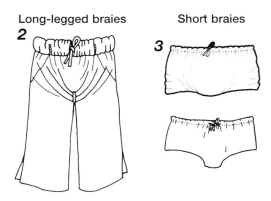

Long-legged braies
2

Short braies
3

Modern fashion linens are rather flimsy compared with the durable shirtings of the past, so choose linen with as dense a weave as you can find, whatever its weight. For frequent use a cotton sheeting may be better, but not unbleached calico, which has the wrong colour and feel. For high quality clothing a fine cotton lawn is better than a loosely-woven handkerchief linen.

Cutting out

Medieval linen was woven quite narrow, from 50 to 90 cm, and the seamstress would use the full width without any waste. Today you may still find a fine cotton or linen only 90 cm wide, but most of it is 150 cm, which affects both the cutting and the sewing. If you use 150 cm width it can be economical to cut two or more garments at the same time, adjusting the dimensions to fit, but first sketch a plan on paper to find the best layout.

Most of the pieces for body linens are cut on the straight grain, so it is worth practising cutting 'to a thread', straight along the weave. If you then fold hems and seams exactly on the weave, the whole garment will keep its shape after washing. On fine materials, draw out a thread as a guide to cut by.

Sewing methods

Oversewing was the traditional method for joining selvedges, hemming for finishing off raw edges, and both were used together (seam-and-fell) for other seams (*Methods*, Figs 1, 2, 6).

As sewing machines can't do oversewing and you probably have no selvedges to work with, shirts and smocks may need to be made up using both hand and machine stitching. There are two ways of machine-stitching linens: the simplest is to make narrow seams and zigzag or overlock the edges. More complicated, but more comfortable to wear because the seam lies flat, is to make run-and-fell seams (*Methods*, Fig 6a), with machine topstitching to secure the folds.

Shirts and smocks continue on p. 71 and are numbered separately.

1. 1430-40, French

Shirt with front slit and possibly a collar. Separate hose rolled down: the pointed flaps are extensions for tying to the doublet at the back. Ankle shoes. (Decameron, Bibliothèque de l'Arsenal, Paris, MS 5070, f.330v).

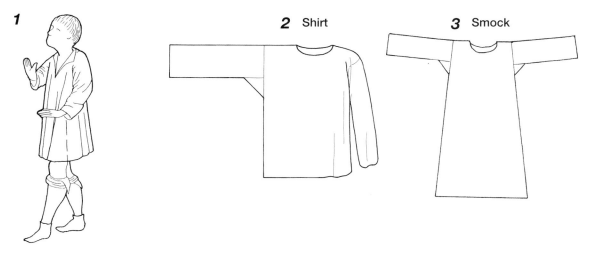

1

2 Shirt

3 Smock

Braies 2

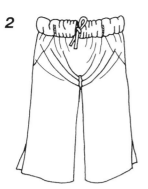

Made from a straight piece of linen, with the girdle enclosed in a waist casing. These are worn tucked into the separate hose. Holes are often cut in the waist casing so the strings for attaching the hose can hang from the breech girdle. The legs can be shortened for wear with longer hose.

This is the basic men's undergarment, also called 'breeches', and later known as 'drawers'. They were not necessarily hidden from view. Working men are depicted stripped down to their braies, or braies and shirt, in hot weather; and any man in a short cote, or cote with a split front, might show them when sitting down.

The most basic form, possibly worn only by working men, was a simple breech clout (Fig 1), wrapped round the body and secured by a tied 'breech girdle'. Better-dressed men in the 13th and early 14th centuries wore a baggy pair of long-legged braies (Fig 2), which were tucked into the tops of the hose (*Hose,* Fig 1). From about the mid 14th century men started tying their hose to the new doublet instead of the breech girdle, and braies became smaller. During the 15th century a baggy form persisted in use, but a much closer-fitting pattern was developed for wear under joined hose (Figs 4, 5; Pl 18).

3. Pattern for Fig 2
The main piece is 170 cm x 68 cm, and folded lengthways. Join the long edges from C to B at each end to form the legs. Leave them open in the middle to form the waist, and add the triangular gussets. Set in the gussets as described for shirt sleeves (*Methods,* Fig 7). Cut a large band and fold it lengthways. Sew it round the waist edge to form a casing for the breech girdle. This band sometimes has two slits at the sides, (faced or blanket-stitched) through which the hose strings pass.

The breech girdle
Until the mid 14th century the breech girdle not only supported the breech clout or braies, but also the hose, and sometimes a purse as well. To avoid cutting into the wearer when tightened to take the strain, early breech girdles were made of thick cord, or a twisted strip of material. Often the spare material at the top of the braies was rolled over the girdle to pad it. The hose were supported by two loops of cord hung from the breech girdle (Fig 1). Where the girdle was inside a casing, this sometimes had slits for the loops, or they emerged from openings at the sides. As the doublet became the normal support for the hose, the breech girdle was reduced to a narrow cord or tape in a smaller casing (Fig 4).

> **Key dimensions**
> Take Seat and Body rise measurements.
> Dimensions shown for the long-legged braies (Fig 3) are only approximate, but plan them generously and allow for seams as they need to be large and baggy. The short fitted braies (Figs 4, 5) need more precise planning. Letters indicate joining points. For abbreviations see p.10.

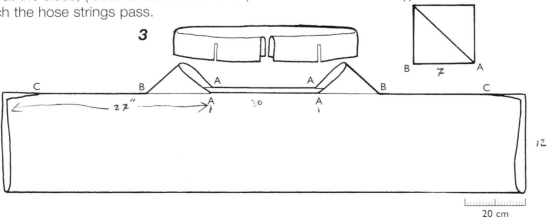

3

20 cm

Short braies

4

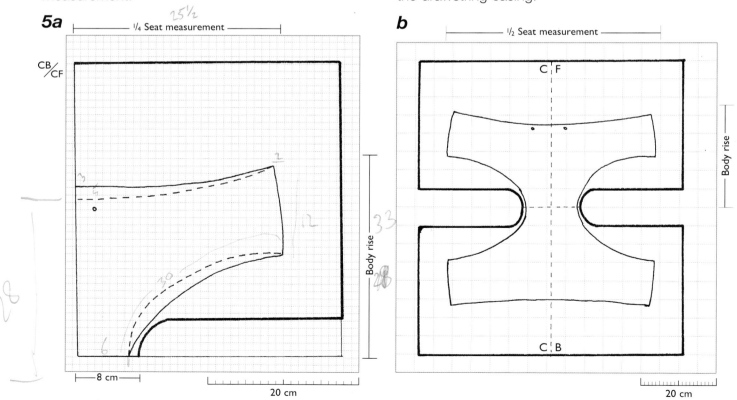

4. Short braies
a. Basic shape, 1350-1500. A loosely fitting garment reaching to the waist. It is held up by a narrow drawstring in a waist casing, which emerges through an eyelet at CF.

b. Fitted braies, 1400-1500. A more shaped version for wear under joined hose. This has two eyelets at the front, 5 to 10 cm apart. The drawstring crosses inside the casing between the eyelets, see *c.*

c. The arrows show the threading of the drawstring.

5. Patterns for Fig 4
The patterns are based on the wearer's Seat and Body rise measurements, and a further measurement round one thigh.

a. Planning a quarter garment
The heavy outline shows loose braies. The width must allow for the leg cut-out, here 30 cm deep and half the Thigh measurement. Back and Front are identical.

The finer outline shows a closer-fitting form. The solid lines show the Back, and the broken lines the Front. The deep shaping of the leg cut-out allows the body to be only slightly wider than Seat measurement.

b. Complete pattern for both shapes
Braies can be cut in one piece, or with Back and Front joined by a seam at the crotch. To make them up, sew the side seams, then hem the leg holes. Work the eyelet(s) through single fabric before turning down the top edge and hemming it to form the drawstring casing.

Shirts and smocks

The male shirt and female smock were essentially the same. They varied only in length and in details of the neck finish. Both were simple garments normally hidden from view: they didn't change significantly during the three hundred years covered here (Fig 1).

Because it was longer, the smock was usually widened with gores to allow free movement. The longer the smock, the wider it should be at the hem. The smock shown (Fig 3) is flared from the shoulder, but the flaring or gores could start from the underarm or waist. Men's shirts could also be made with gores, especially to fit larger figures. A few styles of shirts and smocks had collars, to protect the collar of the garment worn over them.

There is no evidence that medieval shirts had yokes, nor that either garment was fastened by drawstrings at the neck or wrists.

Planning and cutting a shirt or smock

The pieces are simple in shape, so the following instructions don't provide pattern layouts. You may prefer to start with a paper pattern before marking the fabric, or plan a scaled layout on paper before marking and cutting the fabric. If you cut from fabric folded along the shoulder line, note that the Front neck is deeper than the Back. First take the wearer's measurements and work out the dimensions for each pattern part. These dimensions include seam allowances, but be generous – the garments are better loose than tight. Some dimensions make use of other personal measurements (*Blocks*, Figs 1, 2).

continued on p. 72

2a

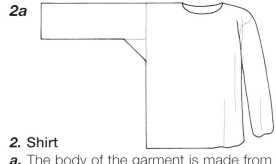

2. Shirt

a. The body of the garment is made from a single piece of fabric folded along the shoulder line, and sewn together at the sides. The sides could be left open at the lower edge to form vents. The neck opening is large enough to slip on easily over the head. The straight sleeves are set on with gussets to give ease under the arms.

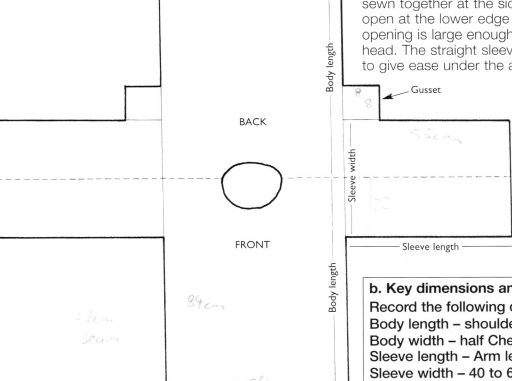

BACK

FRONT

Body width

Body length

Sleeve width

Wrist

Sleeve length

Gusset

20 cm

b. Key dimensions and assembled parts

Record the following dimensions
Body length – shoulder to mid-thigh, or longer
Body width – half Chest + 15 cm, or more
Sleeve length – Arm length, from tip of shoulder
Sleeve width – 40 to 60 cm, according to size
Gusset – 10 to 15 cm square
Close neck – for collar, if required
See also p.10.

Smocks

3a

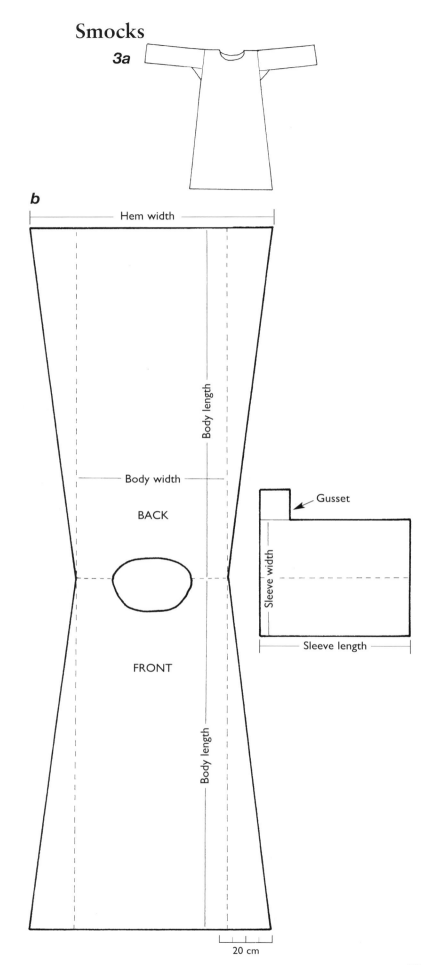

b

Hem width

Body length

Body width

BACK

FRONT

Body length

20 cm

Gusset

Sleeve width

Sleeve length

3. Smock

a. The smock is cut like a longer shirt, with a wider hem produced by flaring or by adding gores. Here the flaring starts from the shoulders, setting the sleeves slightly upwards. This conveniently increases the underarm length.

b. Key dimensions and parts
Record the following dimensions
Body length – shoulder to calf level, or longer
Body width – half Bust + 10 cm or more
Hem width – Body width + twice Gore width
Gore width – half hem increase required over body width, 15 cm or more
Gore length – from waist, underarm or shoulder, to hem
Sleeve length – Arm length, from tip of shouder
Sleeve width – 35 to 50 cm, according to size
Gusset – 8 to 12 cm square
Close neck – for collar, if required
See also p. 10.

continued from p. 71
  Start with the body and fit the other parts to make the best use of the linen. Dimensions can be adjusted slightly to make the pieces fit on the material. The above dimensions *include seam allowances.*
  The bodies for shirts and smocks are best cut along the length of the material; gores can be cut as part of the body or separately in pairs (*Cotes*, Fig 4). The body is normally folded along the shoulders and cut in one piece, but shoulder seams are fine if your material isn't long enough to cut the body in one.
  The sleeves may be cut along or across, provided both are cut the same way; the gussets (and collars) can be fitted in around the main pieces. Fig 4 shows an alternative sleeve made without a gusset and fitting closer than the plain one.

Making up

Body – If you have cut separate gores, sew them to the body as the first step, then sew the shoulder seams, if required. Make the neck opening; see below for neck finishes.
Sleeves – The two ways of making up are:
1. Sew the side seams, then make up the sleeves and gussets and set them into the armhole (*Methods,* Fig 7).
2. Join the sleeves and gussets to the body, then sew side and underarm seams in one (*Methods,* Fig 8).

4. Tapered sleeve

This sleeve is tapered to the wrist and made without gussets. Add 5-10 cm to the straight Sleeve width. Use the Hand measurement for the wrist width.

One sleeve is shown cut whole, and the other with a gore for economy.

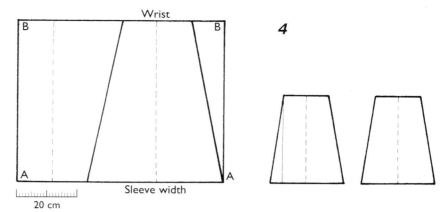

The diagrams show the sleeves going onto a straight-edged body, but the process is exactly the same with the slanted edges (Fig 3a), when the sleeves will slant upwards, improving the underarm ease.

Hem the lower edge and sleeve ends.

Neck finishes and collars

A straight slit (Fig 5a) is the simplest neck opening, but the commonest neck style is a slightly oval opening, deeper at the front than the back and big enough to slip easily over the head (Fig 5b). This is hemmed, or faced with a narrow straight band on the inside. The neck edge of the smock doesn't normally show much above the cote or kirtle.

Men's shirts may also have a close-fitting round neck, with a front slit (Fig 5c). Cut the slit deep enough to pull on easily, and reinforce the base of the slit (*Methods*, Fig 10). This style may be made with a narrow binding extended to form ties (*Methods*, Fig 9c).

Around 1400, when very high gown collars were popular, both the shirt and the smock acquired collars too (Fig 5d), probably to provide a barrier between the gown collar and the wearer's neck. This collar persisted on men's shirts well into the 15th century to protect the high collar of the doublet.

Neck styles

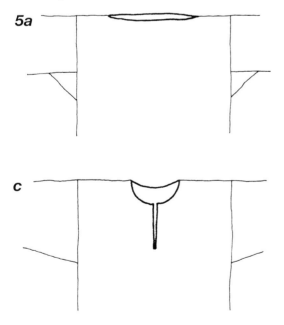

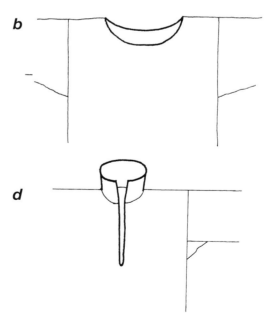

5. Neck styles

a. Straight slash along the shoulder line.

b. Wide oval neck – by far the commonest style.

c. Small neck with front slit, sometimes banded.

d. Straight collar, for wear under a high-necked doublet.

Cut a straight band, 15-30 cm wide, equal to the length of the neck edge + seam allowances for front edges. Hem the front slit, fold the band double, and hem it on to enclose the neck edge. See *Methods*, Figs 9 & 10 for neck binding and finishing slit openings.

Plate 5 Rural workers, early 14th century, English

The six male figures all wear loose cotes of simple cut pouched over belts without any suggestion of
shirts beneath; note the tucking-up of the skirts some of which have front slits. All have well-fitted
hose and ankle shoes and one wears a round hat which is probably felt: he has a button or brooch
fastening the neck of his cote. The others wear hoods with short points, one open and buttoned
under the chin, one thrown back on the shoulders, and one worn on the back of the head. The
ploughman and the driver, top left and top right, both wear divided mittens.

   The two female figures appear to be 'indoors': each wears a loose cote pouched over a belt, with
sleeves which fit well on the forearm and are turned back at the wrists. They are barefoot and
wearing their hair loose, though the one on the left has a narrow barbette and fillet. She is using a
pair of wool combs. The one on the right is spinning from a distaff.

Holkham Bible Picture Book, British Library MS Add. 47682, f.6

Cotes

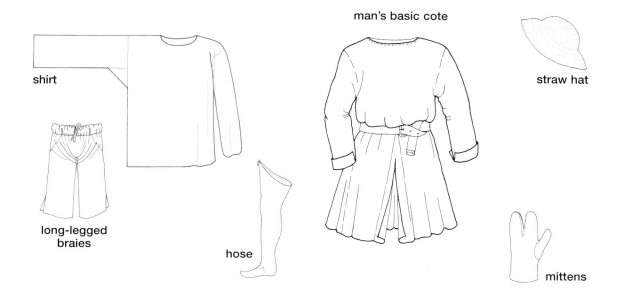

shirt

long-legged
braies

hose

man's basic cote

straw hat

mittens

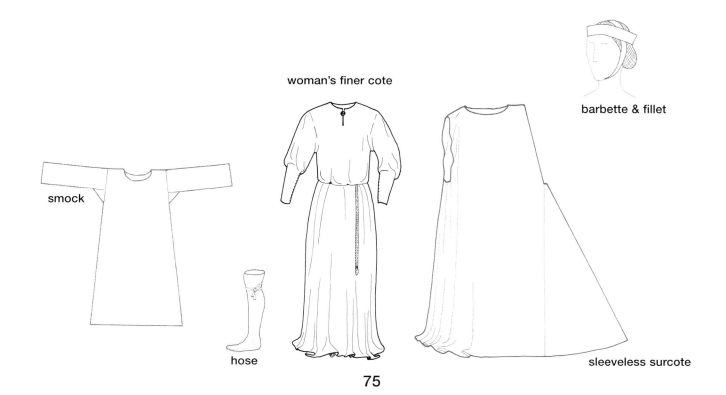

smock

hose

woman's finer cote

barbette & fillet

sleeveless surcote

Cotes

This T-shaped main garment, also known as a tunic, was worn by both men and women of all classes from before the Norman conquest until the middle of the 14th century. It was usually worn over body linen – shirt or smock – (Fig 1) and under a surcote (Fig 2). Because it was universal there was a great deal of variety in the quality of material, in the details of the cut and fit, and especially in the way it was worn and the accessories and head wear which went with it. It was normally worn with a belt.

The shape usually depended on the material and the wealth of the wearer: simple and fitted versions were probably in use at the same time, though in general the cote became more fitted after 1300. The distinguishing feature was the sleeves, so these need special attention. The cote gradually went out of use after 1340 with the new developments in tailoring, but it persisted for working people into the early 15th century. The simple, economical shapes also continued for some children throughout the 15th century.

Cotes and surcotes – The cote is made in the same way as the surcote, which can make identification difficult, though the surcote is an outer garment. Often the only difference is that the surcote is looser and has shortened sleeves. If an inner sleeve is visible it may indicate a cote under a surcote. A cote would be worn over linens, when white or cream might be visible beneath; a surcote would be worn over a cote or kirtle, which might be visible beneath in a different colour. If you can see a belt, or the garment pouched over it, you are probably looking at a cote (Fig 2).

Men's cotes

Men's status was reflected in the length as well as the material and cut of the cote. The king, noblemen and clergy wore them full-length; professional men and older workers wore them calf-length. Workers, and young men in general, wore their cotes to just below the knee (Fig 1; Pl 5). A cote might be split from waist to hem at centre front, and could reveal the braies and hose beneath. Workers often tucked up the two front corners into the belt, leaving the legs free (Pl 5). Calf-length cotes, common for travellers, could be split at the back as well as the front, for riding.

Women's cotes

Women's cotes were always long to the ground, but a working woman would hitch the skirts up in a deep tuck over her belt, well clear of her feet, while a lady ensured her legs were hidden (Fig 2). By 1300 most women's cotes were shaped at the shoulders and underarms and by 1330 the body was likely to be fitted and laced, often indistinguishable from the kirtle which eventually replaced it.

Peasant women wore a simpler, loose cote to 1400 or after. Richer women wore the cote into the second half of the 14th century, later than their men.

The most elaborate styles are well suited to the female figure. These used multiple long gores at the sides, which were shaped above the waist to give a close fit and a dramatic flare over the hips. Some were just loose enough to pull on, but others must have been laced, either at one side or in a slash or seam at the front or back.

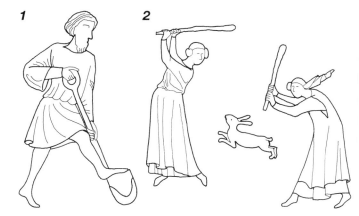

1. Early 13th century. Basic form of short cote, with wide sleeves and slit neck, pouched over a hidden belt. Close-fitting shirt sleeves visible, head bare. (British Library, Royal MS 1 DX f.156).

2. Early 14th century. Women clubbing rabbits
Left Cote pouched over a belt: a long smock is visible at the hem.
Right Sleeveless surcote over a cote, and a fine veil. Both are wearing side buns. (Queen Mary's Psalter, British Library, Royal MS 2 B VII, f.156).

Planning and cutting

The basic cote consists of the body, which is folded along the shoulder line; eight triangular gores, which are sewn one to each side at front and back, and two each in slits at the Centre Front and Centre Back; and two sleeves with or without underarm gussets. Examples of basic cotes are shown in Figs 3 & 5.

Pattern dimensions will vary with the style, weight of cloth, type of sleeve, size of wearer, etc. but are derived from the Key measurements (see box overleaf), so you *must* add seam allowances before making your plan.

Use the dimensions to make a sketch plan on paper of the pieces and layout, like Fig 4. The hem width should be between 2.5 and 3.5 m. For an extravagant long cote add more width by putting in extra side gores. Plan the final pattern pieces on paper, and lay them out on a single layer of cloth, or on calico, which can be fitted and then used as a pattern.

You can adjust any dimension by 1 or 2 cm if it helps make a more economical layout. Check the pattern dimensions match the plan *before you cut*, making sure you have enough length, ease (where required) and seam allowance. Cut out the pattern pieces as nearly as possible along the straight grain (Figs 4, 6). Secure longer bias edges on a stay band.

Body – Fold the cut body in half lengthways and mark the Centre Front and Centre Back lines from hem to waist. Open it out, fold along the shoulder line and mark the neck opening with chalk (Fig 7). Cut along these marks only when you are ready to stitch, to avoid fraying the edges.

Gores – Single gores are cut in pairs from a rectangle. Fold the rectangle diagonally, starting 3 cm in from the corners to allow for the seams, and cut along the fold. For centre gores see Figs 4 & 6.

Sleeves – These vary according to style. A loose cote needs a loose sleeve; on a more fitted cote the sleeve can be shaped. Some are quite close-fitting at the underarm (Figs 8, 9).

Materials

The cote was made of wool cloth, normally without a lining, ranging from thick blanket, through medium-weight twills with perhaps 10-15 threads per cm (the commonest), up to fine worsteds. From the later 13th century more broadcloth was used, which would have made the shaping easier since broadcloth doesn't fray as readily as earlier cloth. A light, draping cloth is needed for the finer cote (Fig 5), while blanket is suitable for a plain, squared-off cote (Fig 3).

It was desirable to have a 'robe' or set of garments, including cote, surcote and hood, made from the same material. A 2 m length of cloth 140-150 cm wide is normally required for a man's short cote, or 3.5 m for a full-length one. Try to avoid a cloth with a nap, or any kind of one-way pattern, since both sides and both directions of the cloth are used.

Making up

Cut and finish the neck opening. Sew the gores to the body, with the side gores straight edge to straight edge. Insert pairs of gores in slashes on the Centre Front and Back. Either set the sleeves on flat and sew the underarm and side seams, with the gussets if used; or, finish the side seams then set in the completed sleeves (*Methods*, Figs 7, 8).

Sew the cote by hand with lapped seams or run-and-fell (*Methods*, Figs 3, 6). Alternatively machine stitch it with open seams and overcast the edges if the cloth seems likely to fray. Finish neck and sleeve ends with a hem, or a narrow facing of linen or silk.

3 Man's basic cote
13th century on

Woman's finer cote
13th-14th century

5

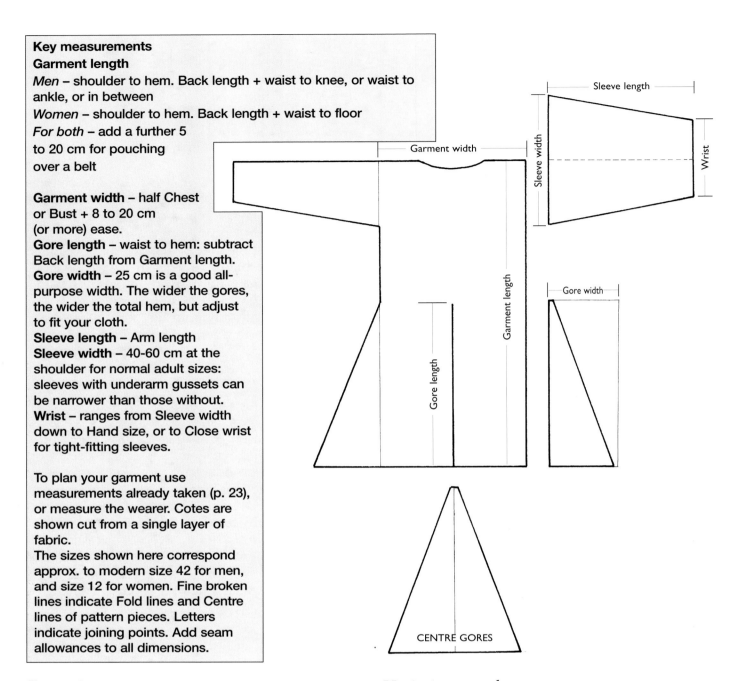

Key measurements

Garment length

Men – shoulder to hem. Back length + waist to knee, or waist to ankle, or in between

Women – shoulder to hem. Back length + waist to floor

For both – add a further 5 to 20 cm for pouching over a belt

Garment width – half Chest or Bust + 8 to 20 cm (or more) ease.

Gore length – waist to hem: subtract Back length from Garment length.

Gore width – 25 cm is a good all-purpose width. The wider the gores, the wider the total hem, but adjust to fit your cloth.

Sleeve length – Arm length

Sleeve width – 40-60 cm at the shoulder for normal adult sizes: sleeves with underarm gussets can be narrower than those without.

Wrist – ranges from Sleeve width down to Hand size, or to Close wrist for tight-fitting sleeves.

To plan your garment use measurements already taken (p. 23), or measure the wearer. Cotes are shown cut from a single layer of fabric.

The sizes shown here correspond approx. to modern size 42 for men, and size 12 for women. Fine broken lines indicate Fold lines and Centre lines of pattern pieces. Letters indicate joining points. Add seam allowances to all dimensions.

Labels in diagram: Sleeve length, Sleeve width, Wrist, Garment width, Garment length, Gore length, Gore width, CENTRE GORES

Fastenings

Most cotes had no fastenings. They were loose enough to pull on, and the bulk was controlled by the belt, and perhaps by a brooch at the neck. Closer fitting cotes were probably laced at the back or side, the eyelets worked through a narrow facing (*Methods*, Figs 16, 17). Tight-fitting sleeves in the 13th century were stitched closed on the arm. This can be done as follows. Leave the seam open below the elbow and hem the edges. Put the cote on and draw the edges together using a needle and strong thread, working towards the wrist; you may need help for this.

By 1300 buttons were replacing sewing on sleeve ends (*Methods*, Figs 19-21; Pls 2, 3). Up to six might be used at first, and later in the century a dozen or more.

Variations to the cote

An enterprising cutter can adapt the simple shapes of the basic cote to vary the form or improve the fit. Techniques for giving a fitted appearance to the top of the cote, probably in use by 1300, included shaping the shoulders and cutting to produce a rounded armhole and sleeve (Fig 8). Long side gores running into the armhole were used to shape the underarm as well as widening the body (see *Surcotes*, Fig 5).

A cote can be made closer-fitting by shaping the body and gores after cutting. The sleeve in Fig 9 (a precursor of the fully-fitted sleeve) is also closer-fitting and matches the shaping of the underarm. It can be used on any cote with this shaping.

Man's basic short cote

3

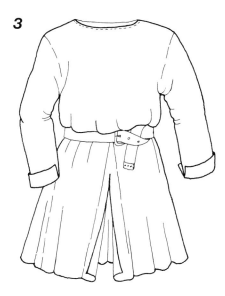

3. Man's basic short cote, 1200 onwards
Made in thick cloth, it has a boat-shaped neck (Fig 7b) and the long sleeves are turned back. The front slit is the open seam between the two front gores. The corners were often tucked up into the belt during work to leave the legs free.

4. Pattern layout for Fig 3

The cote shown is planned on 2.4 m of cloth, 140 cm wide, using almost all the cloth.

Start by sketching a plan of the pattern parts, with the largest and longest first. The 8 gores are quite wide, and the sleeves are extra long. The gores are planned to give both left and right slants, suitable for a non-reversible cloth. One pair of gores has been planned without a seam, to be inserted in the CB slash. Join the straight edges of the side gores to the body.

4

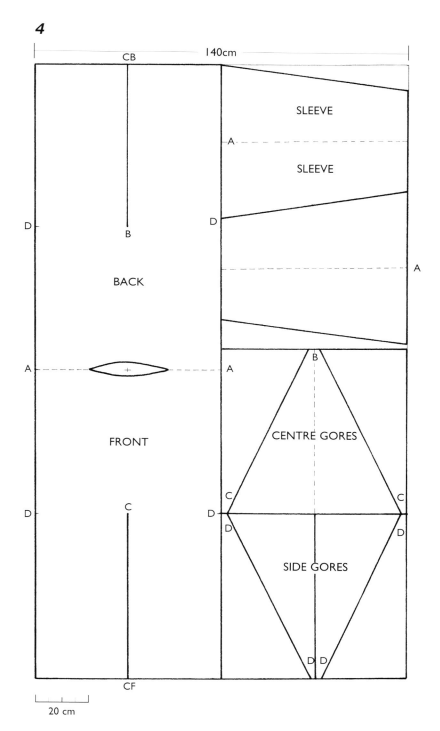

79

Woman's finer cote

5

A full length cote in fine cloth, to fit a small woman. The front slit is secured with a brooch. The sleeves are tight-fitting on the forearm, achieved by stitching the lower sleeve closed on the wearer, and pouched above. Alternatively, this style could have shoulder shaping and a close-fitting sleeve (Fig 9). The cote has extra length to drape over the belt, and to hide the feet.

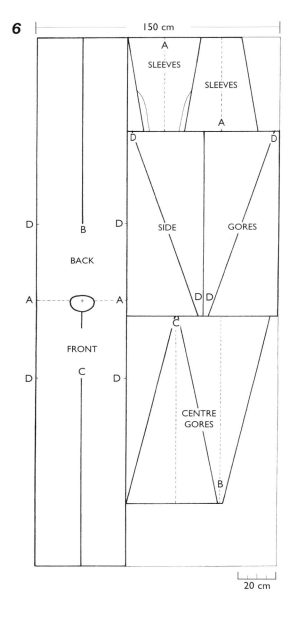

6

150 cm

SLEEVES

SLEEVES

A

A

D   D   D   D

D   B   D   SIDE   GORES

BACK

D   D

A   +   A   C

FRONT

CENTRE
GORES

D   C   D

B

20 cm

6. Layout for Fig 5

The cote is planned on 3.3 m of cloth, 150 cm wide. This is for approximately modern size 12. Larger sizes may require more than twice the garment length. Start by sketching a plan of the pattern parts, with the largest and longest first.

The sleeves are planned fairly wide at the shoulder, tapering to a narrow wrist, and will need fitting on the arms later. The four side gores are planned wider than the two centre gores. Each centre gore can be cut in one piece. The spare cloth could provide an extra gore on each side of the cote, with the straight edges sewn to the Front.

Join the straight edges of all side gores to the body.

Plate 6 Early 14th century cote

This is similar to *Cotes,* Fig. 5, in a medium weight woollen twill. The sleeves are stitched closed on the forearms, so the extra sleeve length forms pouching at the elbows. The long skirts may be hitched over the belt for free movement. She wears a kerchief (*Women's linen head-dresses,* Fig 2b) and a smock whose sleeves are just visible.

Neck styles

7a

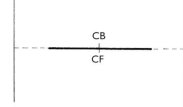

CB
CF

b

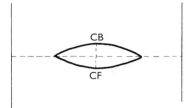

CB
CF

c

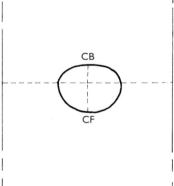

CB
CF

d

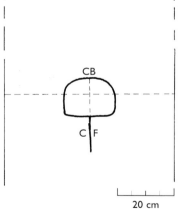

CB
C F

20 cm

7. Neck styles

The neck was often hidden by outer clothing or head-wear.

Ensure the opening is wide enough to pull over the head easily. Centre the neck opening on the shoulder fold. Finish off the edge with a hem, binding, or fancy stitching (*Methods,* Figs 2, 9, 22).

a. Straight slash pulled forwards with a brooch, common in the 13th century.

b. Shallow boat shape with the same back and front shaping.

c. Round neck opening, common in the 14th century.

d. Round back and squared front with slit. Could be fastened with a latchet or button, instead of a brooch.

Shoulder and armhole fit

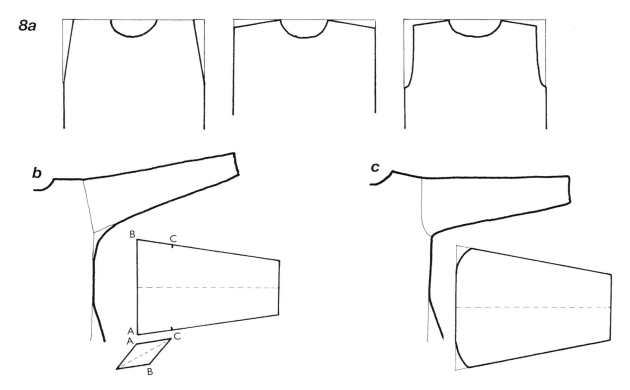

8a

b

c

8. Improving shoulder and armhole fit
The improvement is achieved by adapting the top of the front and back body, and using close-fitting sleeves.

a. Shaping the body. Cut the rectangular body and adjust it by sloping the shoulder seams and/or shaping the armhole a little. Use with sleeves in *b* or *c*, or the transitional sleeve (Fig 9).

b. Narrow tapered sleeve with a lozenge-shaped gusset. This works best with lighter cloth.

c. Partly shaped sleeve head. Adjust a tapered sleeve to fit a shaped armhole by trimming away the corners at the underarm.

9. 'Transitional' sleeve, from 1300
Moving the seam from the underarm to the back offered closer fitting and a better position for displaying the fashionable buttons. This sleeve is suitable for cotes with shaped armholes (Fig 8).

a. Sleeve seen from the back, with gusset and buttons

b. Sleeve plan. Start the pattern from the rectangle, shown by fine lines. The sleeve width should allow an easy fit on the upper arm, not much smaller than the armhole measurement. Plan a slightly curved top edge, and widen it to match the armhole with a triangular gusset in the sleeve seam (heavy broken lines). The highest point of the sleeve lies over the shoulder, with the seam and gusset at the back of the arm. Taper the sleeve below the elbow to the wrist. Try out the pattern in calico first. Fasten the wrist opening with at least six buttons.

9a

b

Sleeve length

Sleeve width

20 cm

Kirtles

smock

hose

kirtle

gown

plait head-dress

belt

84

The kirtle is a shaped and fitted garment which probably appeared in the 1360s. Over the period it became increasingly close-fitting. It could be lined and was worn under an outer garment – at first partly visible under the sideless surcote (*Surcotes,* Fig *9 right*) or the buttoned cotehardie (*Cotehardies,* Fig 7), later mainly hidden under the gown (*Gowns,* Figs 24, 28), or the overkirtle for working women (*Overkirtles,* Fig 2). The kirtle must match the outer garment in date and style.

The kirtle as 'foundation' garment

Throughout the first half of the 15th century, when women of status wore a loose enveloping gown, the kirtle gradually developed into the first 'foundation' garment. Towards the middle of the century, the bodice became tighter in an attempt to control and support the bust, while the skirt was made with a flounce to hold out the heavy skirts of the gown.

The kirtle as working dress

By the early 15th century the basic kirtle seems to have been in general use by working women. Simple to make, practical and graceful, it remained little changed for the rest of the century. Many working women wore two kirtles, one over the other (Fig 1); one on its own seems to have been unusual. The overkirtle is covered in a separate chapter, *Outer working garments.* All the kirtles in this chapter are designed to be worn as the main (inner) garment over a smock.

Planning and cutting

Instructions for planning and cutting kirtles are given as captions to the Figures. They include basic (Fig 2) and flat-fronted with a waist seam (Fig 7) versions. Fig 3 shows how to adapt the neckline of the kirtle so that it will match the outer garment worn with it. Ensure also that the kirtle sleeves match.

Plan paper patterns for Back and Front using the personal Block, and extend the skirts as described in *Blocks,* Fig 27. Don't make the skirts too wide: a 2.5 to 3 m hem is plenty. You can get this out of cloth 140-160 cm wide, folded lengthways (Fig 4). If the skirt is to have a flounce it can be narrower still.

Kirtle skirts must be just short enough to clear the feet. This is important: if the kirtle skirt is clear of the wearer's feet she can concentrate on controlling the much larger skirts of the outer garment.

You may prefer to try the pattern first in calico or sheeting.

To plan your garment use the wearer's personal bodice Block. The fine lines show its original outline. The patterns shown here correspond approx. to modern size 14. Heavy broken lines indicate alternative outlines. Letters indicate joining points. For abbreviations and symbols see p. 10. Check the side seam lines are of equal length and at the same angle. Add seam allowances and balance points.

1. **1480-1500, French.** Countrywomen dancing
Left A close-fitting overkirtle (dark blue, lined in brown) over a light-coloured kirtle with a hem flounce. Her smock shows round the neck. The overkirtle may have a waist seam, or the line might be a fold of its tucked-up skirt. She wears a tailed cap, and the purse is visible.
Right Unusually she is wearing only her kirtle, with short sleeves and flounced hem. The front lacing shows her smock; a white apron hides the waistline. One smock sleeve looks gathered at the wrist, but not the other. She wears an old-fashioned scarlet open hood over a white cap or kerchief.
(Bibliothèque Nationale, Paris, MS Latin 873, f.21r)

1

Materials

Outer fabric – use medium or lightweight woollen material or worsted; in a good strong colour for wealthier women, or an undyed, light or muted shade for working dress. Linen may also have been used and is certainly cooler under a gown in hot weather.

The kirtle with a waist seam (Fig 7), for wear under a gown, can be in two materials: strong linen or canvas for the bodice (which should be lined) and a lightweight cloth, or even heavy silk, for the skirt (which can be unlined). This skirt would be visible, so was often made of patterned material to show under a plain-coloured gown.

Lining – use another lightweight wool, or linen, or leave unlined with faced edges.

Making up

Most kirtles consist of backs, fronts and sleeves, with an opening for lacing, normally at CF. Assemble the body and set in the completed sleeves. If the kirtle is unlined you can face the neck, CF opening and sleeve ends with narrow straight strips of linen (p. 51). For a flounced hem see below. If the kirtle is lined, make up the lining like a separate garment and insert it by hand (p. 51).

The flat fronted kirtle with a waist seam (Fig 7) is more elaborate. Make up the bodice and skirt separately. The bodice must be interlined, with extra stiffening at the front, and lined (*Methods,* Figs 11-13). Pin and tack the shaped side fronts, easing them carefully onto the front panel between the balance marks AB. Leave one side seam open for lacing (*Methods,* Figs 16-18).

Make up the lining and insert it into the bodice, clean-finishing all the edges, including the waist.

Make up the skirt by sewing all the panels together, with an opening to match the bodice opening. Turn in the seam allowance on the waist edge and oversew it to the waist edge of the finished bodice, pleating the skirt to fit, and matching CF and CB.

Hem flounce – Leave this until you can try on the nearly finished kirtle. Adjust the skirt length so the flounce is clear of the floor all round.

Join the pieces of the flounce into a loop and hem one edge. Using pins for markers, divide the raw edge by folding it into halves, quarters, etc., down to 1/16 or 1/32. Divide and mark the lower edge of the skirt in the same way, then with the right sides together match up the pins. Sew the flounce to the skirt taking up the fullness in small regular pleats.

Fastenings

Kirtles are normally fastened by lacing, usually at the front but sometimes at the side or back. Keep the eyelets no more than 3 cm apart (*Methods,* Fig 16). For a fitted kirtle, tie the middle of the lace into an eyelet at waist level. Lace one end up the bodice and the other one down the skirt; this will improve the fit. Long sleeves are normally fastened by buttons, especially in the late 14th century when there may be a dozen or more (*Methods,* Figs 19-21; Pls 2, 3).

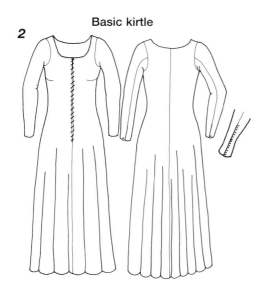

2   Basic kirtle

7   Flat-fronted kirtle

Basic kirtle

2

2. Basic kirtle, later 14th century onwards
The shape follows the personal bodice Block, and two different sleeve styles are shown. The body is cut in four panels with the skirt flaring from the hips and laced at the front from neckline to hip. The neck is cut fairly low, though it would be higher for older women, and should be adjusted to match the garment worn over it. It was often filled with a kerchief or wimple. The plain sleeve, from the sleeve Block, is fastened with one or more buttons.

3. Bodice for Fig 2
Trace the personal Block and ensure that the neckline of the kirtle matches that of the garment to be worn over it and plan low-necked styles together. Several alternatives to the plain kirtle neckline are given.

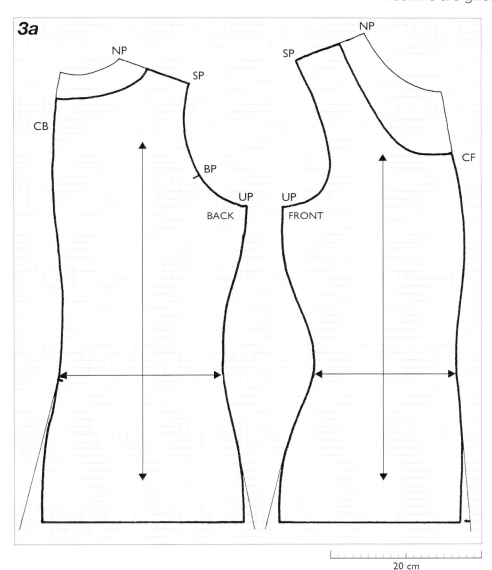

a. Basic or working kirtle with a plain neckline. Lower the back and front necklines: by 5 cm at CB, from NP at the shoulder and 10 cm at the CF. These measurements will vary with the wearer. Mark the waist level clearly – it is needed for planning the skirts. Mark the centre of the waistline on Front and Back and rule the SG line through this point as shown. Use this line as the construction line to plan the skirts and use the thin lines at the sides as a guide for the flare.

continued overleaf

20 cm

87

b. Wide but shallow neckline to match the surcote in *Surcotes,* Fig 9. Lower the neckline by 3(4) cm at CB, 4(7) cm from NP at the shoulder and 1(2) cm at CF. Figures in brackets are for the lower neckline, shown by broken lines.

c. Wide neckline to match the cotehardie in *Cotehardies,* Fig 7. Lower the neckline by 3 cm at CB, 7 cm from NP at the shoulder and 7 cm at CF. Don't reduce the width of the shoulder seams to less than 4 cm.

d. A low front neckline to match the flared gown in *Gowns,* Fig 24. Lower the neckline by 3.5 cm at CB, 5 cm from NP at the shoulder and 9 cm at CF. The V-neck of the gown may be filled with a fine kerchief or a stomacher to conceal the front of the kirtle.

As the armholes are unaltered you can use your sleeve Block for a basic sleeve, or plan one of the alternatives from Fig 5 or 6.

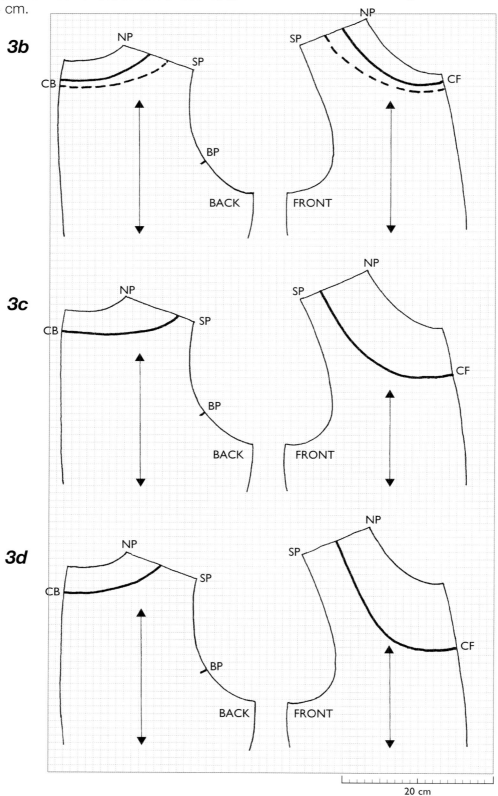

20 cm

88

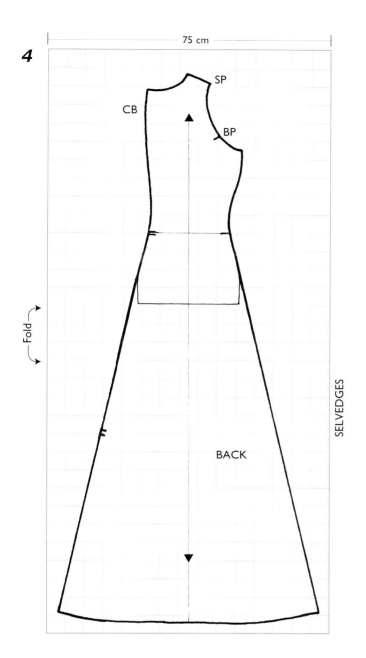

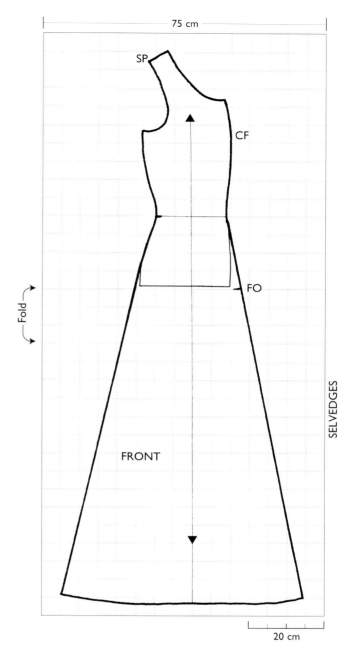

4. Full pattern and layout for Fig 2

The patterns are shown on 150 cm wide cloth folded lengthways. Front hem is 63 cm wide, the Back hem 68 cm, giving a total hem width of 262 cm. For a wider hem either add width at the CB or add an equal amount to all seams.

Back – Extend the bodice construction (SG) line to hem level and mark off the Waist to floor measurement, here 107 cm.

Centre the hem width, here 68 cm, on the construction line. Draw the CB line from hem to waist and the side seam line from hem to hip curve, using the thin side lines on the bodice, Fig 3, as a guide to flaring. Mark off the hem curve by measuring the Waist to floor length from several points on the waist.

Front – Repeat the process for the Front, but plan the hem width slightly off centre, here 29 cm towards CF and 34 cm towards the side seam line.

No additional hem allowance is needed; the Waist to floor length, when turned up, will lift the hem clear of the ground. Cut out the completed patterns, ready for laying on the cloth. Make sure that the side seams on both Front and Back are the same length and are cut on the same angle. Mark the end of the front opening (FO) at hip level.

For small sizes, you can cut both sleeves from the spare fabric on the left. For larger sizes, open out the fabric after cutting the Front, and cut one sleeve from the spare fabric. Cut the other sleeve similarly from the spare of the Back.

89

5

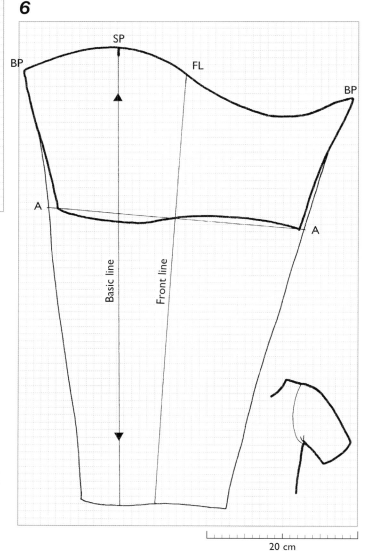

20 cm

5. Sleeve with mitten cuff for Fig 2 (Pls 2, 3)

Trace the sleeve Block, extending the Front line, shown broken, by 10-12 cm.

Measure round the wearer's knuckles, across the widest part of the hand, and plan the new sleeve end. Both edges of the cuff are the same shape and are centred on the Front line. Make the wrist and cuff close-fitting, and leave the seam open for 10-15 cm up the arm from the wrist, shown by balance marks. Fasten with 12 or more buttons.

6

20 cm

6. Short sleeve for Fig 2

This later sleeve reaches about halfway down the upper arm, and is seen on kirtles worn for work.

Measure the required length down the back of the arm.

Trace the sleeve Block. Measure the required length from BP down the back seam lines and rule a construction line AA.

For a loose fit, simply follow the Block outline and draw a shallow curve for the lower edge of the sleeve.

For a closer fit, take in the sleeve a little on both edges, as shown.

Flat-fronted kirtle

7

7. Flat-fronted kirtle, mid 15th century onwards

This kirtle was worn under the tighter and more revealing gowns of the middle and late 15th century (*Gowns,* Fig 28). It is tighter, lower-necked and sleeveless. The flat front panel and side lacing produce the characteristic high cleavage. The bodice is interlined with firm canvas, including a double layer in the front panel if necessary, and lined. It is cut and made up separately from the skirt with its pleated flounce (Fig 9).

8

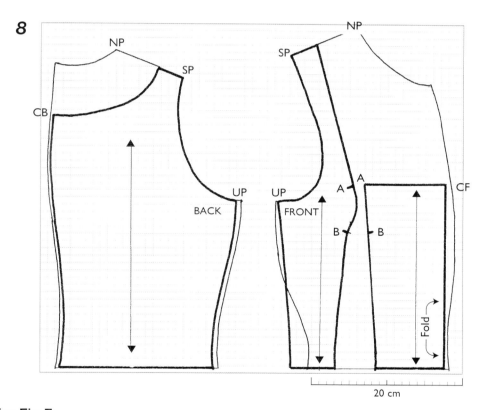

20 cm

8. Bodice for Fig 7

Trace the personal Block to waist level. Plan the front panel on a straight CF line, to be cut on the fold. Plan the Front side piece and Back with no ease at all on the waist. Reduce the bust size to slightly less than the actual Bust measurement. Use the Under Bust measurement to determine the shaped part of the side panel seam, AB. When making up, this section must be eased carefully onto the straight edge of the front panel, AB.

You will need to check the fit of this bodice carefully, preferably trying it first in calico. It should fit closely round the waist and ribcage while supporting the bust. Hollow out the armhole at the side seams if it is uncomfortably tight. For making up see p. 86.

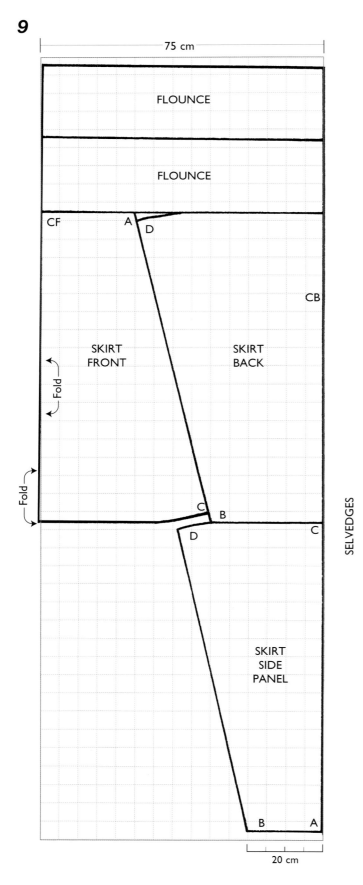

75 cm

FLOUNCE

FLOUNCE

CF   A
      D

CB

SKIRT
FRONT

SKIRT
BACK

Fold

Fold

C
  B
D
        C

SELVEDGES

SKIRT
SIDE
PANEL

B   A

20 cm

9. Skirt pattern and layout for Fig 7

Shown on 150 cm wide fabric folded lengthways. The flounce is 10-25 cm deep: subtract this from the Waist to floor length to give the skirt length. Make the total hem of the skirt 2 to 2.5 m, and the flounce 1¼ to 1½ times the hem. Cut the flounces and Front on the fold. The top edge of the skirt pieces combined should be 20-50 cm wider than the total waist edge of the bodice; more width will make the skirt too bulky. For making up see p. 86.

Doublets

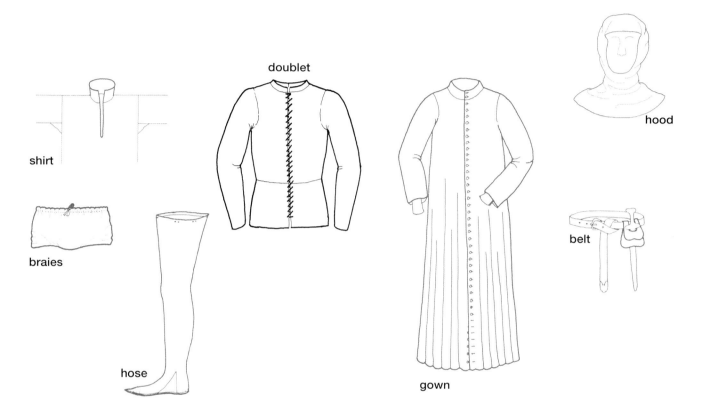

shirt

braies

doublet

hose

gown

hood

belt

Doublets

The doublet almost certainly began as a military garment, the close fit making a secure foundation for armour. It appears to have been the first garment made by fitting on the body, rather than by building up panels with gores and gussets in the old way, and it introduced an era of closer fit and increasingly sophisticated cutting.

The doublet was adopted for civilian wear towards the mid 14th century. By 1500 it was in general use by men, under various outer garments. The body and sleeves were close-fitting, and the shoulders and sleeve heads were cut to allow freedom of movement (Fig 1). The neck band of the earlier versions grew into the standing collar of the 15th century, visible above the neckline of the gown (Fig 2). Occasionally the 15th-century doublet had detachable sleeves tied on with points at the shoulder. Instructions for a sleeveless doublet are given with Fig 5.

The paltok – As a rule the doublet was hidden by the outer garment with only parts of the sleeve, and later the collar, visible. Between about 1370 and 1400 smart young men sometimes appeared in a more elegant version of the doublet, the paltok, worn on its own (Fig 3). This often featured a deeply-cut armhole, and one or both sleeves could be made of different material. It was worn with a belt round the hips, often a 'knightly girdle' of metal plates on a leather or canvas backing.

Doublet and hose (see also *Hose*)

Before the doublet, men wore separate hose (stockings) tied to the breech girdle of their braies (*Braies,* Fig 1). Tying them to the lower edge of the doublet applied more tension to the hose, pulling them to fit further up the legs. The early doublet (Fig 4) reached to the groin, so the hose came no higher than the top of the leg. By the end of the 14th century, however, the doublet was sometimes shortened and worn with hose joined into a single garment cut to reach above the groin.

Although the long doublet persisted in use, for much of the 15th century the fashionable doublet and hose met about 10 to 15 cm below the waist, and towards the end of the century the junction moved higher, almost to the waist (Pls 7, 8).

Points – The points (ties) which secured the hose were at first stitched inside the doublet. In the early 15th century the points began to be threaded through eyelets in its lower edge and around the top of the hose, so the two garments butted together instead of overlapping. Nine pairs of eyelets were usually spaced round the lower edge of the doublet (*Methods*, Figs 16, 18).

1. 1430-40, French
Executioner in long fawn-coloured doublet, his shirt or braies visible at the side. Separate hose (stockings) of scarlet cloth rolled down; scarlet bag-hat and black shoes. (Decameron, Bibliothèque de l'Arsenal, Paris, MS 5070, f.201).

2. 1468, Flemish/Burgundian (Pl 9)
Smart young man with an open gown. Doublet with cut-away front, high collar and puff sleeves; joined hose, ankle shoes and acorn cap. (Chroniques du Hainaut, Bibliothèque Royale, Brussels, MS 9243 f.72)

3. c.1400, English
Nobleman in elaborate high-necked doublet (paltok) with one contrasting sleeve. Separate scalloped cuffs, knightly girdle round the hips, footed hose with one leg red, the other green. The hat is unusual. (Lincoln Cathedral Library, MS 218).

Materials

Outer fabric – use lightweight (but firm) woollen or worsted cloth, closely-woven linen or furnishing union (cotton/linen mixture). Twill-weave linen or flannelette sheeting can be used in place of the medieval fustian. Elaborate doublets could be in taffeta, satin, patterned silk or embroidered silk. Some 15th-century doublets had the collar or sleeves made in a finer material or richer colour than the body, which was largely covered by the outer garment.

Lining – use linen or another light wool.

Interlining – use canvas or calico. Use stiffer canvas for standing collars.

Padding – use layers of soft woollen cloth

Planning and cutting

Instructions for planning and cutting specific doublets are given as captions to the Figures. They include basic (Fig 4) and fashionable (Fig 6) versions.

Cut all the pattern pieces in the outer, interlining and lining materials, noting instructions for the different sleeves. For edges which are to have eyelets or buttonholes – sleeve openings, fronts and lower edges – cut the interlining to the fitting line, but cut the outer material with extra seam allowance to fold back over the interlining (*Methods*, Fig 12). You can cut the lining shorter along these edges to avoid working the eyelets through extra layers of seam allowances.

To plan your garment use the wearer's personal bodice Block. The pattern shown here corresponds approx. to modern size 42. The fine lines show original Block outline. Heavy broken lines indicate alternative outlines. Letters indicate joining points. For abbreviations and symbols see p. 10. Add seam allowances. The four bodice pieces must be cut accurately for a proper fit.

Making up

Doublets are built up from several layers of light or medium weight materials to produce a firm, structured effect. The same result will not be achieved with a single thicker layer, so there are no short cuts.

Interlining – Tack the interlining to the wrong side of all outer material. The high 15th century collar needs an interlining of stiff canvas.

Bodice – Make up the bodice, including the hip sections and under collar. For collars see *Methods*, Fig 14.

Sleeves – Make up the sleeves including the linings, with puffs if used. Finish the wrist ends with any fastenings, and tack all layers together round the sleeve head.

Set the finished sleeves into the doublet body, matching the SP and BP.

For sleeveless doublets (Fig 5) finish off the neck and armholes.

Padding – The bodice of doublets can be padded with extra layers of soft cloth over the shoulders and upper chest. Add them at this stage, stitching them lightly in place along the seam lines, then stitch down the edges of the outer material on the inside, over all interlining. Padding of sleeve puffs is described in Fig 9.

Bodice lining – Stitch the facing to the collar. Make up the complete lining for the Back, Front and hip sections.

Pin the lining into the bodice (*Methods*, Fig 12), matching up the seam lines; turn in the allowances round the armholes and edges. Hem round the armhole seams, then hem or stab-stitch round the front, neck and lower edges (Pl 1). To make the garment firmer or hold any extra interlining in place, catch the lining through the seam turnings of the outer fabric, stitching along the seam lines from the inside so the stitches are not seen on the outside.

continued overleaf

Basic doublet

4

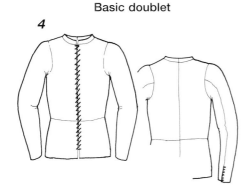

Fashionable doublet

6

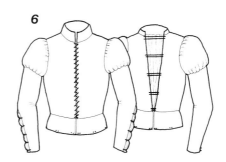

Basic doublet

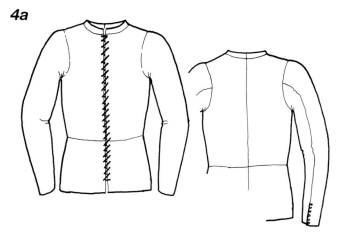

4. Basic doublet, mid 14th century onwards

a. The neck can be plain or have a narrow band collar. Hip sections are long, with side vents, and have points stitched inside for separate hose. The sleeves are quite plain and tight at the wrist: in the 14th century they were fastened with a dozen or more buttons. Later they had just one or two. The body is laced closed. The whole garment could be lightly padded and quilted.

Fastenings – see *Methods*, Figs 16-21

Most doublets were laced at the front (Fig 4a) and buttoned at the wrists, but sometimes they were buttoned at the front (Fig 4b). Despite the close fit of the doublet, no extra width needs to be added for fastening, as the buttons and holes are very close to the edge (Pls 2, 3). The number of buttons on each sleeve varied, from a dozen or more in the 14th century to one or two by the middle of the 15th.

For tying a doublet to hose see *Methods,* Fig 18.

b. The standing collar with characteristic V back was usual for the 15th century. The front is fastened with buttons, though lacing was still more common. The hip sections might be shortened for joined hose, and have eyelets for trussing.

5. Pattern for Fig 4 ⟶

a. Bodice. Trace round the personal bodice Block. For a sleeveless doublet use the lowered neckline for the round collar and the larger armholes indicated by the broken lines.

Hip section – Add balance marks to the side seams for the vents. The broken line shows a shorter version for wear with joined hose. See Fig 7 for eyelet positions.

Round collar (Fig 4a) – Lower the neck line by 3-4 cm all round. Trace off the back and front neck pieces above the new line and cut them out. Slash each piece in two or three places from the inner curve almost to the outer. On a fresh piece of paper position the back and front pieces together at a. Open out the slashes slightly on the neck edge to lengthen it by 1-2 cm. Draw round the pieces to make a pattern for half the collar, which will have a seam at CB.

b. Standing collar (Fig 4b). This is a two piece collar, planned on the Block but cut separately. Plan the new neck line. From 5-10 cm down the CB line rule a slanting line to the shoulder, 2-4 cm away from NP. From the corresponding point on the front shoulder draw a curved neck line which can dip slightly to CF. Measure the length of the new neck line.

For the collar itself, draw a CB line initially following the shaping of the back, then running straight to 5 cm above the Block neck line. Mark the SG. Rule another slanting line from CB to about 20 cm beyond the shoulder line, spacing it 0.5 cm from the new neck line at the shoulder. Mark off from CB the total neck line to define the neck edge of the collar to CF. The balance mark shows where it meets the shoulder seam.

Make a trial sketch of the collar upper edge, trace off the collar pattern and make a calico toile for fitting. If it is too tight, adjust the front collar section as shown by the fine outlines. This lengthens the upper edge while keeping the neck edge the same. Its approximate front shape is outlined by the fine broken line.

Sleeve – Use your sleeve Block unaltered.

5a

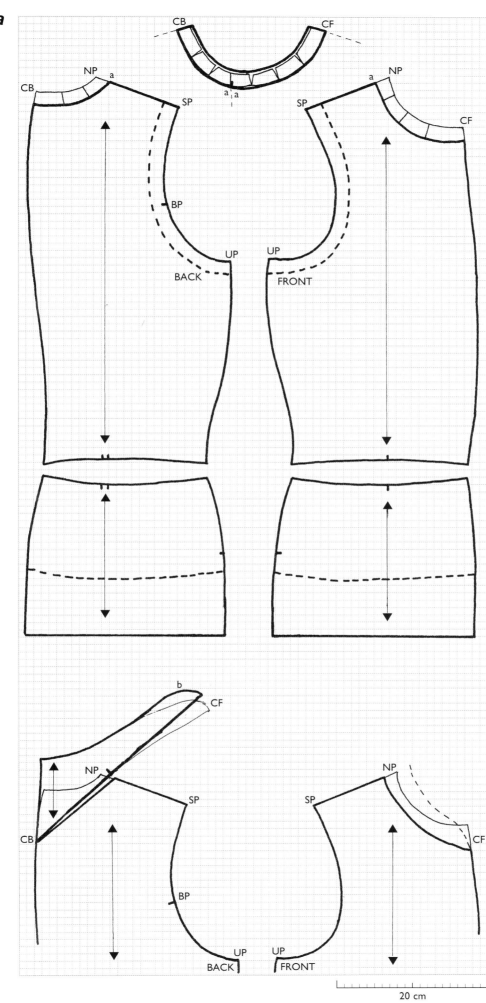

20 cm

Plate 7 **Mid-15th century doublet and hose**

A fashionable doublet (Fig 6) with joined hose (*Hose,* Fig 8) in black serge. Note the close fit of both garments, still allowing free movement, but with unavoidable wrinkles at the knees. The doublet is worn over a linen shirt, which would normally have a high collar. The doublet will be fastened close to the hose with the points. The pointed shoes are laced on the inside.

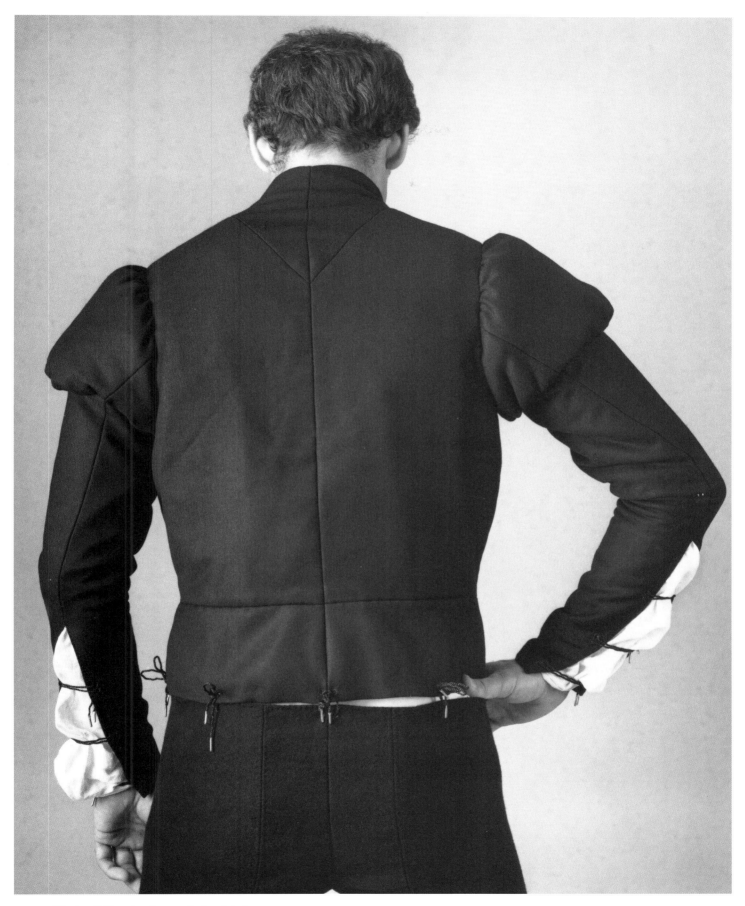

Plate 8 Back view of doublet
This shows the characteristic V-back of the collar, sometimes made from finer fabric than the body. The sleeve puffs reach over the shoulder joint; the lower sleeves are cut away to show off the shirt and tied with points.

6. Fashionable doublet, mid to late 15th century

The collar was high and stiff. After 1470 it became noticeably lower and its V-shape at the back went out of use. The hip sections are short, with eyelets to support joined hose. The sleeve puffs supported the full sleeves of a gown worn on top.

Left The shirt sleeve protrudes between the latchets of the cut-away sleeve (Pls 7, 8).

Right The cut-away front is drawn together with latchets. A fine linen breast-kerchief is worn behind them.

7. Pattern for Fig 6

Trace round the personal bodice Block.

Body and hip section – Shorten the hip sections to 10-12 cm. For a cut-away front use the broken line as a guide: it joins the neck line about 5 cm from CF. Eyelet positions are shown on edges.

Fashionable doublet

6

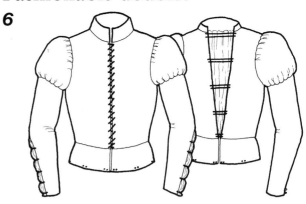

Collar – A higher version of the standing collar in Fig 5b, also planned on the block and cut separately, but in 4 pieces. Lower the neck line as described in Fig 5a.

Back collar – Draw the collar CB slanting in slightly from the vertical, 5-10 cm above the Block neck line. Draw the neck edge, the same length as the body, leaving a 0.5 cm gap at the shoulder. Draw the top edge at least a fifth of the Neck size, and the slanted side seam 5-10 cm long.

Front collar – Draw the neck edge curve shallower than the body neck but equal in length. Rule the vertical CF 5-10 cm high. Plan the side seam and top edge to match the back collar. The combined top edges of back and front collar on the pattern should equal half Neck size plus 1-2 cm ease.

Mark the SG on both sections (the Front is on the bias) and trace off the patterns. Make a calico toile for fitting. For a cut-away front shorten the front collar to match the new neck line (see broken lines). You could also use the round collar from Fig 5a.

Sleeve – Use your sleeve Block unaltered, or see Fig 8 for a puff sleeve.

7

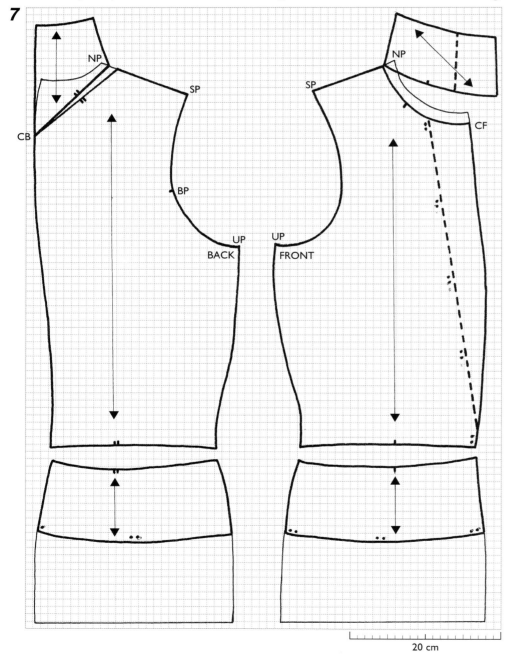

20 cm

100

8. Puff sleeve for Fig 6

The sleeve is in two parts: the *lower section*, made up with interlining and lining using the whole pattern; and the *puff* with its interlining, stitched to the made-up lower section.

Lower section – Trace round the personal sleeve Block. Plan the curved seam line as follows: measure 12-15 cm from BP down the Back seam lines and rule a construction line A-A. Plan the curved seam line dipping slightly before the Basic line, and rising to within 4-6 cm of the underarm. Trace off the lower sleeve pattern below the seam line.

For the cut-away style, which will require eyelets for fastening (*Methods,* Fig 16), follow the broken lines on the lower sleeve.

Puff – Draw the grid and number the pieces (to keep track!). Trace off, and cut along the grid lines. Spread the pieces as shown in (*b*), leaving wider gaps at the shoulder than at the underarm, and draw a smooth outline round them to make the puff pattern. The puff should be about 20 cm wider than the Block and up to 10 cm deeper on the Basic Line. A larger puff would be difficult to pad firmly.

Cut the outer fabric only up to the seam line AA (remember seam allowance!), but cut the lining and interlining using the whole sleeve pattern. Cut the puff pattern (*b*) from the outer fabric, and a firm interlining. See Fig 9 for making up.

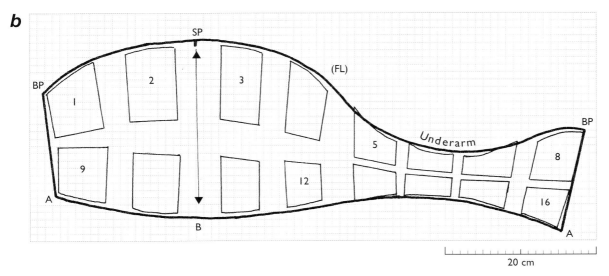

101

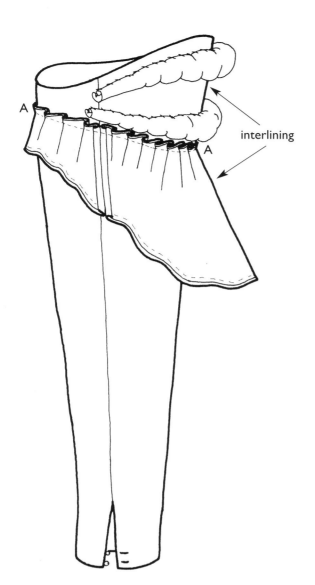

interlining

9. Making up the puff sleeve (Pls 7, 8)

Make up the lower section by combining the interlining and lining for the whole sleeve length with the outer fabric up to AA (Fig 8). Complete the wrist fastening.

Tack the interlining of the puff to its outer fabric and stitch the ends of the puff together. With right sides together pleat the lower edge of the puff onto the top edge of the outer fabric. Tack and stitch through all layers.

Make two firm tapered pads by rolling up soft woollen cloth, or by stuffing cotton wool into a calico tube. The upper roll should be larger. Tack them in position at the base of the puff and over the crown of the sleeve, just below the seam allowance. Draw the puff up over them, stuff with more padding if required, pleat it to fit, and tack it to the top of the sleeve. Set the complete sleeve into the doublet.

Plate 9 Scene from mass baptism, 1468, Flemish/Burgundian

The lady on the left is wearing the characteristic form of the gown without its belt, and the straight neck edge of a kirtle can be seen beneath. The gentleman at centre front is slipping off a fashionable lined gown with little fullness, revealing a tight, high-waisted doublet. This is cut away at the front and has a contrasting collar and puffed sleeves. The joined hose is tied to the doublet well below waist level and the codpiece is just visible. The man seated on the right of the font is having his hose removed. These have striking zigzag seams at calf level, and stirrup feet. Points for tying the hose to the doublet hang from the hose waist.

Chroniques du Hainaut, Bibliothèque Royale, Brussels MS 9243, f.72

103

Hose

All forms of leg covering in general use were known as hose, and all hose covered at least the lower leg. Many enclosed the feet as well, and some reached right up the leg to become joined hose – a form sometimes likened to tights. In practice it is better to think of separate hose as a pair of heavy stockings (Figs 1-3), and joined hose as very close-fitting trousers (Pl 9). The close fit was achieved by modelling the hose pattern as a toile on the wearer – a process similar to that described for personal Blocks – and maximum 'stretch' obtained by cutting the woollen cloth on the bias.

Women's hose
Women wore short separate hose (Figs 3, 4b) held up by garters just below the knee. These usually had plain feet for wear with shoes.

Men's hose
Separate (stocking) hose
Up to the late 14th century all hose consisted of two separate legs. The early form (Figs 1, 4a) fitted closely up to the knee, then widened, the front rising to a point with a button on it. Such hose were worn with loose braies (Fig 1) which were tucked into the hose. A breech-girdle supporting the braies (*Braies*, Fig 1) also held up the hose by a loop of cord passed round the button. This was sometimes supplemented by garters.

From about mid 14th century the hose could be tied to the doublet by laces ('points'), stitched inside the doublet (*Doublets,* p. 94) and tied through eyelets at the top of the hose. Hose soon became longer and more closely fitted round the thighs (Fig 4c). Separate hose continued to be worn throughout the 15th century by workmen, and by older men with long gowns.

Separate hose without feet, like leggings, were often worn by peasants. They were slightly loose and were held on by garters at the calf and ankle. They could also be worn over another pair of hose for warmth. 'Boot hose', an extra pair of hose worn inside long riding boots, were used in the 15th century. Different combinations were used to suit the wearer's needs.

Joined hose
These were probably introduced before 1400. They were much harder to cut and fit well than separate legs, and how widely they were worn is uncertain. Joined hose were made with a codpiece, and were usually worn with a shorter doublet reaching to hip length or above (Pl 11).

Joined hose were commonly worn with shoes, using stirrups – a simple loop of cloth under the foot – to maintain the tension. The most elegant joined hose with full feet had leather soles and were worn without shoes. Pattens (see below) were worn over them out of doors. These hose were not used for working dress as their tight fit restricted the wearer's movements.

1. Late 13th century, English
Thresher in blue shirt and white coif. Ankle boots and separate (stocking) hose which are drawn up over loose braies or a breech clout and secured at the front. (English calendar, Bodleian Library, Oxford, MS Corpus Christi, 285, f.6v)

2. c.1465, Flemish
Mason at work with separate (stocking) hose unlaced from his doublet. His braies fit more closely than their earlier counterparts. Stylish acorn cap. (Histoire de Charles Martel, Bibliothèque Royale, Brussels, MS6, f.554v).

3. Late 15th century, French
Woman being pulled by the hair, revealing her hose and shoes. Russet gown worn over white smock, with black hose held up by garters (Roman de la Rose, Bodleian Library, Oxford, MS Douce 195, f.66v).

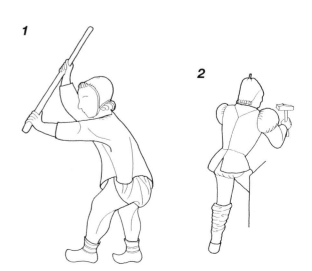

Footwear

Most men and women wore shoes over their hose, but shoemaking is beyond the scope of this book. They can be ordered from re-enactment traders and theatrical suppliers. Medieval shoes were made with left and right shaping, usually with slightly pointed toes and without built-up heels. Points more than 5 cm beyond the end of the foot were not worn by ordinary people. Although coloured leather was available, most illustrations show them as plain black.

How often people wore socks inside their shoes is not clear and certainly many men with stirrups to their hose had nothing else between foot and shoe. Some examples show short socks above the shoe top, so perhaps they were sometimes worn for warmth. Socks for regular washing would be of linen rather than cloth, made like short footed hose.

Pattens were wooden soles held on the foot with leather straps; they were usually worn with soled hose and were commoner for men than women. They were made of aspen or poplar wood for lightness.

Materials

The best fabric for hose is pure wool of light to medium weight, and with little or no 'finish' – the weave should be plainly visible on at least one side of the cloth. Twill weave is usually best, but a tabby weave may be springy enough. The stretch of the fabric is important, so test it by tugging across the bias (at 45° to the weave): if it stretches well and springs back, it is suitable.

You will need 1 to 1.5 metres of 150 cm wide cloth for a pair of separate hose, and 1.5 metres or more for joined hose.

Linen can be used for short hose or socks, for both men and women, but though cooler and easily washed it will never give quite as good a fit. For authentic hose avoid jersey (knitted) fabric, even in wool, which can be too close-fitting: wrinkles are a normal feature of properly made hose.

To plan your garment you will need to:
- select your foot style
- take body measurements
- prepare a toile and model it on the wearer
- adjust it, and draw a working pattern
- refit as necessary, then draw the final pattern
- align the pattern SG on the SG of the fabric

Letters on patterns indicate joining points. For abbreviations and symbols see p. 10.
Remember to add seam allowances.

Preparing your pattern

It is best to start with separate hose before attempting the more complicated joined version. If you have not already modelled and prepared a personal bodice Block you should read about this first (see *Blocks*) as the method is similar.

Foot style – Select from the styles shown in Figs 4, 7, 10. To model the feet, which are shaped for left and right, follow the captions.

3

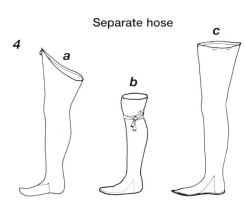

Separate hose

4   a

b

c

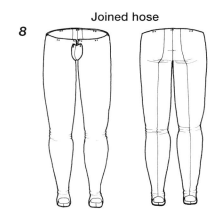

Joined hose

8

Separate hose

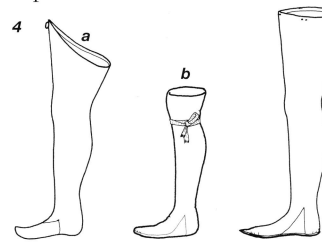

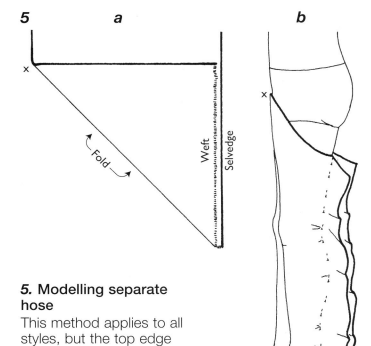

4. Separate hose, 1200-1500

The foot styles are interchangeable: they could also have stirrups as shown in Fig 10.

a. Early form of man's hose, with point at front and button (wood or cloth) for string tied to breech girdle. Upper legs are cut wide to fit over long braies.

b. Woman's hose; often seen folded down over the garter.

c. Later form of man's hose reaching to top of the leg, with eyelets for lacing to long doublet.

Separate hose, Fig 4

Measurements – Width: round the thigh at the widest point.

Length: from top of thigh to floor, when standing, plus the requirements of the chosen foot style.

Preparing and modelling the toile, Fig 5 – You need to cut the two pieces of calico for the toile on the bias, one for each leg. First tear across the weft end of the calico to ensure it is on the straight grain. Find the bias line by folding the material diagonally so the weft end lies along a selvedge. Measure the length along the bias and the width across it. Mark a Centre line down each piece on the bias. Cut out each toile with plenty of spare and model it on the wearer.

The model must stand, bare legged and bare footed. Finish fitting and pinning one leg before starting the other. You can expect the calico used for the toile to have less stretch than the finished hose. Be careful with the pins! Pointing them upwards makes it safer for the model when you remove the completed toile.

For adjusting the toile and drawing the working pattern see Fig 6. For making up see p. 111.

5. Modelling separate hose

This method applies to all styles, but the top edge and foot style correspond to Fig 4a.

a. Fabric folded to find the true bias before cutting. The corner *x* will lie at the top of the leg.

b. Modelling the leg Position the toile with the centre line running down the front of the model's leg, pinning it to the clothing at the top of the leg for support during fitting.

Draw the edges back round the knee and lower thigh until they fit fairly closely, but not tightly, and pin the back seam from the knee upwards. Next draw the edges back round the calf and pin them to fit behind the knee, over the calf muscle and down to the ankle, always keeping the line on the toile straight down the front of the leg. The toile should fit closely enough to stay in place by itself, but don't pull it tight round the ankle or it will not come off over the heel.

The foot – As soon as the toile starts to drag over the top of the foot, fit the chosen foot style. This figure and Fig 6 show the method for making an upper (or vamp) and sole in one.

Cut the toile to form a short pointed flap on top, and bring two extensions under the heel, continuing the back leg seam.

Lay another piece of fabric over the foot, pinning it first to the flap, then down the sides of the heel extensions. Trim away the surplus. Bring both sides under the model's sole, pinning them together from heel extensions to toes. You won't get a close fit with this style, and the pattern tends to form a 'peak' at the toes, but it is simpler than other enclosed feet, and useful on thicker cloth.

106

Checking the fit – Check up the back of the leg
and mark the shape of the top edge. Men's early
hose (Fig 4a) reach halfway up the thigh at the back
and rise to a point, *x*, at the Centre line on the
working pattern, Fig 6. Men's later hose (Fig 4c)
reach to the top of the leg all round. Women's hose
(Fig 4b) reach about 10 cm above the kneecap.

Ease the completed toile off the leg. If it won't slip
over the heel, move the pin out slightly. Repeat for
the other leg.

6. Pattern for Fig 4a

Remove the fitted toiles, mark the fitting lines onto
both sides of each and remove the pins. Rule a
Centre line onto paper and trace the outlines of
both toiles *(Blocks: From toile to Block)*, each
centered on this line. Fold the paper along this
Centre line, and trace a final back seam line from
the four toile fitting lines. Your final pattern should be
symmetrical along the Centre line for the length of
the leg down to the ankle.

To make up first sew the foot section to the leg,
matching the letters, then sew the leg and
underfoot seams in one.

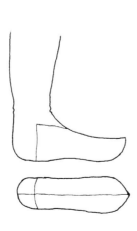

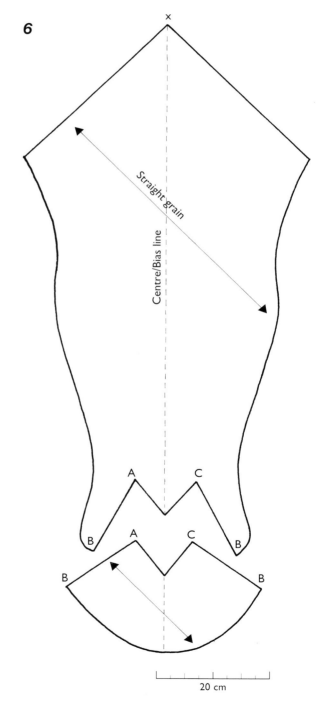

20 cm

107

7. Foot styles for Figs 4b&c

a. Style for Fig 4b This has heel extensions as in Figs 5 & 6, and combined half-sole and side gussets. With careful adjustment it can give a good fit. Before starting, ensure your toile is long enough to reach beyond the model's toes.

Leg – Fit the toile as·described in Fig 5. When it begins to drag over the foot, snip into the fabric on each side over the ankle bone, and slash straight down. Draw the back edges of the toile under the foot to enclose the heel, trimming away the surplus. The front section of the toile will form the vamp.

Sole – Take another piece of fabric with a straight edge (AC) on the straight grain. This will form the sole and gussets. Place it under the foot and bring the straight edges up to match the slashes (marked " on the pattern) and pin in place.

Smooth the toile over the foot towards the toes to form the vamp. Work round both sides of the foot, smoothing the vamp down and pinning it all round to the sole. Any folds formed will be eased onto the sole when you make it up.

When you reach the slashed edges of the vamp, mark the position of the sloping edge of the gussets on the sole piece. Trim away the surplus round the foot before removing the toile. Plan a pattern from the toile and refit if necessary. Repeat for the other leg.

Making up – First sew the back leg seam to B, then carefully pin and stitch the sole and gusset piece, matching the letters. Ease the curved vamp onto the sole.

7a

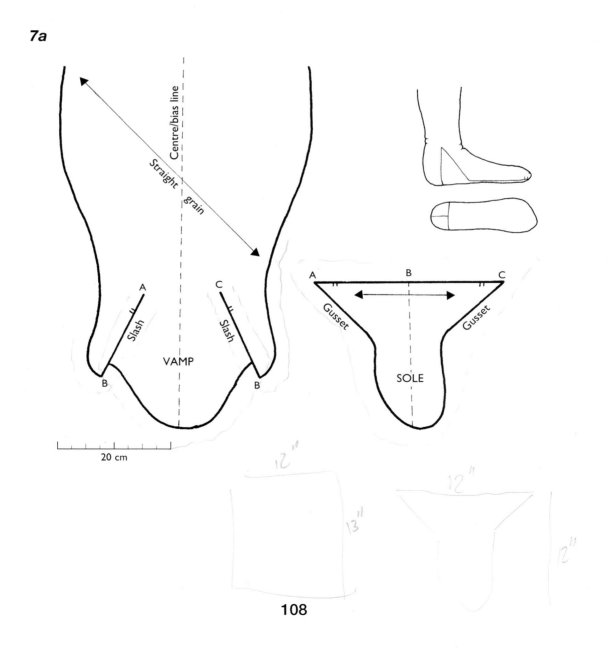

20 cm

b. Style for Fig 4c This is the best style for soled hose and has a one-piece sole, with no seams under the foot. With skilled fitting it can give a 'skin-tight' fit. Before starting ensure that your toile is long enough for the extended toes.

Sole – First make a sole pattern by drawing round the model's bare feet, with the pencil slanting under the foot. Overlay the two outlines, trace a common shape, and plan extended toes to produce a pattern. Cut out two soles with generous seam allowances for the fitting.

Leg – Fit the toile as in Fig 5. When it starts to drag over the foot, snip into the fabric on each side over the ankle bone and slash straight down. Place the fabric sole under the foot. Fit the back edges of the toile down to the back of the heel and pin them to the sole, trimming away the surplus.

Vamp – Smooth the front of the toile over the foot and pin it to the sole to form the vamp, as described for the previous style. Leave a gap on each side where the ankle slashes open out, to be filled later by separate gussets. Remove the toile. Repeat for the other leg.

Gussets – To make a pattern for the gussets, measure each edge of the slash, and the gap on the sole between them. If the gap is different on the inside and outside of the foot, make a pattern for each side. Hollow out the front edge of the gusset slightly to improve the fit.

For a long extension, as shown, cut the upper part 0.5-1 cm shorter than the sole and stretch it onto the sole when you sew them together: this will make the point curl upwards slightly.

Plan a pattern and refit if necessary. This style reaches the top of the leg and is finished with a facing and eyelets (*Methods*, Fig 16).

Making up – First set the gussets into the slashes, then stitch the back leg seam, and finally stitch on the sole.

For soled hose, use the pattern to cut two soles in leather, without seam allowances. Oversew them to the completed hose.

If the style fits closely the foot must be put on by turning it inside out and easing it over the heel.

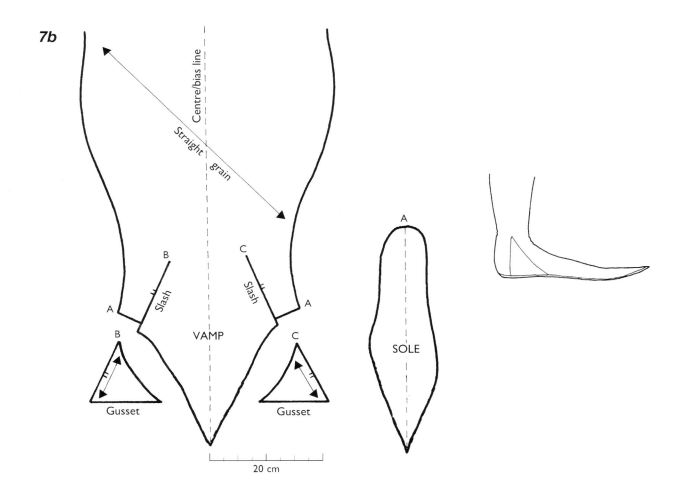

7b

20 cm

Joined hose

8

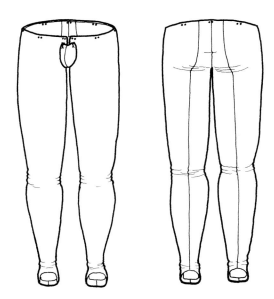

8. Joined hose, 15th century

These meet the doublet 10-15 cm below the waist, though the level moved up gradually towards the waist in the late 15th century.

The CF edges are finished by the breech lining and left open (Fig 12), to be covered by the codpiece. The opening can be fastened with a lace close to the waist, using two pairs of eyelets, one on each edge. The codpiece is made up separately: its lower end is sewn to a gusset at the breech seam and its top is tied to the hose through eyelets on either side of the front opening.

The stirrup feet shown were the commonest form, and the easiest to make.

Joined hose, Fig 8

A wrinkle-free fit is possible but will restrict movement, so most hose are baggy at the seat and knees. Freedom of movement is gained by lengthening rather than widening the legs: note the horizontal wrinkles in Fig 8. Aim for a good fit round the calf, and looser round the ankle to slip over the heel. Start with an easy-fitting pair: a closer-fitting version can follow with practice.

Measurements – Width: round the thigh at the widest point, or half the Seat measurement if this is greater.

Length: from waist to floor at the side, when standing, plus the requirements of the chosen foot style.

Preparing and modelling the toile, Fig 9 – You will need help to model joined hose. Cut two pieces of calico on the bias, as for separate hose. Make them wider than the Thigh measurement at one end, and a little narrower at the other. Mark a Centre line down each piece on the bias.

Read the caption to Fig 5 for separate hose, then study the pattern for joined hose (Fig 10). See also the *Note on fitted garments,* p. 23, which applies here. Although hose don't

necessarily fit skin-tight, they follow the body more closely than modern trousers. Start by fitting the leg, as for separate hose, then fit the breech section as described below. The codpiece and its supporting gusset are drafted separately (Fig 11), not modelled as part of the toile.

Position the centre line of the toile down the model's leg and pin it to his clothing at waist level. It is best to fit the toile to waist height, then reduce the length of the final pattern to match the length of the doublet. When each leg is fitted (Fig 5) move up to the crotch or breech section. The wearer may prefer to handle the scissors himself, with the assistant to pin the Back extension.

Two points are important for the fit of the breech.
• The toile must fit well up to the groin at the inside thigh, with extra length for freedom of movement.
• The edge of the breech cut-out must be long enough to allow sitting down or stooping in comfort: note its shape in Fig 10.
For adjusting the toile and drawing the working pattern see Fig 10.

---

9. Modelling joined hose

Prepare the toile and fit each leg as described for separate hose and in Fig 5. In this case it will be modelled to waist height and the finished pattern shortened to match the length of the doublet. This diagram and the pattern (Fig 10) show a stirrup foot. It is formed by hollowing out the toile round the heel and instep to leave a strip of fabric which is joined under the foot.

Breech – Fit and pin the seam up the back of the thigh until the material begins to drag between the legs.

At waist level, fit the toile across to the CF of the model's body and pin it to the undergarment. Fit the toile round the side of the waist, smoothing upwards and round and pinning at waist level, until the outer edge of the back seam runs from the thigh up to the waist.

Return to the CF. Slash straight down to genital level, then curve the slash line to fit under the body, round the top of the leg and through to the back, smoothing the material up to the top of the thigh. This will form the Back extension (Fig 10). If you run out of toile at this point, cut a strip on the straight grain and pin or staple it on to complete the extension.

At the back, trim away the surplus material above the slash line, leaving a narrow strip from the CB to the Back seam. Leave the CB edge slightly baggy. After fitting the second leg, pin the two together at the CB and ensure there is enough ease. Ask the model to snip into the edge of the toile, on both legs, at the base of the genitals: this will define the position of the codpiece (A in Fig 10).

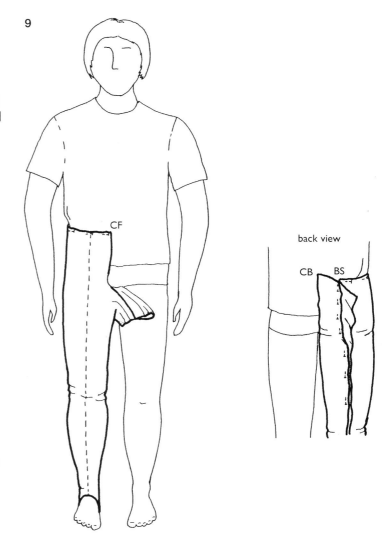

Making up separate and joined hose

The long seam up the back of the leg must 'give' with the stretch of the cloth, so use a narrow zigzag stitch if you are machine sewing it, or a slightly slack backstitch if hand sewing. Silk thread has more stretch than cotton. Catch down the raw edges with running stitch to make a triple-run seam (*Methods,* Fig 5) or make a run-and-fell (*Methods,* Fig 6). The different feet are described in the captions.

Separate hose – The top edges may be finished in different ways. For women's gartered hose, turn over the tops and hem them. On the early form of men's separate hose (Fig 4a), sew a large shanked wooden or cloth button at the top of each point to support them. For the longer separate hose (Fig 4c) face the top edge with a narrow strip of linen or canvas to reinforce it, and work eyelets through both layers to match the points or eyelets on the doublet (*Methods,* Figs 16, 18).

Joined hose – Make up the legs, and feet if present, then sew the legs together round the breech seam, inserting the codpiece gusset. Cut a strip of canvas on the straight grain, 2-3 cm wide, and tack it inside the waist edge of the hose to reinforce the eyelets.

Joined hose are best made with a lined 'breech' or seat area. Use light cloth or linen for this, and the outline in Fig 10 as a guide for cutting. Allow a little extra fabric if it is not as stretchy as the hose cloth. Make up the lining as for the hose, with a gusset, hemming the leg ends. Insert the lining into the hose, and turn in the edges round the waist and Centre front opening. Oversew or topstitch together all round before working the eyelets and making and attaching the codpiece (Figs 11, 12).

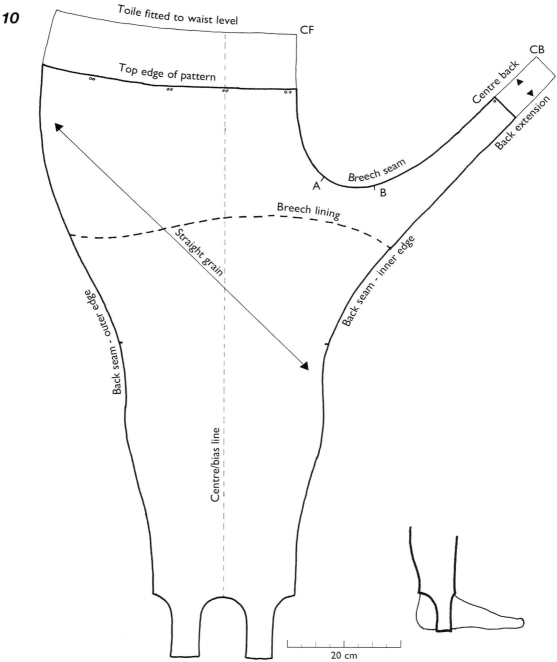

10. *Toile fitted to waist level*

CF

CB

Centre back

Top edge of pattern

Back extension

Breech seam

A   B

Breech lining

Straight grain

Back seam - inner edge

Back seam - outer edge

Centre/bias line

20 cm

10. Pattern for Fig 8

Remove the fitted toiles carefully, remove the pins and mark the fitting lines onto both sides of each. Proceed as in Fig 6.

The legs should be symmetrical on either side of the Centre line, from the stirrup foot to above the knee, marked by balance points. Above this the inner edge slants out into the extension. Check the two back seam edges are about the same length, though the outer edge can be 1-2 cm longer. Ease this extra length in when sewing the seam.

The fit of hose always needs adjustment, so be prepared to try out your working pattern in calico more than once before making a final pattern. The commonest problem is too narrow a breech curve, giving insufficient ease between the legs: widen the curve by increasing the angle and length of the Back extension.

When the fit is satisfactory, make your final pattern on paper. Lower the waist edge to match the length of the doublet. Mark the line for the breech lining, and the SG at 45° to the Centre line. Point *A* on the breech seam is the lower edge position for the codpiece, transferred from the toile: point *B* is the approximate position of the back end of the codpiece gusset. Plan the codpiece and gusset as described in Fig 11.

The pattern for a complete leg is large, and awkward to lay out for cutting: open the cloth out to a single layer, and if it has a right and wrong side reverse the pattern for the second leg. You may have to 'piece' the pattern as described in *Blocks*, Fig 28.

11. Codpiece and gusset

The codpiece is there to enclose and support the genitals, and cover the front opening.

Gusset – This provides a base to attach the codpiece to the hose. Cut a strip on the bias, 3-5 cm wide and 10-15 cm long, plus seam allowances. Ease it into the breech seam when making up the hose, with the back end tapering to B and the front end finishing at A just under the genitals (Fig 10).

Codpiece pattern – The codpiece is made in two halves with a curved CF seam, and lined. Scale up the pattern, adding seam allowances, and try it out first in calico. Check it doesn't reach above the top edge of the hose.

Making up – Cut the pattern twice in the outer fabric, then again in the lining. Sew the CF seams of each, then turn in all the raw edges and stab stitch outer and lining together (Pl 1). Work pairs of eyelets in the top corners.

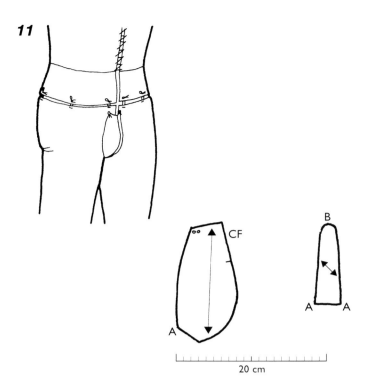

20 cm

12. Making up Fig 8

Made up hose, with breech lining and codpiece gusset in place. Work eyelets (*Methods,* Fig 16) as follows:

    On the top edge, the usual nine pairs to tie the hose to the doublet

    On either side of the front opening a vertical pair (if needed) to fasten the front of the hose.

Attaching the codpiece – Tack and stitch it in place across the base of the opening so that it overlaps *AA* on the outside. Position the horizontal eyelets on the hose to secure the top corners.

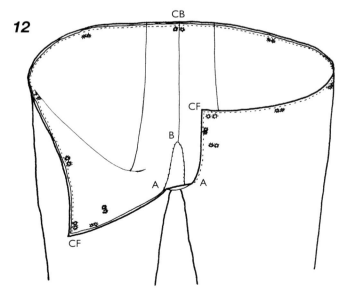

113

Surcotes

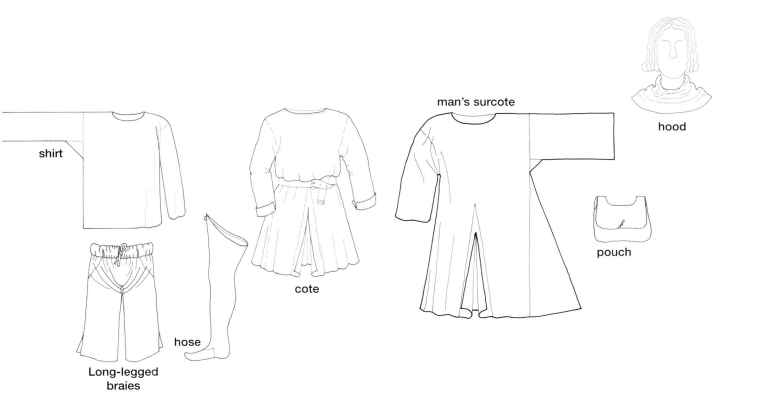

shirt

Long-legged braies

hose

cote

man's surcote

hood

pouch

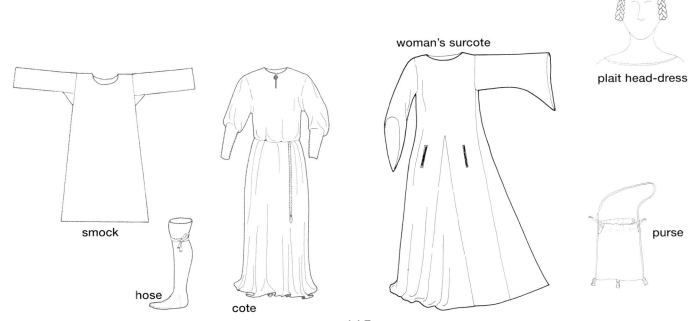

smock

hose

cote

woman's surcote

plait head-dress

purse

Surcotes

'Surcote' is used here to describe a range of early outer garments worn over a main garment by both men and women. Most were related to the cote in both cut and construction, but the cote was normally worn with a belt, while the surcote was worn loosely over it. Like the cote, men's and women's versions showed some differences.

Men's surcotes

In the 13th century men wore either sleeved or sleeveless surcotes (Figs 1, 3). They abandoned the sleeveless form in the early 14th century just as women adopted it. Surcotes were usually at least calf length, but longer for older men or those of higher status. The surcote of the first half of the 14th century had the same elbow-length peaked sleeves (Fig 2; *Frontispiece*) as on women's, which gradually became more pronounced. Openings in the side seams gave access to the belt. Older men continued to wear this surcote until the later 14th century, though more fashionable men seem to have abandoned it by the middle of the century.

The neckline, frequently hidden by the cape of the hood, was usually round and large enough for the surcote to be pulled on without a front slit opening. The skirts could be slit at the front and back for riding.

Women's surcotes

Surcotes with sleeves – During the 13th century women's surcotes usually had sleeves, three-quarter length or longer, wide enough to show the sleeve of the cote (Fig 1). In the early part of the century the sleeve developed a 'peak', an extension below the forearm (Fig 2). By the 1370s the cotehardie or gown can be seen in place of the sleeved surcote.

1. Early 14th century, English. Woman going to market
A simple loose surcote over a long-sleeved cote. Bare feet; cloth veil over wimple. (Book of Hours, British Library, MS Stowe 17, f.67).

2. c.1340, English. Man removing surcote
Loose surcote with peaked sleeves, its edges bound or bordered. The cote within is loose enough to pouch over the unseen belt, but well fitted over the shoulders and upper arms. Well-fitted hose and ankle shoes. (Luttrell Psalter, British Library, MS Add 42130, f.198)

3. c.1340, English. Woman in sleeveless surcote
The surcote is slit at the side and here worn with a belt. The cote sleeves are narrow but not buttoned; a single kerchief is swathed round head and neck. (Luttrell Psalter, British Library, MS Add 42130, f.158).

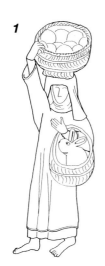

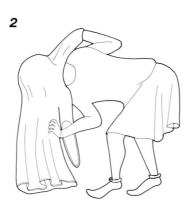

Sleeveless surcotes – These were commonly worn from about 1300 (Fig 3). At first they appear loose and unshaped. By the middle of the century they became more fitted, with some showing the cut-out armholes which developed into the sideless surcote (Fig 9). The deeply cut-away sideless surcote, worn over a kirtle, is one of the best-known medieval garments. It is often seen on effigies but was mainly for court and ceremonial wear. The surcote went out of general use by the early 15th century.

The skirts of the surcote were generally cut wider than for the cote and might be worn longer or shorter. Some 14th century peasant women, however, had long slits at the sides of their skirts, suggesting a narrower, more economical garment, slit for greater ease of movement (Fig 3). The round or boat-shaped neckline, large enough to slip over the head, was often hidden by the wimple or veil. The wide, revealing necklines, shown on richer women from the 1330s, would have been matched on the cote beneath.

Materials
Outer fabric – Use wool cloth, choosing the quality to suit the wearer – thick and heavy for a warm, simple surcote, or fine and flowing for a lady. The quality should be better than for the cote beneath, since it is more visible. Wealthier people might have a set, of cote, surcote and hood, made from the same cloth. In the mid 14th century it was fashionable to make the two halves of the surcote in contrasting colours. The very rich might wear a surcote made from imported patterned silk, or decorated with fine embroidery.

Lining – Use a lining of thick cloth or fur for warmth; or fine cloth, linen or silk for a neat inside finish, together with a flash of contrasting colour. If left unlined, apply facing round the neck and armholes or sleeve ends.

continued on page 119

Man's sleeved surcote

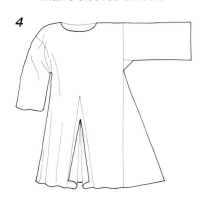

4

Woman's fashionable surcote

5

Planning and cutting

The range of surcotes included here covers both sleeved (Figs 4, 5) and sleeveless (Figs 7-9) versions, from simple garments to more elaborate fitted ones, for both men and women.

Plan the surcote as described for *Cotes*, p. 77. If you haven't already made a cote, you will find more details of the methods there. The open sided surcote (Fig 9) is based on the personal Block, like the kirtle.

Refer to the Key measurements. Ensure that Garment width and Sleeve width will be an easy fit over the cote beneath. Most surcotes were quite ample, so if in doubt make it bigger.

Use the dimensions to make a sketch plan on paper of the pieces and layout, like Fig 4b. For a fuller surcote add more width by putting in extra side gores. Plan the final pattern pieces on paper, and lay them out on a single layer of cloth, or on calico, which can be fitted and then used as a pattern.

You can adjust any dimension by 1 or 2 cm if it helps make a more economical layout. Check the pattern dimensions match the plan *before* you cut, making sure you have enough length, ease and seam allowance. Cut out the pattern pieces as nearly as possible along the straight grain (Figs 4b, 5b).

To plan your garment use measurements already taken (*Blocks*, Figs 1, 2), or measure the wearer, but plan the surcote in Fig 9 from the personal bodice Block. Fine broken lines indicate Fold lines and Centre lines of pattern pieces. Heavy broken lines indicate alternative outlines. Letters indicate joining points. For abbreviations and symbols see p. 10. Add seam allowances to all dimensions.

Key measurements

Garment length

Men – shoulder to hem. Back length, + waist to knee, or waist to ankle, or in between

Women – shoulder to hem. Back length, + waist to floor

For both – add a further 5 to 20 cm for pouching over a belt

Garment width – half Chest or Bust + 8 to 20 cm (or more) ease

Gore length – From waist to hem: subtract Back length from Garment length.

Gore width – 25 cm is a good all-purpose width. The wider the gores, the wider the total hem, but adjust to fit your cloth.

Sleeve length – Arm length

Sleeve width – 40-60 cm at the shoulder for normal adult sizes: sleeves with underarm gussets can be narrower than those without.

Sleeve end – depends on style

Simple sleeveless surcote

7

Man's sleeveless surcote

8

Women's open surcote

9

Sleeved surcotes

4a

continued from page 117

Making up

Cut and finish the neck opening. Sew the gores to the body, with the side gores straight edge to straight edge. Insert pairs of gores in slashes on the Centre Front and Back. Either set the sleeves on flat and sew the underarm and side seams in one, with the gussets if used; or, finish the side seams then set in the completed sleeves (*Methods*, Figs 7, 8).

Sew by hand with lapped seams or run-and-fell (*Methods*, Figs 3, 6), or machine stitch with open seams. Finish unlined surcotes by overcasting the seams if the cloth seems likely to fray. Finish neck and sleeve ends with hems or narrow facings of linen or silk.

For lined surcotes cut and make up the lining as the outer fabric. Insert it and finish the neck, hem, and armholes or sleeve ends (Pl 1), perhaps with a fancy stitch in a contrasting thread (*Methods*, Fig 22).

Fastenings

Most surcotes simply pull on over the head (Fig 2); a few have a front neck opening with a couple of buttons (*Methods*, Figs 19, 21). Fitted examples may be laced at the back or side (*Methods*, Figs 16, 17).

4. Simple sleeved surcote, 13th and early 14th century

A loose, square garment with plain elbow-length sleeves.

a. **Calf-length man's version** with gores and front slit. It could be lengthened for a woman (Fig 1).

b. **Cutting layout** for *a*, shown on 2.5 m of single layer cloth, 150 cm wide, with seam allowances included. Garment width is 75 cm – a generous fit on modern size 42 (Chest 105 cm). The side gores reach to the base of the separate sleeve gussets, *D*. The centre gores, at front and back, are quite short and cut in one. The front gore is slit for most of its length as shown.

b

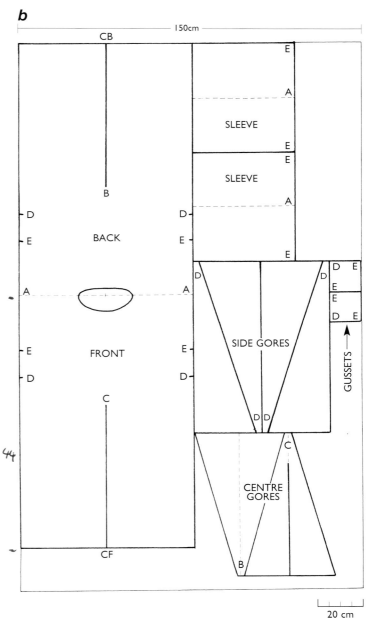

5a

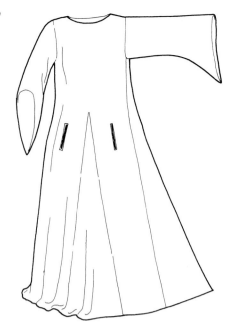

5. Woman's fashionable sleeved surcote, mid 14th century

***a.* Style.** The body has shaped shoulder seams and armholes, and long side gores (modern size 12-14, Bust 90 cm). The slightly peaked sleeves and the fitchets (slits for access to the purse) are typical of the period.

***b.* Cutting diagram for *a*.** Shaping is shown by fine lines. When the Back and Front are shaped at the shoulders they can be cut separately, as shown here. The long side gores can be used as they are, or shaped at the top for a closer fit. The sleeves are flared at the end, and shaped at the top (Fig 6b). Alternatively a 'transitional' sleeve (*Cotes,* Fig 9) could be used.

The fitchets are not shown on the plan; it is best to complete the garment and fix their position on the wearer (*Methods,* Fig 10; Pl 1).

b

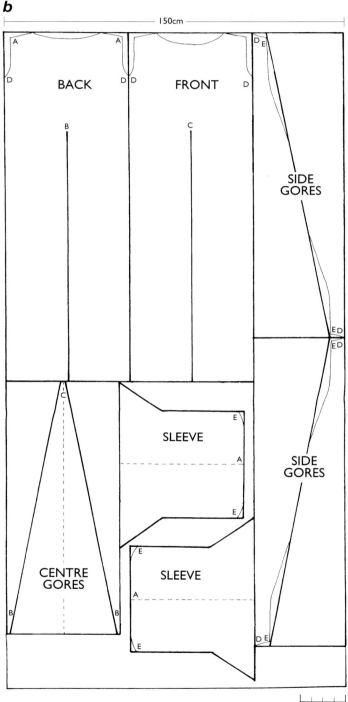

6. Peaked sleeves for surcotes, first half of 14th century

a. Fairly loose sleeve with gusset and slight peak, shown by solid lines on the pattern.

b. Sleeve with shaped sleeve head and extended peak, shown by heavy broken lines. See also *Cotes*, Fig 8.

c. Fitted sleeve (back view) with long peak (tippet). See also *Cotes*, Fig 9.

When planning a fitted sleeve *c*, make sure the peak or tippet is at the underarm. The visible parts of sleeve ends were probably lined.

Fine broken lines follow the top of the sleeve, leading to SP.

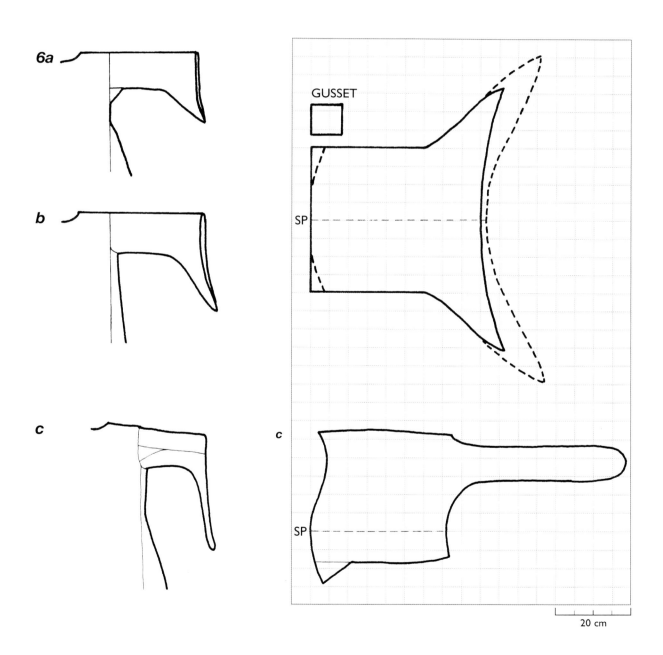

20 cm

121

Sleeveless surcotes

7a

b. Pattern and cutting layout for _a_, shown on a single layer of cloth 140 cm wide, 270 cm long. This voluminous style should be cut generously. Here the Back and Front panels are each 70 cm wide.

Plan the Back and Front either as separate panels, to be joined at the shoulder as here, or in one piece as in Fig 4b. The neck is wide and shallow and the sides slant out to form a deep arm opening.

Plan two pairs of side gores to reach from _B_ to the hem. Their narrow top ends will form the base of the arm openings. Set on the gores with straight edge to straight edge.

7. **Simple sleeveless surcote, 13th to mid 14th century, Pl 10**

_a._ Style worn by men and women, here shown full length for a woman. Men might also wear a shorter form. The simple cut is suitable for thicker woollen cloths. For a garment in finer cloth use the example in Fig 8.

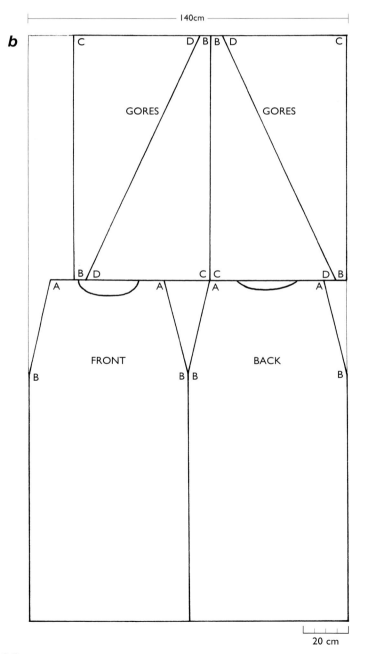

Plate 10 Early 14th century surcote
A simple sleeveless surcote (Fig 7) in medium weight, plain weave wool. It is unlined and the neck and arm openings are finished with facings of silk. The cote from Plate 6 is worn underneath, and its belt can be used to hitch up the cote skirts, and to hang a purse safely.

123

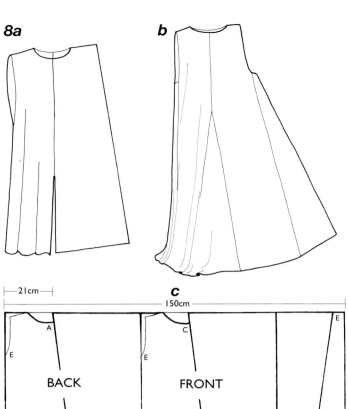

8a   **b**

8. Sleeveless surcotes, 13th to mid 14th century

A more elaborate cut than Fig. 7, and suitable for different weights of cloth. It is unsuitable for fabrics with a nap, wrong side or one-way pattern since the panels are cut and reversed.

a. Man's calf-length surcote, without gores but with slits for riding

b. Woman's surcote, with added gores

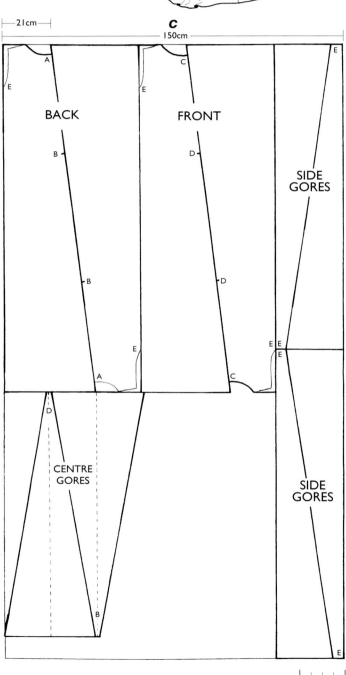

c

├─21cm─┤

├──────150cm──────┤

BACK

FRONT

SIDE GORES

CENTRE GORES

SIDE GORES

├─┬─┬─┤
20 cm

c. Pattern and layout

This shows the woman's surcote, and the fine lines indicate the shoulder and armhole shaping. Use the same layout for a man, but with the appropriate dimensions and without the gores.

The examples, for a man (Chest 100 cm) and woman (Bust 90 cm), are only for guidance. Actual dimensions will depend on how loose a fit you want, as well as on body size. Start with a scale diagram before making a full-size pattern, or try out the pattern in calico.

Plan the Back and Front as two rectangles, each equalling Garment length by Garment width (Garment width is from two-thirds to three-quarters Chest or Bust measurement). Divide each rectangle diagonally. The diagonal lines will form the CF and CB seam lines, after the four panels are joined bias to bias and straight edge to straight edge.

Ensure that the narrow ends of panels, which form the shoulders, are at least a quarter Bust/Chest size, to give enough width round the torso. If the shoulders are very wide they can be trimmed and shaped after cutting. Secure bias edges on a stay band.

Man's surcote – Garment length 120 cm, Garment width 75 cm (three quarters Chest size). The shoulder ends are 26 cm giving a wide, square shoulder. The straight side seams are left open 30-35 cm down from the shoulders, to form armholes; the seams at CF and CB are left open 40 cm up from the hem.

Woman's surcote – Garment length 160 cm, Garment width 60 cm (two thirds Bust size). The shoulder ends are only 21 cm: extra width is provided by the gores. The side gores reach to the underarm, adding both armhole shaping and flare to the hem.

Women's open surcotes

9

9. Women's open surcotes, mid 14th century on

Later surcotes are worn over a kirtle and based on the personal Block. They are cut for fit above the waist, and for flare below. Although out of fashion by the late 14th century, both styles persisted into the 15th.

Left The simple style replaced the gored surcote in general wear. It might have quite small armholes, or deeper openings as shown. Working women might still wear it in the 15th century.

Right The sideless surcote appeared for court and ceremonial wear about 1370. It was worn by royalty for many years but was not part of ordinary dress. The main picture shows an English version, and the detail shows a French form with a white fur front. The front buttons are ornamental.

10. Bodice for Fig 9

The solid line is for Fig 9 *left* and the broken line for Fig 9 *right*.

Trace the personal Block and plan the shape of the surcote neck, shoulder and armhole. Ensure that Back and Front match up and the neckline matches that of the cote or kirtle worn underneath; see *Kirtles,* Fig 3. As the garment will be flared, the final width along CB and CF will be greater than on the Block. Use the prepared bodice to plan the complete pattern on paper as shown in Fig 11. If necessary the side or armhole openings can be cut deeper at fitting.

10

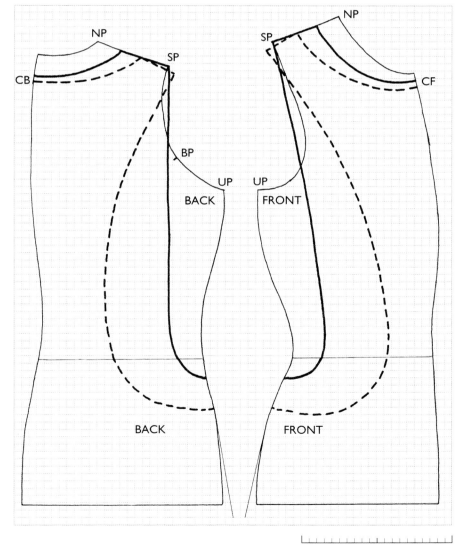

20 cm

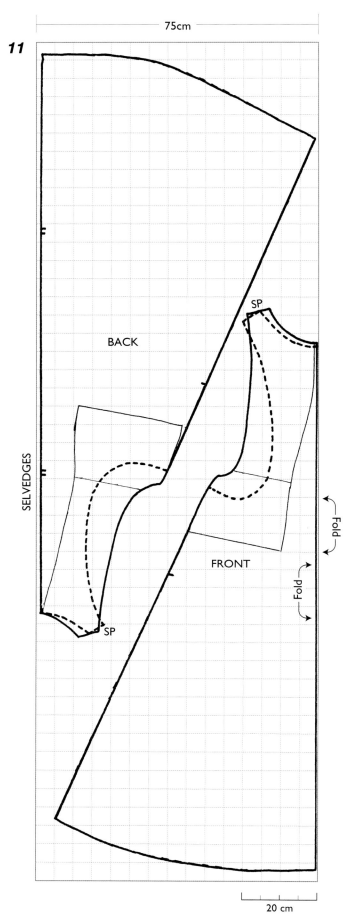

75cm

11

SP

BACK

SELVEDGES

SP

FRONT

Fold

Fold

20 cm

11. Full pattern and layout for Fig 9

Front – Rule a CF line. Lay the Front bodice just touching it at the neck, and 5-10 cm away from it at hip level. Plan the skirt with the side seam flaring from the hip (*Blocks,* Fig 27).

Back – Rule a CB line. Lay the Back bodice with the neck just touching the CB line, with the hip slightly further away than for the Front to create more flare. This pattern shows a skirt with a slight train on the Back. It is best to try out the pattern first in calico.

The pattern is shown laid out on cloth 150 cm wide folded lengthways, with the Front cut in one piece on the fold and the Back on the selvedges, giving a CB seam.

Cotehardies

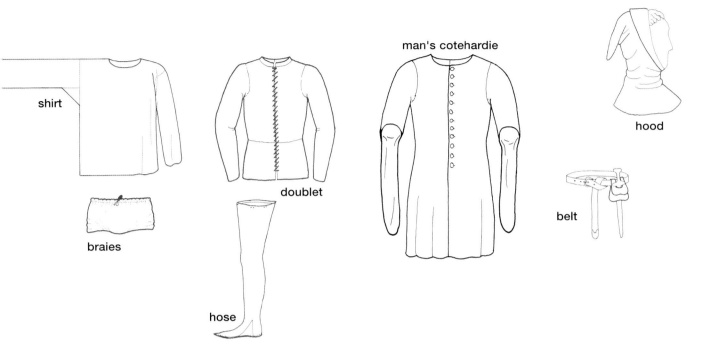

shirt

braies

doublet

hose

man's cotehardie

hood

belt

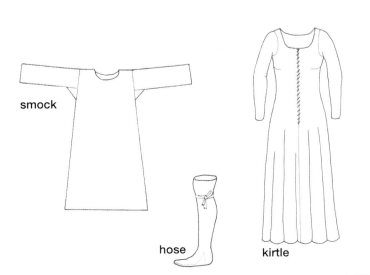

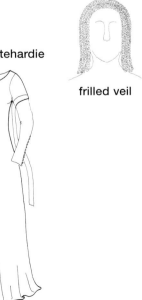

smock

hose

kirtle

woman's cotehardie

frilled veil

Cotehardies

The cotehardie tended to be worn by younger people of means. With its close fit and extravagant button fastening it represented the new approach to tailoring which appeared around the middle of the 14th century. Older men and women continued to wear the more established surcote, or later the gown.

Men's cotehardies

The cotehardie appeared at about the time of the doublet and was worn over it, often with peaked sleeves revealing the doublet sleeves at the lower arms (Fig 1). It was open at the front and the belt was worn outside, emphasising the slim line (Figs 1, 2). The skirts soon became shorter. The hem might be dagged (Fig 2), often echoing the dagging of the hood worn with it, so the neck of the cotehardie was rarely seen.

The sleeves could be short, with streamers (added round the sleeve ends as facings) or 'tippets' (long peaks). Sometimes they were long and buttoned at the wrist.

Later in the 14th century young men gradually abandoned the cotehardie for the gown. A longer version, worn by older merchants and provincial gentry, persisted into the early 15th century.

Women's cotehardies

Women seem to have adopted tailored garments later than men, but for a short period about the 1370s they are seen in cotehardies. From the hips up they were similar to the male version (Fig 3); the front was buttoned down to hip level where the bodice flared into long skirts. It was worn over a kirtle with a matching low neck, and long buttoned sleeves. A belt is not normally seen, though sometimes the cotehardie had fitchets or slits (*Surcotes,* Fig 5) through which to reach a hanging purse. A stacked, frilled veil, resting on the bare shoulders was often worn with it (*Fashionable head-dress,* Fig 5).

Materials

Good quality wool, preferably a broadcloth, is best, especially for a dagged hem (*Methods,* Fig 24). The cotehardie can be made in two colours. Note that parti-coloured garments are normally divided vertically, not horizontally – halved, but not quartered. It can be lined with linen, lightweight wool, or fur, or left unlined for a closer fit. The visible parts of sleeve ends were probably lined. Sleeve streamers (Figs 4, 7), often light-coloured, are made from doubled strips of lightweight cloth. Make the buttons from the same cloth as the garment (*Methods,* Figs 19-21), or use shanked metal buttons.

1. c.1340, English. Drummer
The earliest form of cotehardie, with buttons only to the waist. Long peaks (tippets) reveal doublet sleeves to the wrists; the neckline is hidden by the large hood. (Lutrell Psalter, British Library, MS Add 42130, f.176).

2. c.1350, English
Youth in narrow cotehardie with dagged hem. The neckline and upper sleeves are hidden by the hood, but the sleeves are probably part of the cotehardie, perhaps with a sleeveless doublet beneath. The hood is tight round the face, probably with buttons under the chin. (Detail from misericord, Gloucester cathedral).

3. c.1360-80, English. Iseult
She wears a low-necked, buttoned cotehardie with extended cuffs which must be buttoned to fit. Her head-dress is a stacked, frilled veil. (Detail from misericord, Tristram and Iseult, Lincoln cathedral).

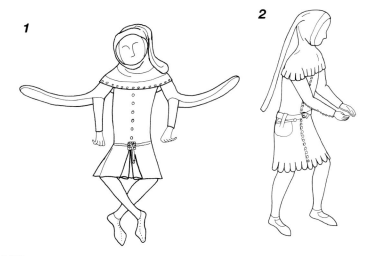

Planning, cutting and making up

The patterns are adapted from the personal Block (*Blocks*, Figs 25-27). The alterations are shown with each pattern; for men (Fig 5) and for women (Fig 8). To adapt the neckline of a woman's cotehardie to that of a kirtle worn underneath, see *Kirtles*, Fig 3c.

The order of making up is described in *Methods*, p. 46.

For an unlined garment, finish the neck and front edges with narrow facings (p. 51). Sleeves with long peaks (Fig 6a) may need to be lined (p. 51). If the sleeves have streamers, add them as facings round the sleeve ends (Fig 6b).

To plan your garment use the wearer's personal bodice Block (see *Blocks*). The patterns shown here correspond approx. to modern size 42 for men and size 14 for women. The fine lines show the original Block outline. Letters indicate joining points. For abbreviations and symbols see p. 10. Add seam allowances and balance points. The four bodice pieces must be cut accurately for a proper fit. Check the side seam lines are of equal length and at the same angle. Secure long bias edges on a stay band.

Fastenings

No extra width is allowed for button fastenings as the edges barely overlap. Sew the buttons to the right edge of the finished garment and work the buttonholes close to the left edge (*Methods*, Figs 19-21; Pls 2, 3): this applies for both men and women. The main thing is to have plenty of buttons: they should normally be no more than 3-4 cm apart and can be packed so close together that they touch. On men's cotehardies the buttons are sometimes seen closer together above the waist than below.

3

Men's cotehardies

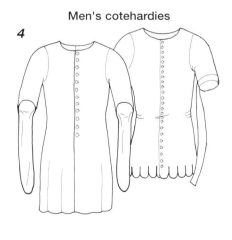

4

Woman's cotehardie

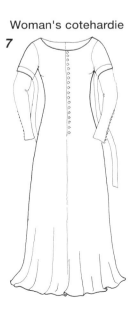

7

Men's cotehardies

4

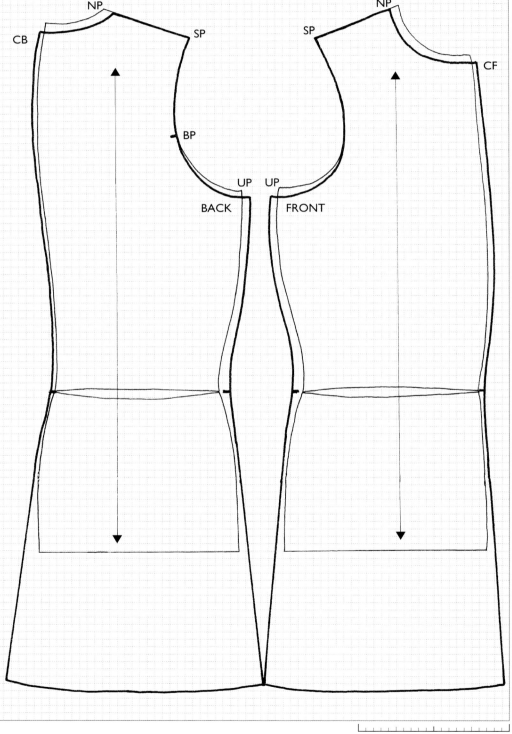

4. Men's cotehardies, mid 14th century

Cotehardie sleeves were commonly short enough to reveal the doublet sleeves beneath. The hem is knee-length or shorter and the edge may be dagged. The neckline is normally covered by a hood, which may be dagged to match and in a different colour. A belt is normally worn.

Left Characteristics of the early style: buttons ending at waist level and long peaks cut in one with the sleeves.

Right Later, shorter style. The buttons reach to the dagged hem, and streamers are sewn onto the short sleeves.

5. Pattern for Fig 4

The body is tight-fitting and needs to follow the shape of the doublet closely.

Trace the personal bodice Block. Lower the neck line and underarm by 1-2 cm. Add a little ease all round for freer movement: here 0.5 cm ease at CB, and 1 cm on each side seam and at CF.

Mark the required length of the skirts below the waist, and flare them slightly.

For parti-coloured garments, cut one Back, Front and sleeve in each fabric, taking care to cut the sleeves to match the correct halves.

5

CB NP SP BP UP UP BACK FRONT SP NP CF

20 cm

6. Sleeves for Fig 4

Trace the personal sleeve Block. Enlarge the sleeve head by slashing down FL almost to the wrist and spread the parts to match the enlarged armhole, as in *Blocks,* Fig 25.

a. Elbow-long sleeve with a long peak. Measure 25-35 cm from BP down the Back seam lines and rule a construction line *AA*. Plan the peak at the underarm following the sleeve line as shown, extending it to the desired length. Complete the new sleeve edge with a shallow curve. Complete the new pattern by marking SP, SG and seam allowances.

b. Short sleeve with separate streamer. Measure 15-20 cm from BP down the Back seam lines and rule a construction line *AA*. Plan a short sleeve as shown and complete the pattern as above.

  Make the streamer from a doubled strip of lightweight cloth – it is usually light-coloured. Sew this as a facing round the edge of the sleeve, with the hanging end at the back.

  Alternatively plan long sleeves with buttons, or mitten cuffs as described in *Kirtles,* Fig 5, which are also seen on men's garments.

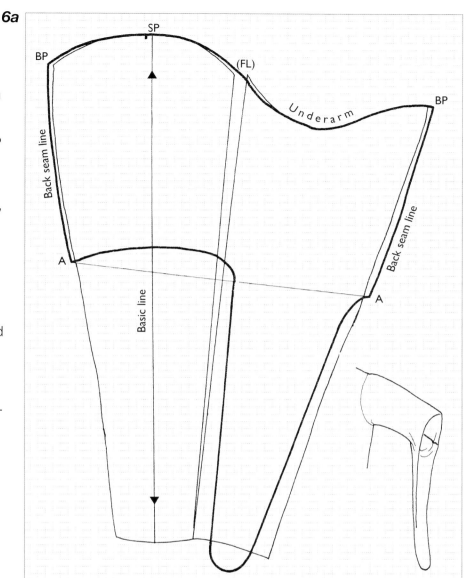

6a

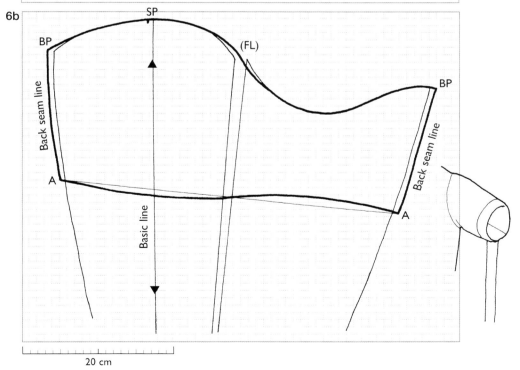

6b

20 cm

131

7. Woman's cotehardie, later 14th century

This short-lived but distinctive form echoes the men's style. The front is open to hip level, and buttoned: note that it buttons left over right, as for men. The sleeves are short, with streamers, showing the buttoned mitten cuff sleeves of the kirtle. Alternatively the cotehardie might have long sleeves (*Kirtles,* Fig 5). It sometimes has fitchets, or pocket slits, like those on the surcote (*Surcotes,* Fig 5).

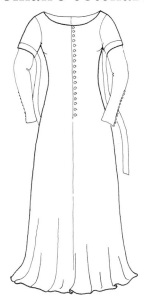

Woman's cotehardie
7

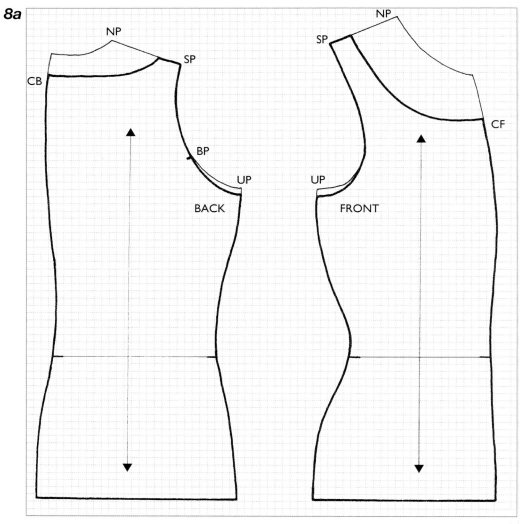

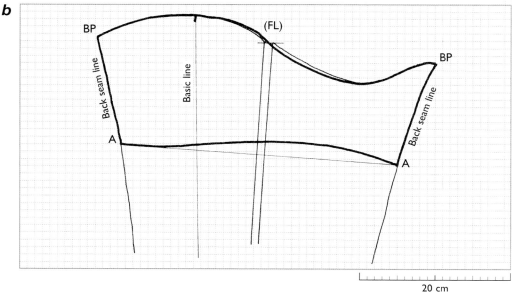

20 cm

8. Bodice and sleeve for Fig 7

The cotehardie is cut to fit closely over the basic kirtle (*Kirtles,* Figs 2, 3c), and the two garments should be planned together. In wear the two layers function almost as one, though the kirtle skirts should be shorter and less full.

***a.* Bodice.** Trace the personal Block. Make sure the kirtle and the cotehardie patterns have the same low, wide necklines. A matching neckline pattern is given in *Kirtles,* Fig 3c. Here the neckline is lowered by 3 cm at CB, 7 cm from NP at the shoulder, and 6 cm at CF. The only other adjustment for the cotehardie is to hollow out the underarms by 1 cm, as shown, to give a little ease over the kirtle sleeves. Trace off the adapted bodice.

***b.* Sleeve.** Measure the enlarged armhole and widen the sleeve Block along the FL to match, see *Blocks,* Fig 25. Here it is widened by about 1 cm, which can all be added at FL. Plan a short sleeve. Measure 15-20 cm from BP down the Back seam lines and rule a construction line *AA*. Draw a shallow curve, as shown, and trace off the pattern.

Make the streamer as a doubled strip of lightweight cloth. Sew this as a facing round the edge of the sleeve, with the hanging end at the back.

9. Full pattern and layout for Fig 7

The patterns are shown on 150 cm wide cloth folded crossways. This layout permits generous hem widths without piecing, though you may need extra length for the sleeves.

Plan the skirt as shown in *Blocks,* Fig 27, by extending the vertical construction line to the required length. Plan the hem with the fullness towards the side and CB as shown. Referring to your kirtle pattern (*Kirtles,* Fig 4) make the cotehardie 10-15 cm longer with a total hem at least 30 cm wider. Here the Back hem is 84 cm and the Front hem is 80 cm, giving a total hem of 328 cm.

You may prefer to try out the pattern first in calico.

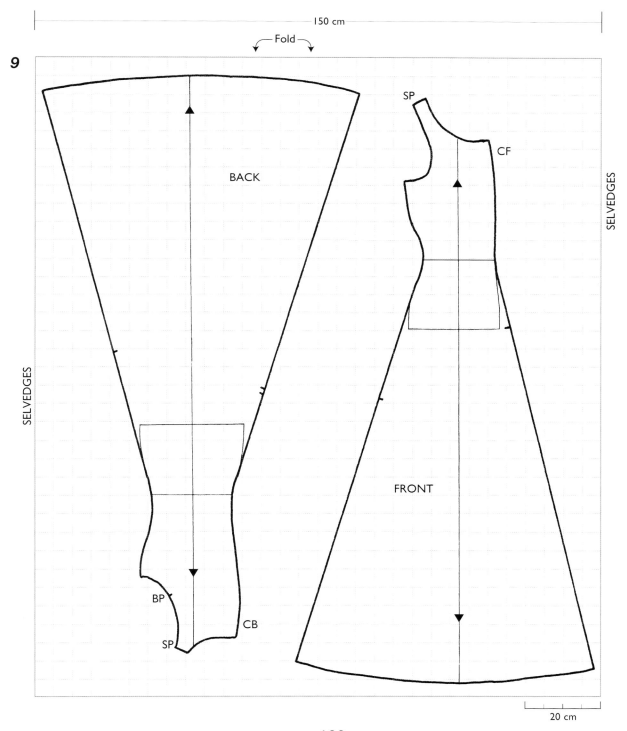

Plate 11 Court dance, 1465, French

The king wears his crown round his hat, and a ceremonial mantle over a long fur-lined gown with pleats at the centre front. The queen wears a tight gown trimmed with ermine, its neckline filled with a fine scarf, and an old-fashioned wide horned head-dress which seems to amalgamate her coronet with the padded roll.

The gentlemen wear joined hose and long piked shoes. The one on the extreme left wears a short mantle which reveals the top of his hose and the form of his tight doublet with its puffed upper sleeves. The man on the left with his back to us wears a very short gown edged with fur, over a doublet with a high collar, and no belt. His gown sleeves are slashed at the back, revealing open doublet sleeves caught together over his shirt. The fullness and pleating at the sleeve head indicate puffed doublet sleeves supporting the gown sleeves. The men's hats are tall and almost brimless.

The lady nearest the queen wears a fitted garment, with no belt, which may be a cotehardie with a train. The other ladies wear typical gowns with wide V-fronted necklines, the collars dipping over the belts at the back, and skirts with perhaps a metre of train.

The lady to the left with her back to us shows how the wide belt was worn with the buckle at the back: her left sleeve shows a long mitten cuff worn down over her hand. Of the five ladies, two wear tall steeple hennins with black velvet frontlets and bindings, and transparent veils; two wear shorter truncated hennins, also with long veils, and one wears an upright horned head-dress. It is likely that the different head-dresses represent different ages or social and marital status.

Roman de la Vidette, Bibliothèque Nationale, Paris, MS FR 24378, f.5

Gowns

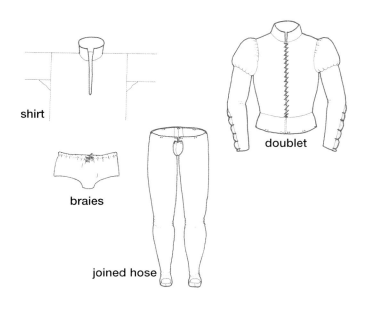

shirt

braies

joined hose

doublet

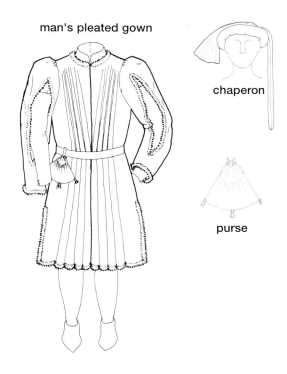

man's pleated gown

chaperon

purse

smock

hose

kirtle

woman's flared gown

padded roll
head-dress

belt

Gowns

The gown, or *houppelande* as it was also called through much of the period, first appeared about the 1360s. The same style was worn by both men and women as an alternative to the tight-fitting cotehardie. It was loose and often buttoned from neck to hem (Fig 1). It was worn with or without a belt. This early simpler form persisted well into the 15th century among the merchant class and gentry.

The gown had undergone some changes by the beginning of the 15th century. It became more voluminous, with folds falling to a wider hem, and ranged from full length (Fig 1) to about hip level (Fig 8). Sleeves became more elaborate and collars higher for both men and women (Fig 3). The front opening was buttoned or laced closed to the chest, or reached down to the hem. The body was drawn in with a belt worn by men at natural waist level, and by women high up under the bust. Contemporary illustrations indicate a careful arrangement of the fullness under the belt. An elaborate example for the wealthy of both sexes is shown in Fig 12, for a woman.

In the first quarter of the 15th century, men's and women's styles started to diverge into distinct garments, as described below.

Men's gowns

Changes in the gown were brought about by tailors' increasing skill in manipulating pattern and fabric. Fig 16 illustrates an elaborate gown of the mid 15th century. This might be open for its full length and fastened with concealed hooks and eyes (Pls 12-13). The gown was usually calf-length or longer, sometimes with slashed sleeves, and lined or edged with fur (Fig 18), though worn very short by some fashionable young men (Pl 11). The garment became slimmer in shape, and from the 1470s was worn open to show the inner clothing.

The early plain shape, still fastened from neck to hem, persisted to the end of the century among merchants, wealthier townsmen (Fig 17), and workmen with one gown for best.

Men wore the gown over doublet and hose, though sometimes only the ends of the doublet sleeves were visible. Often the gown neck was

1. 1400, English
Elderly merchant displaying the 14th-century passion for buttons, which fasten every visible garment. His hood lies on his shoulders over a mantle, thrown back to show a plain buttoned gown, with very long doublet sleeves emerging. A handsome belt supports a short sword. (Brass, Northleach church, Gloucestershire).

2. 1395-1400, French
Three men in short gowns with very high collars edged with fur and a variety of sleeves. Note the regular pleats under their belts. The central figure wears an early bag-hat. Although this is an era of excessively long toes, all three wear plain shoes or soled hose, perhaps because they are out of doors. (British Library, MS Royal 20, C VII, f.60v).

3. c. 1410, English
Merchant and his wife in similar gowns. Both have bag sleeves and buttoned neck openings, but her outfit has a wider collar and longer inner sleeves. He is bareheaded; she has a fillet looped round side buns of plaited hair, and a draped veil.
(Brass, Southfleet church, Kent).

1

2   *3*

cut away to show the doublet collar as well. Even the earliest men's gowns were usually belted and the belt was worn at waist height. Men in gowns usually wore a bag-hat or chaperon (*Men's hoods*, Figs 4-6) rather than a caped hood.

Women's gowns

Significant changes occurred to the gown in the 15th century, which can be seen in the neck opening, the sleeves and the shaping of the waist (Figs 3, 22, 23). The collar became lower and the neck opening deeper and wider. The bodice and sleeves became more fitted, and the fullness moved downwards to the hips (Fig 23).

The popular image of the 15th-century lady's dress is a high-waisted, V-necked gown topped with a huge head-dress (Fig 22). This image, from about 1460, reflects just one stage in the development of the gown from an ample belted garment to a figure-hugging one.

Plain gowns, cut like the early gowns, continued to be worn by the less affluent, but also by older women of all classes. These retained fairly high necklines and loose sleeves for most of the century.

By the early 15th century most women above peasant status probably owned a gown. A lady or rich merchant's wife might have worn them regularly, but a craft worker would have worked in a kirtle (Pl 16) and kept her gown for best.

Related garments – The gown was worn over a kirtle, which in its fashionable early form had long mitten cuffs buttoned to the knuckles (*Kirtles*, Fig 2). The kirtle skirt could be seen when the gown was lifted for walking. While a plainer gown could be slipped on over the day-to-day kirtle, the more fitted shapes from 1450 required a carefully fitted kirtle to match.

With the deeper V-neck a stomacher might be used. This can be a nice bit of silk or scarlet cloth, mounted on a lining and pinned to the kirtle (*Methods*, Fig 15).

The neckline of the gown was often filled in with a fine linen or gauze scarf, tucked in at the back with its ends drawn forwards to form an inner V-neckline (Fig 22; Pl 11).

A belt was worn above the natural waist. For much of the period it was 5 cm or more wide, worn high under the bust, often with the buckle at the back (Fig 22; *Accessories*, Fig 2). In the later 15th century the waistline dropped to its natural level, and a much narrower belt was worn loosely on the hips (Fig 23).

Head-wear – The high collar of the early gown affected the style of head-wear: the frilled veil was replaced with a caul or templers (*Fashionable head-dresses*, Figs 5, 6, 9). A frilled veil, or possibly small side buns or templers might be worn with a plain early gown (Fig 4), and an elaborate caul with the gown in Fig 12.

The 15th century was the era of the dramatic head-dress and as with the gowns themselves, different head-dresses were in use at the same time (Fig 22; *Fashionable head-dresses*, Figs 11, 13, 15). A horned head-dress might be worn with Fig 24, and a butterfly or late form of black hood with Fig 28.

Early gowns

Early buttoned gown

Men's short gowns

Fashionable gown

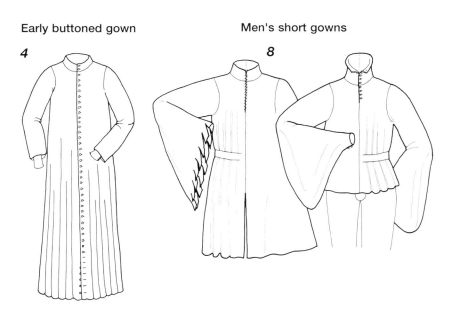

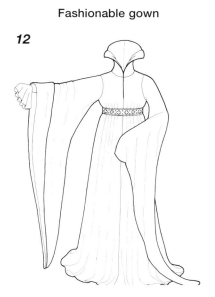

4

8

12

Materials

Outer fabric – Use woollen cloth. A firm Melton will make a warm gown, but for a man's gown with heavy pleats, finer cloths can be used interlined with blanket or canvas. The woman's later fitted gown (Fig 28) needs a lighter woollen cloth. Use worsted for a lighter gown.

Lining – All gowns should be lined. Use soft woollen cloth, worsted, or linen; or silk for a grand gown. Linings may be visible and a contrasting colour can be effective. Fur linings were worn for warmth by both men and women: for economy, line the gown with blanket and edge it with fur (*Materials,* p. 65; *Methods,* p. 53).

Women's gowns in the 15th century show turned-out collars and cuffs of fur or contrasting fabric. They can be a continuation of the lining, or separate facings in a different material.

Quantities, using 140-160 cm wide material – A man's medium-length or short gown, or a long gown in plain style, will need twice the garment length (adding a hem allowance), plus the sleeve length. Small sleeves may come out of the garment length. This will give a total hem of about 3 m.

A woman's gown with a hem of over 4 m will take three times the garment length, plus sleeve length. A wide gown of 6 m hem will take four times the length though the sleeves will probably come out of this. Add generous hem allowances.

If the material has a nap or one way pattern, you must allow enough to cut all pattern pieces in the same direction.

Men's gowns

16. 1460-65, French

Chamberlain or steward in a knee length gown which is edged and probably lined with fur. The gown has the fashionable structured look to the pleating, which is stitched in place. The doublet collar shows at the neck. The pleated sleeve heads are probably supported by padded doublet sleeves. He has long pointed toes, and wears an 'acorn' cap. (Histoire de Helayne, Bibliothèque Royale, Brussels, MS 9967).

17. 1490, English

Prosperous merchant in a conservative gown, without much fullness in the body or sleeves, edged and probably lined with fur. The doublet collar and sleeves are visible. Note the round-toed shoes of the late 15th century. The liripipe hanging over his shoulder probably supports a chaperon. He carries a large purse and a rosary on his belt.
(Thomas Andrewe, brass, Charwelton church, Northamptonshire).

Pleated gowns

16

17

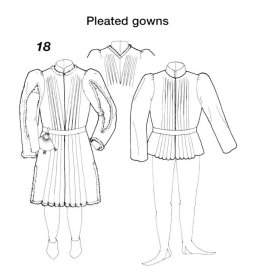
18

Planning

Gowns are planned by adding skirts to a bodice adapted from the personal Block (*Blocks*, Figs 25-27). The gown fits over the shoulders and flares towards the hem, which can be wide. They are cut in four panels with seams at CF, CB and sides. Most gowns are simply flared at the side seams. The basic steps are outlined below except for the gowns of Figs 18 & 28, which are planned by different methods, as explained in their captions.

The gowns described include Early buttoned and Short (Figs 4, 8), Early fashionable (Fig 12), Men's pleated (Fig 18), Woman's flared (Fig 24), and Woman's later fitted (Fig 28) versions. Instructions for each gown are given in the captions.

Men's gowns were usually calf- or ankle-length, or long enough to reach the ground, but could be as short as hip level. Women's gowns were long enough to lie on the ground all round and often had extra length at the back extending into a train.

It is safer to make a complete pattern rather than plan directly on the cloth. If you make your pattern on calico, rather than paper, you can tack it up for a fitting to try out the shape. If you work on paper, mark lightly in pencil until the shape is right; on fabric use pins, and chalk the final outline. The full pattern pieces are shown laid out on cloth, with the straight grain indicated.

continued overleaf

Women's gowns

22. 1460-65, French

The older woman, *left*, wears a fur-lined gown and horned head-dress covered in a stiffened transparent veil. The younger woman, *right*, has a more fitted tight-sleeved gown and hennin, also with transparent veil. The line inside her gown neckline may be the edge of a sheer kerchief, or a cord supporting a pendant. Both wear their belts above the natural waist, and show different amounts of kirtle front or stomacher inside the gown neck. (Histoire de Helayne, Bibliothèque Royale, Brussels, MS 9967).

23. 1485, 1490, English

Left Late style of gown with separate collar dipping below the bodice edge at the front. There might be a waist seam under the wide belt, which is at waist level. Note the generous length of her skirts. She wears an elaborate necklace and a 'butterfly' or truncated hennin head-dress. (Brass to Isabella Cheyne, Blickling church, Norfolk).

Right Less fitted version of the late style, pulled in by a belt. The flounced kirtle skirt is visible. The head-dress is a form of combined cap and hood. (Brass, Charwelton church, Northamptonshire).

22

23

24   Flared gown

28   Late medieval fitted gown

139

To plan your garment use the wearer's personal bodice Block (see *Blocks*). The patterns shown here correspond approx. to modern size 42 for men and size 14 for women. The fine lines show the original Block outline. Fine broken lines indicate Fold lines. Heavy broken lines indicate alternative outlines. Letters indicate joining points. For abbreviations and symbols see p. 10.

Measure on the wearer the shoulder to hem length required, or take the Back length plus the Waist to knee, Waist to ankle or Waist to floor measurement.

You will need plenty of space to spread the work out, and a long tape measure. Trace the personal bodice Block to *waist only* and enlarge it to fit over the doublet or kirtle (*Blocks*, Fig 25-27). This is a simple enlargement with vertical CB and side seams; the CF seam may slant out slightly on larger figures.

Plan the collar: details are given with the patterns. Measure the enlarged armhole and plan the sleeve to match, either by adapting the sleeve Block or using one of the sleeves shown. Decide on the total hem for the gown, see *Quantities* above and the captions. The hem on each panel will be one quarter of this amount.

Plan the Front first, then the Back: the method is the same. Draw a CF line equal to the garment length required. At the top, square out a short construction line. At the bottom, square out a construction line equal to the hem width, and from here draw a short vertical guideline.

Position the front bodice on the CF line, with the short construction line passing through the shoulder. Measure straight down from UP to the hem: this will be the side seam length.

Use this length to draw the side seam line from UP to the vertical guideline at the hem. Draw the curved hem line: the wider the hem, the longer the curve.

Plan the Back by the same method using the side seam length from the Front.

To add extra length to the back skirt on women's gowns see Figs 26, 30.

Check that the side seams are the same length and at the same angle to the construction line on Back and Front. Add seam allowances, and balance points on side seams, BP, *at waist* level on *all seams*, and at the base of the CF opening, if appropriate. Trace round the whole pattern, marking details such as fold lines and, for Fig 20, pleat positions. The gown will hang better with a seam at CB even if CB falls on a fold in the layout.

Cutting and making up

Cut out Back, Front, sleeves and any collar from the outer fabric. If using a patterned fabric ensure you have enough material for repeats and that the designs on left and right sides match. Ensure that any pile or nap also matches on left and right sides. You can use wheel pieces (*Blocks*, Fig 28) on the side seams for economy.

Identify all pattern pieces on the wrong side. Use the same patterns to cut the lining, and interlining if required, matching the SG. Cut the interlining for the collar, and separate facings if used (*Methods*, p. 52, 53). Secure bias seams and edges on a stay band.

Follow the usual assembly procedure (p. 46): tack in the interlining; sew the shoulder, side and CB seams, and part of CF if required. Make up and attach the collar, noting the methods for different collars (*Methods*, Fig 14); make up the sleeves and set them in; make up the lining and set it in (p. 51; Pl 1).

For men's pleated gowns use tailor's tacks to mark the pleat positions at waist level (Fig 20). Secure the pleats on the finished gown to a stay band as described for Plate 14.

Fastenings

These must match the style. Buttons (*Methods*, Figs 19-21) were used for short neck and full-length openings up to the early 15th century; lacing was sometimes used for short openings (*Methods*, Fig 17). After that hooks and eyes became usual for men's gowns. In the 15th century the opening of women's gowns was often controlled by the belt, though later fitted gowns had concealed lacing.

Early gowns, worn by both men and women

4. Early buttoned gown, late 14th/early 15th century

Here shown as a man's version, worn by merchants and minor gentry. It was worn in the same form, though longer, by women. The body, fitted round the shoulders and upper chest, is slightly flared and buttoned for its full length. It has a small two-piece collar and plain straight sleeves. Worn with or without a belt. This style was also worn by children into the 15th century and beyond.

Buttoned gown

4

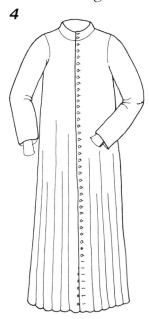

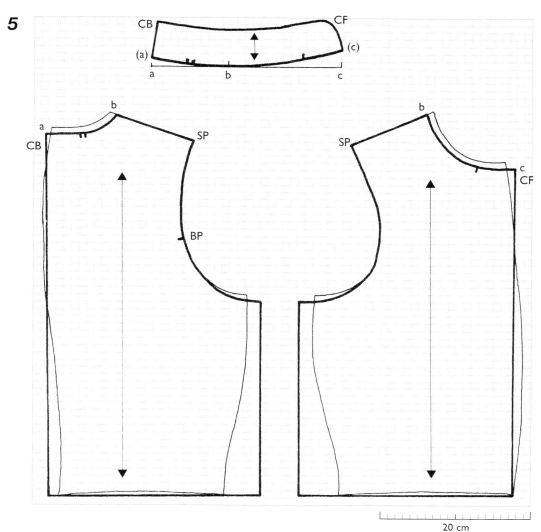

20 cm

5. Bodice and collars for Fig 4

This example is based on the man's Block, for a woman's Block see Fig 13a.

a. Bodice with round-necked collar

Trace the bodice Block to waist only. Draw straight CF and CB lines starting 0.5-1 cm outside the Block neckline. The CB line should be vertical but the CF may slant out if it would otherwise be more than 2 cm inside the Block waist.

Draw straight side seam lines starting 2-3 cm outside and 1-2 cm down from UP. Re-draw the armholes to match.

Collar – This 2-piece collar has a seam at CB. Draw new back and front neck curves, 0.5-1 cm below the Block neckline all round. Using a tape on edge, carefully measure the new back and front necklines, here totalling 25 cm.

Rule a horizontal construction line to the same length and measure along it the new back neck size *a-b*, and front neck size *b-c*. Point *b* will meet the shoulder seam when the collar is set on. At 1 cm above *a*, mark point *(a)*, and 2 cm above *c*, mark point *(c)*. Join them by a gentle curve as shown and check the length still matches the gown neck. *(a)* and *(c)* should be lower for small collar sizes.

From *(a)* draw a straight CB line, slanting slightly inwards to the required collar height, here 5 cm. From *(c)* draw a straight or rounded CF shape the same height. Draw the outer edge of the collar following the curve of the neck edge. Check the outer edge is 1-2 cm longer than half Neck size. Measure and mark balance points on the neck edges. Mark SG and trace off the collar.

For making up the collar see *Methods*, Fig 14a.

continued overleaf

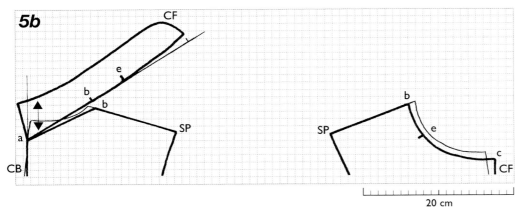

5b

b. V-necked collar

This two-piece collar has a seam at CB. Start the new back neckline at *a*, 2-5 cm below the Block neck, and run it straight to the shoulder at *b*, 0.5-1 cm down from the neck. ⟶

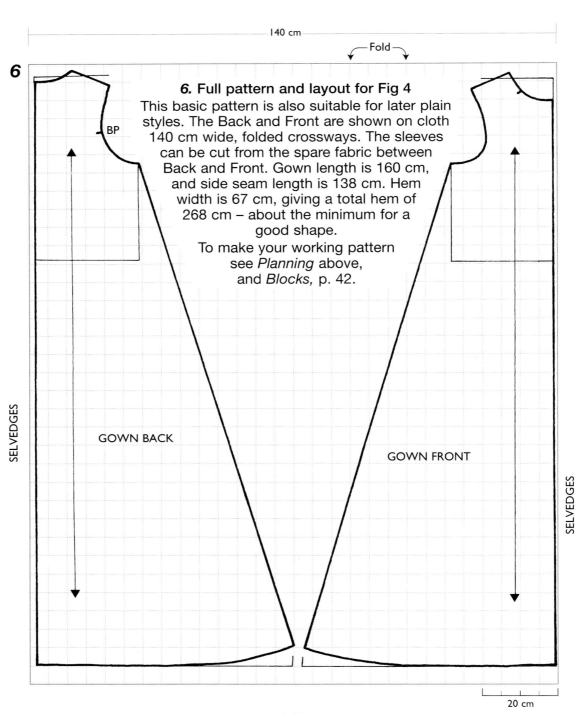

6. Full pattern and layout for Fig 4

This basic pattern is also suitable for later plain styles. The Back and Front are shown on cloth 140 cm wide, folded crossways. The sleeves can be cut from the spare fabric between Back and Front. Gown length is 160 cm, and side seam length is 138 cm. Hem width is 67 cm, giving a total hem of 268 cm – about the minimum for a good shape.

To make your working pattern see *Planning* above, and *Blocks,* p. 42.

GOWN BACK

GOWN FRONT

SELVEDGES

SELVEDGES

Lower the new front neckline by the same amount. Measure the new neck edge of the bodice, back plus front. From *a* on the new CB neck, rule the CB line of the collar slanting out slightly and about 5 cm long. From *a* rule another line about 25 cm long, passing 0.5 cm above the neck point of the block, *b*.

On this line measure off the length of the back neck edge and mark it *b*: this point will meet the shoulder seam when the collar is set on. From *b* measure off the length of the front neck edge and mark it *c*. Draw a slightly curved line from *b* ending 1-2 cm above *c* as shown.

Measure off and mark a balance point, *e*, on both the Front neck edge and front collar edge, 10 cm from *b*. Draw the top edge of the collar 4-5 cm above the lower edge to *d*, checking that it is 1-2 cm more than half Neck size. Mark the SG and trace off the collar.

For making up see *Methods*, Fig 14a.

7. Sleeve for Fig 4

A plain gown sleeve for men and women, enlarged from the sleeve Block.

Measure the armhole of the gown bodice. Add the increase, here 3 cm, as in *Blocks*, Fig 25. Combine the enlarging of the sleeve head with widening the wrist, here by 15 cm, to make a tubular sleeve. Trace the Block and slash down the Front line.

Front line – Rule a new FL on a fresh piece of paper. At the sleeve head, position the two pieces half the total increase apart (here 2.5 cm) on either side of the new FL. At the wrist, position the halves about 5 cm apart. Stick down the two halves.

Seam lines – To complete the sleeve head move BP out by half the remaining increase (here 1.25 cm) on each side and redraw the curve. To complete the wrist, measure about 5 cm out on each side and mark this. Rule new seam lines from BP to wrist, checking they are of equal length, and draw a new wrist edge which may be slightly longer than the Block.

Trace off the pattern and mark the new SP, shown by the balance mark.

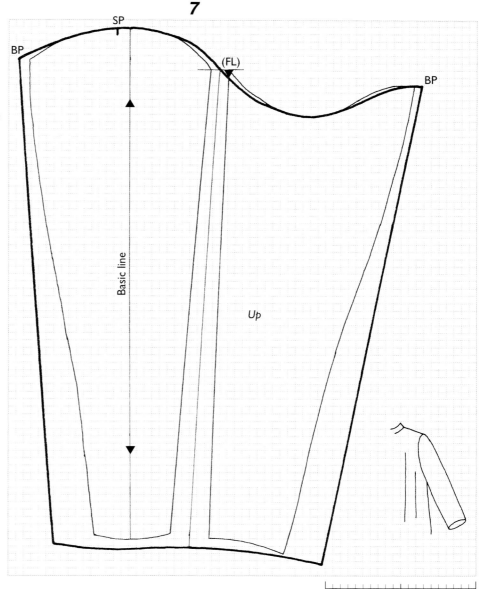

20 cm

143

Men's short gowns

8

8. Men's short gowns, late 14th/early 15th century

The flare is pulled in by a belt, but the folds are not stitched in position. This early style can also be made full-length.

Left Calf-length gown with standing collar. Short laced opening at neck, and vent at hem. Open sleeves (Fig 15) with square dagging.

Right Short gown with high standing collar. Short buttoned opening. Large bag sleeves with tight, buttoned wrists (Fig 11).

9

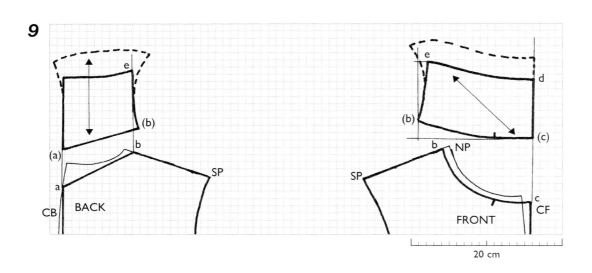

20 cm

9. Upper bodice and collar for Fig 8

Bodice – Trace and enlarge the bodice Block to waist only, as for Fig 5.

Collar – This is a 4-piece collar, shown in two heights. A 2-piece alternative is shown in Fig 5. Draw vertical construction lines by extending the CB and CF lines upwards – if the CF is slanted, draw up vertically from CF at the neck. Add a third line up from the Back neck point *b*.

Back collar – From *a* at the CB measure up 5 cm and mark *(a)*. Measure up and mark the top edge 8-10 cm above *(a)*.

From the Back neck point *b*, measure up 3 cm. Rule a line from *(a)* through this point and measure off from *(a)* the length *ab*, to mark *(b)*. From near *(b)* measure 6-8 cm up the construction line and mark e. Draw the side seam to here, curving in from *(b)*. Draw the top edge of the back collar curving it slightly up to e. Mark the vertical SG.

Front collar – From the extended CF line at *(c)* rule a horizontal construction line, running just above the

Front neck point. From *(c)* draw a curved line to *(b)*, about 2.5 cm above the horizontal line, with *(c)(b)* equal in length to the Front neck edge. Measure 6-8 cm up from *(c)* and mark *d*. Measure and mark the same distance vertically up from *(b)* to match the side seam of the back collar.

With a tape measure on edge, measure the top edge of the back collar and subtract this from half Neck size. Use this difference plus 1-2 cm ease for the top edge of the front collar *de*. This collar should fit closely, so the two top edges together should equal half Neck size plus about 2 cm ease. Adjust the size if necessary, by moving in the point e.

Draw in the side seam and top edge, and mark the SG on the bias as shown. Mark matching balance points on the neck edges of bodice and collar. Trace off the collar patterns.

The higher collar with the rolled edge is shown by the broken outline: extend the existing pattern upwards as shown, flaring it out to form the roll. See *Methods,* Fig 14c for making up the collar.

10

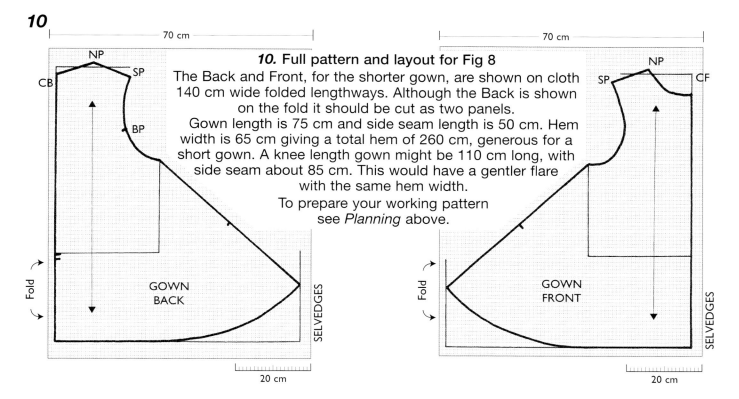

10. Full pattern and layout for Fig 8

The Back and Front, for the shorter gown, are shown on cloth 140 cm wide folded lengthways. Although the Back is shown on the fold it should be cut as two panels.
Gown length is 75 cm and side seam length is 50 cm. Hem width is 65 cm giving a total hem of 260 cm, generous for a short gown. A knee length gown might be 110 cm long, with side seam about 85 cm. This would have a gentler flare with the same hem width.
To prepare your working pattern see *Planning* above.

11

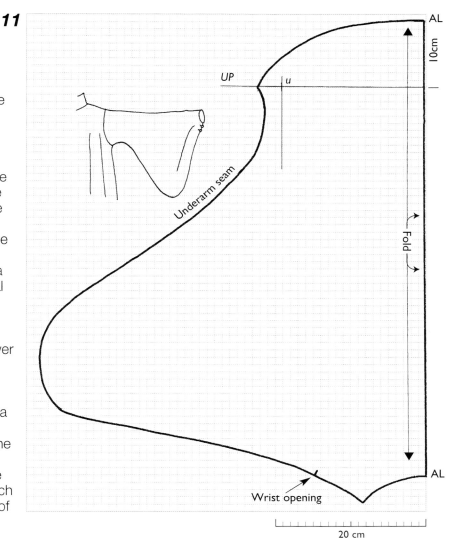

11. Bag sleeve, late 14th to mid 15th century

A wide, loose shape with the seam at the underarm, not based on the sleeve Block.

On the right of the paper, rule a vertical line equal to Arm length (AL) and parallel with SG. This will be the fold line of the finished sleeve. Measure the gown armhole. From (AL) measure down 10-12 cm and square out to the left. Along this line measure off and mark half Top Arm plus 5 cm, to *u*. The UP must lie beyond this point.

Using a tape measure on edge for a guide, sketch the sleeve head to equal half the gown armhole. Start by squaring out from the shoulder, then curve gently down to UP, outside *u*. If UP lies more than 5 cm outside *u*, lower UP slightly to bring it nearer.

Plan the shape of the underarm seam, keeping outside *u*. The outline shows the fashionable deep bag with a tight buttoned wrist; check against Wrist size. The balance mark shows the short wrist opening along the seam.

Cut each sleeve in one piece on the fold. When setting into the gown, match the underarm seam to the side seam of the body: the fold line will normally fall forward of the shoulder seam.

Fashionable gown

12

12. Fashionable gown, end 14th/early 15th century

This was the last common style before men's and women's gowns diverged into distinct garments. The high belt identifies this as a woman's gown. Men wore it with the belt at waist level.

The body is full and the folds round the waist need careful arrangement to achieve the correct look. The collar is very high and the short front opening is fastened by concealed hooks and eyes. This style of gown is later depicted on women with the collar falling onto the shoulders or lying flat (Fig 13b).

The wide and extended open sleeves can be worn covering the hands, or folded back as a cuff as shown, revealing the circular cuff of the kirtle sleeve (*Blocks* Fig 26c). This style of gown was also worn with large bag sleeves (Fig 11).

13. Bodice and collars for Fig 12 ⟶

Bodice – Trace the bodice Block to waist only. For a woman enlarge the Block as follows. Draw straight CF and CB lines starting 0.5-1 cm outside the Block neckline. The CB line should be vertical but the CF may slant out if it would otherwise be more than 2 cm inside the Block waist.

Draw straight side seam lines starting 1.5-2 cm outside and 1 cm down from UP. Redraw the armholes to match. Start the new back neckline at *a*, 2-5 cm below the Block neck, and run it straight to the shoulder at *b*, 0.5-1 cm down from the neck. Lower the new front neckline by the same amount. For a man enlarge the Back and Front as in Fig 5.

Collars

a. For the very high collar, follow Fig 9 and extend it upwards to form a funnel shape: try it out in spare fabric to check the shape. The top edge may need a wire sewn into it, to hold its form.

b. For this flat collar plan a *round back neck*, instead of the V. Lay the Back and Front bodice so the shoulder seams touch at the neck and overlap 2-3 cm at SP. This produces a collar which rolls at the neck: for a completely flat one omit the overlap.

Plan the round collar shape 10-15 cm deep, and trace it off as a single pattern piece. Cut it as a 2-piece collar with a seam at CB. It may be faced with the gown fabric or a contrasting one (see *Methods,* Fig 14) .

A matching linen collar can sometimes be seen lying over it. Use the gown collar pattern to cut one. Attach it to a linen neck band, or to a smock with a high neckline (*Linens,* Fig 5c).

13a

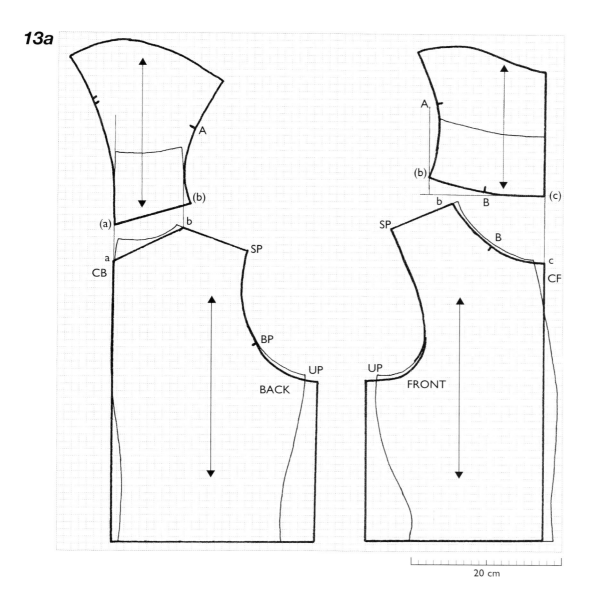

20 cm

13b

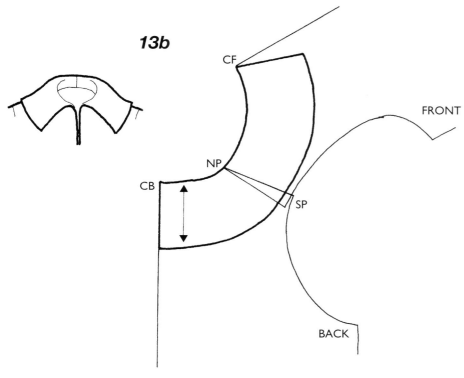

147

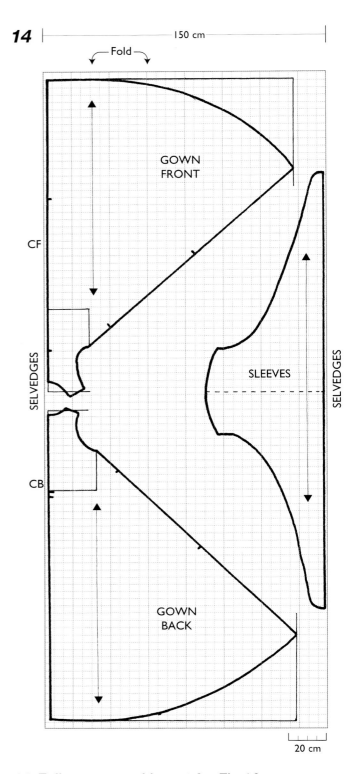

14. Full pattern and layout for Fig 12

The Back and Front, together with a large open sleeve, are shown on cloth 150 cm wide, folded crossways. The full sleeve pattern was obtained by tracing off the pattern of Fig 15 along its fold line. Note the small scale!

Gown length is 170 cm, and side seam length is 145 cm. Hem width is 130 cm, giving a total hem of 520 cm.

To prepare your working pattern follow instructions in *Planning* above and *Blocks,* p. 42.

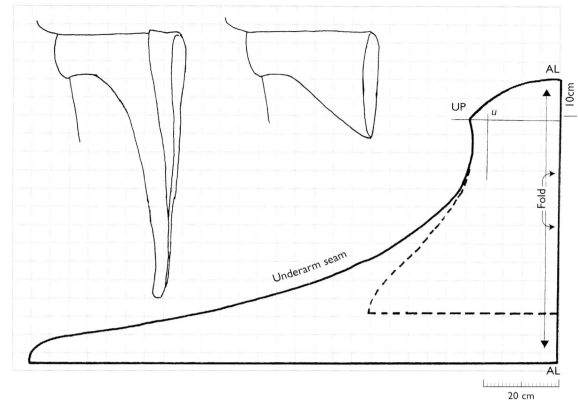

15. Open sleeve for Figs 12 & 8 *left*

To plan the construction lines and sleeve head see instructions for the bag sleeve, Fig 11.

Plan the shape of the underarm seam, keeping outside *u*. If extra length is needed over the hand, extend AL.

The broken outline is for the dagged sleeve in Fig 8. For dagging see *Methods,* Fig 24.

Cut each sleeve in one piece on a fold. When setting into the gown, match the underarm seam to the side seam of the body: the fold line will normally fall forward of the shoulder seam. As the sleeve lining will be visible, you could use a finer fabric than for the body lining, such as silk.

Pleated gowns

18

18. Pleated gowns, middle 15th century

This style could be short, calf length (Pls 12, 13) or full length, depending on the age and status of the wearer. The shape has been achieved by placing the side seam lines of the flared bodice pattern on the Straight grain, and the CF and CB on the bias. Tubular pleats, formed by the wide flaring, follow the direction of the slash lines on the pattern, either diagonally or vertically. They are stitched in place inside at the waist, to a stay band (Pl 14).

The full length front opening is often hidden by the pleats and fastened by hooks and eyes. The neckline is plain or edged with fur, leaving the doublet collar visible, though the gown might still be made with a standing collar (Fig 9). Sleeves are straight or tapered, sometimes slashed (Fig 16) with pleats at the shoulder which are supported by the padded sleeves of the doublet. This style was often lined or edged with fur (*Methods,* p. 53).

Making this style of gown requires considerable experience and care.

19. Bodices for Fig 18

a. Enlarged bodice with four slanted slashes from the shoulder, for the calf-length style.

b. Enlarged bodice with five vertical slashes, for the short style.

Bodice – Trace the bodice Block to waist only. Enlarge it as described in Fig 5. Plan 3 or more slash lines, either slanted or vertical, as shown. On the finished gown the pleats will form along these lines.

Collar – Leave the neckline plain as shown, or use a collar from a previous pattern.

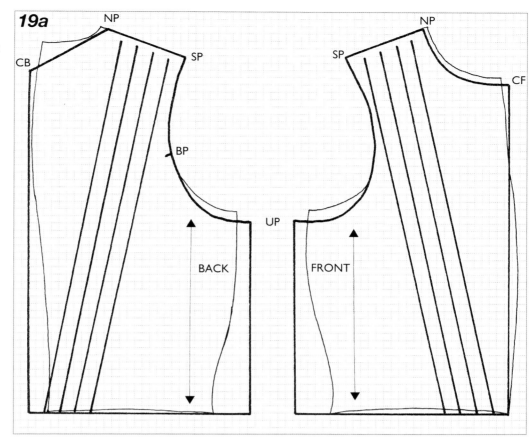

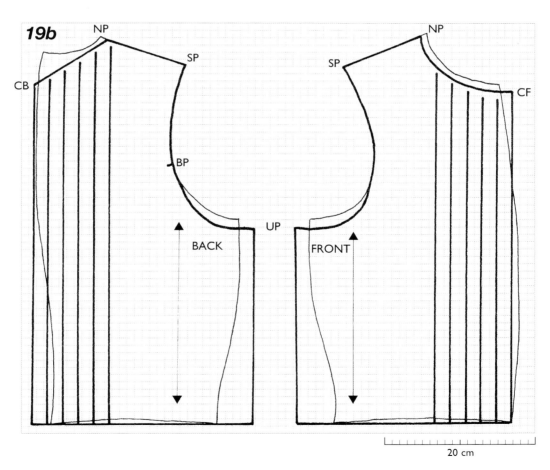

20 cm

151

Plate 12 Mid 15th century pleated gown
Gown similar to Fig 18, in good quality woollen cloth with fur edging, showing well-defined pleating. He is wearing a chaperon (*Men's Hoods,* Fig 6); the white at the neck is a breast kerchief. The slashed sleeves show off both doublet and shirt.

152

Plate 13 Back view of pleated gown

The back pleating is the same as the front; the fur edging outlines the side openings. The back neckline is cut in a *V*, corresponding to the doublet collar. The chaperon was often carried over the shoulder in this manner, the weight of the liripipe keeping it in place.

153

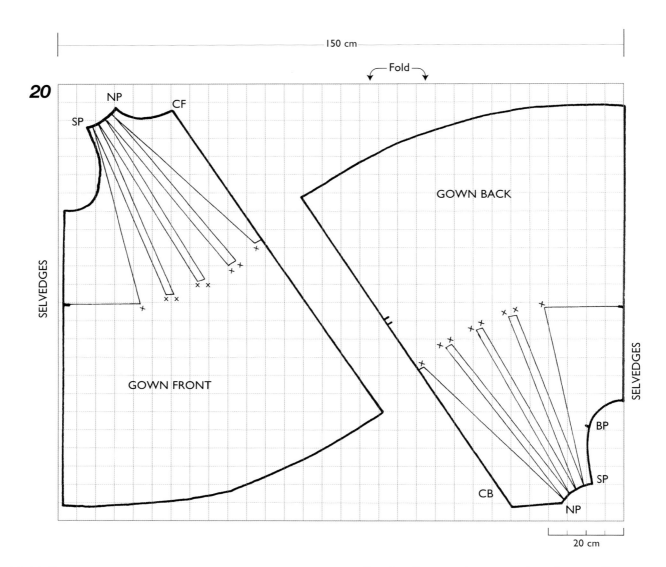

150 cm

Fold

20

NP
SP
CF

SELVEDGES

GOWN FRONT

GOWN BACK

SELVEDGES

BP
SP
CB
NP

20 cm

20. Full pattern and layout for Fig 18

The patterns are shown on cloth 150 cm wide, folded crossways, with both side seam lines on the selvedges and the CB/CF lines on the bias.

Measurements – The following measurements are for the calf length style, but the method of planning and layout applies to any length.

Find the gown length by adding the shoulder-to-waist and waist-to-hem measurements. Here the total length is 110 cm, and waist-to-hem is 55 cm. The Back and Front hems are each 90 cm wide, giving a total hem of 360 cm.

Front – Rule a line and place the side seam line of the enlarged bodice Front along it. Continue the side seam line to the required hem length. Cut and open the slash lines equally, 6-10 cm at the waist, or up to 12 cm for a short gown.

Rule the CF seam line from neck to hem. This line will slant out sharply. Check the hem width and adjust the spacing of the slashes if necessary, securing them provisionally in position.

Plan the hem curve by measuring off the waist-to-hem length from several points on the waist. Mark the final pleat positions (x..x) at the end of each slash line.

Back – Repeat the procedure for the Front, checking that the side seams are the same length on each. Trace off the patterns; see also *Blocks,* p. 42.

Note: The greater the gown length, the less the slashes need to be opened to achieve the same hem width. To form good pleats, however, they must be opened at least 6 cm at the waist, so allow a generous hem width for a pleated gown.

After cutting, mark the pleat positions (x..x) with tailor's tacks on both outer fabric and lining. This will act as a guide when stitching the pleats to the waist stay band (Pl 14). Also reinforce the bias edges with stay bands.

154

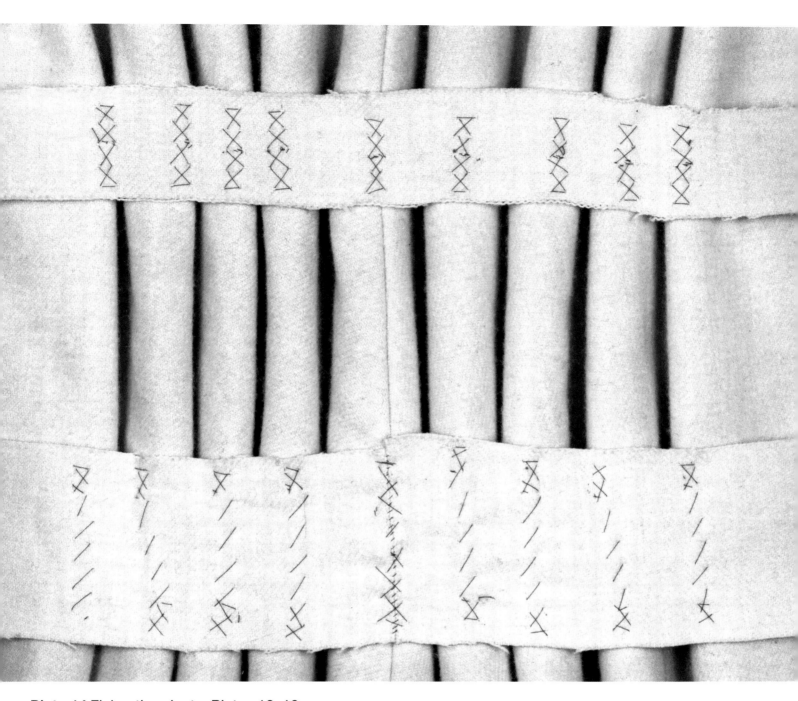

Plate 14 Fixing the pleats, Plates 12, 13

First make up the gown. Put it on a sturdy hanger or dress stand, to fall into shape. To make a waist stay cut a strip of cloth or canvas 5 cm wide and 10-15 cm longer than the wearer's waist size. Mark the half and quarter points with pins, and pin these at waist level to the CB and side seams inside the gown. Pin the ends of the stay to the CF edges.

    Work from the outside, through all layers of the gown together. Starting from the side seams, on the Back and then the Front, pin the stay flat to the fabric as far as the first pleat. Arrange the pleats evenly using the tailor's tacks as a guide, and pin each pleat to the stay.

    Leave overnight on the hanger to see if the pleats distort or twist, and adjust if necessary before stitching firmly through the stay into each pleat. Stitch the stay in place on the seams and front edges. A further stay at a different level, as illustrated, will add stability.

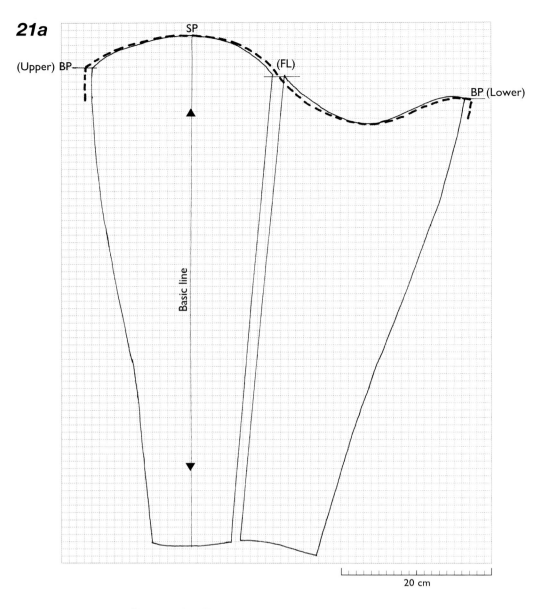

21a

SP

(Upper) BP

(FL)

BP (Lower)

Basic line

20 cm

21. Sleeve for Fig 18

A tapered sleeve with pleats at the shoulder, drafted in two stages from the sleeve Block.

a. Stage 1 Enlarging the sleeve head to match the armhole

Measure the armhole and add the increase, here 3 cm, as shown in *Blocks,* Fig 25. Add half the increase at FL, opening it for its full length. Divide the other half between the upper and lower BP. The provisional sleeve head shape is shown by the broken line.

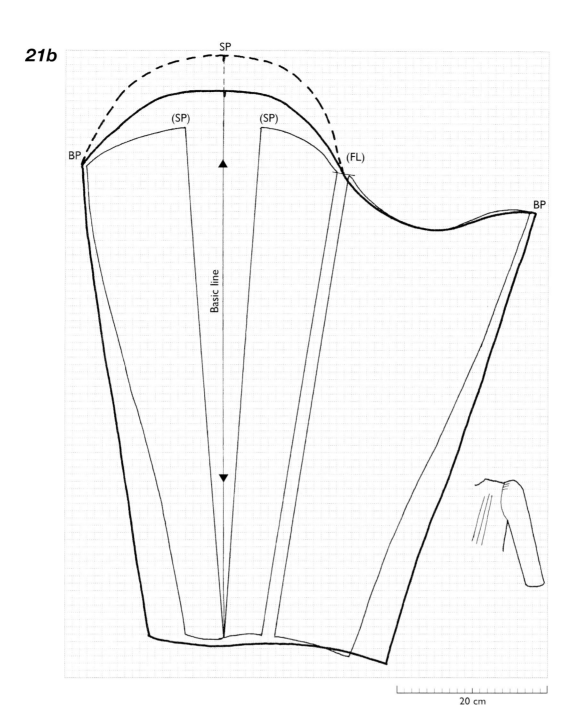

21b

SP

(SP)   (SP)

BP

(FL)

BP

Basic line

20 cm

b. Stage 2 Adding fullness to the sleeve head and wrist

On a fresh piece of paper rule a new Basic line. Slash the enlarged sleeve pattern (Stage 1) down its Basic line, and open it at SP by at least 10 cm, centring the opening on the new Basic line. For a higher crown (shown by the broken line) widen it up to 25 cm. Paste down the opened pattern.

Raise the SP by 3-5 cm on the new Basic line, or up to 10 cm for a very large sleeve head, and draw a new upper curve, starting flat, across the crown.

Widen the wrist, here by 5 cm on each side, as shown. Draw new seam lines from BP to wrist, checking they are of equal length. Trace off a new copy.

To set in the finished (lined) sleeve, match BP and SP to the armhole, pin the underarm curve in smoothly and pleat in the fullness over the shoulder. Tack firmly, and fit, before stitching. A strip of interlining, sandwiched between the sleeve and its lining along the sleeve head, will support the pleats.

For slashed sleeves, see *Methods,* p. 49 & Fig 9a; Pl 1.

Flared gown

24

24. Flared gown, early to late 15th century

This is cut like the early gown. The extended shape of the back collar appeared towards 1450. The fashionable neckline was low enough to show the front of the kirtle, or later a stomacher. A fine kerchief might be tucked inside the neckline. The front opening extended to hip level and was often clearly visible. It had no fastenings. The gown has no waist seam, but with careful adjustment it is possible to get a smooth fit above the belt and an even flare below.

Straight fitted sleeves became increasingly common, though early wider forms were still used. This basic gown shape persisted to the end of the century for older and less fashionable women, with a small collar and a looser sleeve.

Plate 15 Detail from Plate 9

This characteristic gown, with a train, is seen here without a belt. It is lined or edged with fur, which is also seen on the mitten cuffs of the fitted sleeves. The square neck opening of the kirtle beneath is filled with a sheer kerchief. A 'flowerpot' head-dress with black loop and fillet completes the outfit.

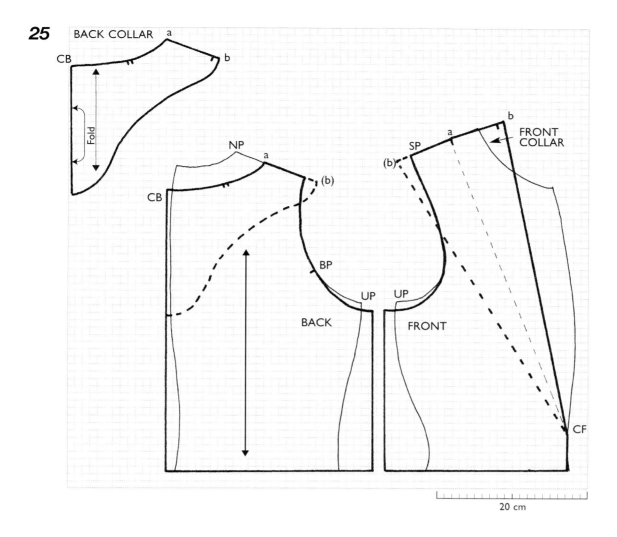

25. Bodice and collar for Fig 24

Bodice – Trace the bodice Block to waist only. Draw a vertical CB line starting 0.5-1 cm outside the Block neckline. The short vertical CF line runs from the Block waist to the base of the collar. The collar is shown as a deep V-shape, which could be shortened. Draw straight side seam lines starting 1.5-2 cm outside and 1 cm down from UP. Redraw the armholes to match.

Draw the new curved back neckline 2-5 cm below the Block neck. Measure from NP to *a* on the back shoulder, and mark *a* on the front shoulder to match. Rule the front collar fold line from *a* to CF (fine broken line).

Collar – This is a 3-piece collar. The back is cut separately in one piece on a fold, and the fronts in one with the gown Fronts. For making up see *Methods,* Fig 14. For contrasting facings see *Methods: Collars and cuffs.*

Back collar – Plan the shape, shown by the heavy broken line, on the bodice Back. The collar extends slightly beyond the gown shoulders. Trace off the pattern, to be cut on the fold.

Front collar – Measure off *a-(b)* on the Front shoulder to equal *a-(b)* on the Back. Rule from *(b)* to CF (heavy broken line). Fold back the pattern paper along the fine broken line, *a*-CF. Trace off the shape of the front collar and open it out again, marking *b* as shown. The line *ab* may slope up or down. It may help to fit the collar and Front in calico at this stage, before tracing off the working pattern.

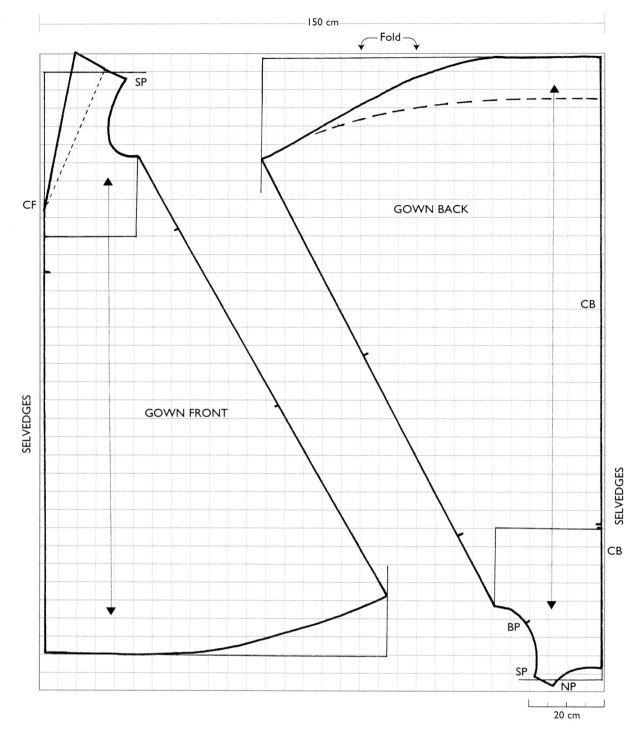

150 cm

Fold

SP

CF

GOWN BACK

CB

SELVEDGES

GOWN FRONT

SELVEDGES

CB

BP

SP

NP

20 cm

26. Full pattern and layout for Fig 24

The Back and Front are shown on cloth 150 cm wide folded crossways.

Gown length is 160 cm. Add 10 cm to the length at CB to give a slight train, as shown. Side seam length is 138 cm and hem width is 90 cm, giving a total hem of 360 cm.

To prepare your pattern see *Planning* above and *Blocks,* p. 42.

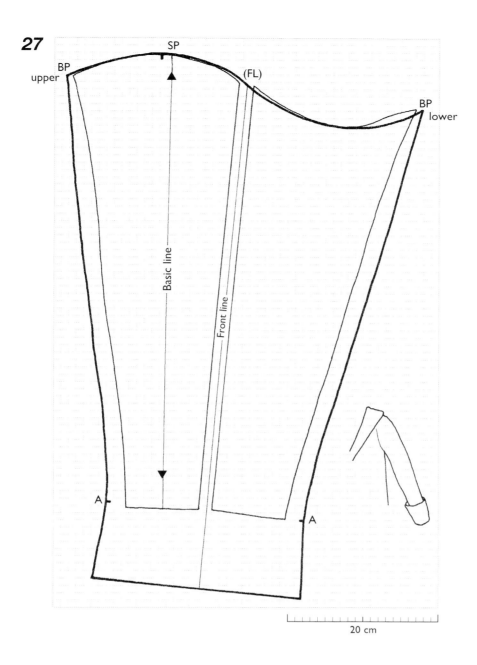

27. Sleeve for Fig 24

This narrow sleeve has an extension forming a cuff, which may be worn over the hand or turned back, showing the lining or a contrasting facing.

The sleeve is adapted from the Block, with the wrist widened (here by 5 cm) to a slip-on fit. Measure the armhole of the gown bodice to find the sleeve head increase, here 4 cm.

Trace the Block and cut it in two along the Front line. Rule a new extended Front line on fresh paper. Centre the cut pieces on this line, half the sleeve head increase apart (here 2 cm) all the way down, and paste them in position.

Divide the other half of the increase between the upper and lower BP (here 1 cm at each) and redraw the sleeve head. Widen the wrist just enough to slip over the hand, and mark the balance points, A. Draw new seam lines, BP-A, checking they are of equal length.

Lengthen the sleeve below the wrist by 10-15 cm. Make the cuff end wide enough to flare when turned back over the sleeve. Check on the pattern by folding it back at the wrist, then trace it off. For a tight-fitting sleeve see Fig 31.

Fitted gown

28

This fashionable gown fits the body to hip level, worn over the tight kirtle (*Kirtles,* Fig 7). To achieve this look it is planned like a kirtle or cotehardie. The belt is worn lower to emphasise the new look. The edge-to-edge front opening is laced to hip level through concealed metal rings (*Methods,* Fig 17c). The collar, often of fur, dips below the neckline at the front. The gown was sometimes worn without a collar. The tight sleeves with conical cuffs are shown in Fig 31.

31

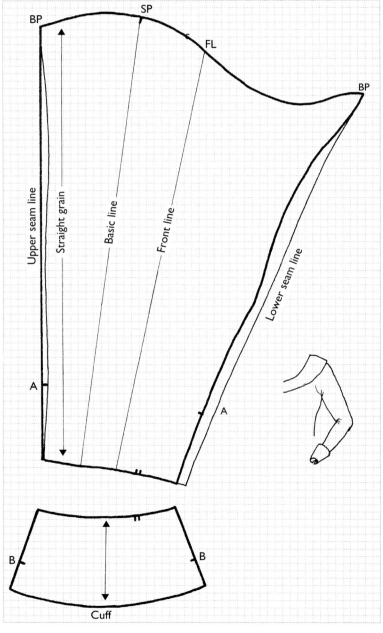

Cuff

20 cm

31. Sleeve for Fig 28

This sleeve is adapted from the Block to give a tight fit. It has a wrist opening, fastened by hook and eye, and a separate cuff. It is best to try out the fit in calico before cutting the cloth.

Measure the gown armhole. Trace the sleeve Block. Add any increase needed on the sleeve head at BP on the upper curve. None was required here. Rule a straight upper seam line from BP to wrist and a new SG parallel to it.

Reduce the sleeve width from BP to wrist along the lower seam line, as shown, referring to the measurements in *Blocks,* Fig 3. Try out the fit on the wearer in calico and adjust if necessary. Draw the final pattern, marking an opening on the seam at *A*, 10-15 cm from the wrist.

Plan the cuff pattern using the 'slash and flare' method (*Blocks,* Fig 26) with the wrist edge of the sleeve as a guide. Make the cuff 10-15 cm deep and not too flared. Cut the cuff in the outer fabric, interlining, and lining or facing. Make it up and attach it to the wrist edge, with its side edges either caught together at the balance point *B,* or left open (p. 52).

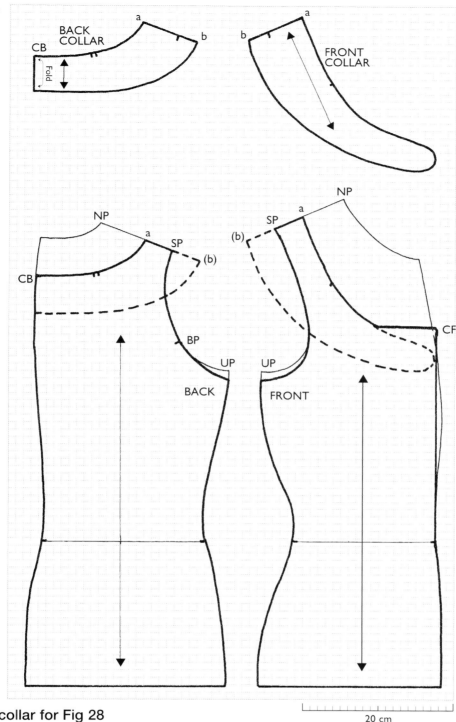

29. Bodice and collar for Fig 28

Bodice – Trace the bodice Block to hip level: little alteration is needed. Rule a vertical CF line upwards from the Block waist, but leave the CB unaltered. Lower the armhole at UP by 1-2 cm.

Plan a low, curved neckline on Back and Front, here 5 cm below the Block neck at CB and 6 cm from NP to a at the shoulders. The front neckline should meet the CF at right angles, well above bust level to cover the kirtle front.

Rule a vertical construction line centred on the waist line on Front and Back.

Collar – This 3-piece collar is made up separately and sewn to the gown. It is 6 cm deep at CB, 7.5 cm at the shoulder, narrowing to 2.5 cm at CF.

Use these measurements to draw the outer edge of the collar, shown by heavy broken lines. Broadly follow the back and front necklines, but dip and round the end at CF. Trace off the pattern and add the SG and balance marks, as shown. Cut the back in one, on a fold, and the front as separate pieces. Make up the collar, with interlining and lining, finishing all the edges. For light materials use edge stitching (*Methods,* Pl 1). For heavier fabrics and velvet follow *Methods,* Fig 13. For fur see p. 53. Tack and hand stitch the finished collar in place round the finished gown neck.

163

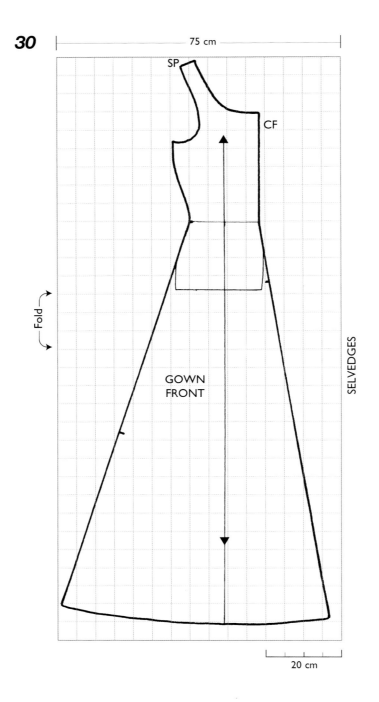

30. Full pattern and layout for Fig 28

The patterns are shown on 150 cm wide cloth, folded lengthways for the Front, and crossways for the Back. This gown is planned as in *Blocks,* Fig 27.

Measurements – Waist to hem is 110 cm. The front hem is 70 cm, the back hem is 115 cm, giving a total hem of 3.7 m. Gown length is given from waist to hem because the flaring is added from the waist or below.

Front – Extend the bodice construction line using the waist-to-hem measurement. Mark off the hem width on either side of the construction line: 25 cm towards CF and 45 cm towards the side seam line. Now draw the CF and side seam lines from the hem to join the bodice pattern on the curve of the hip. Plan the hem curve by measuring off the waist-to-hem length from several points on the waist.

150 cm

⌐ Fold ⌐

SELVEDGES

SELVEDGES

SP

CB

BP

GOWN BACK

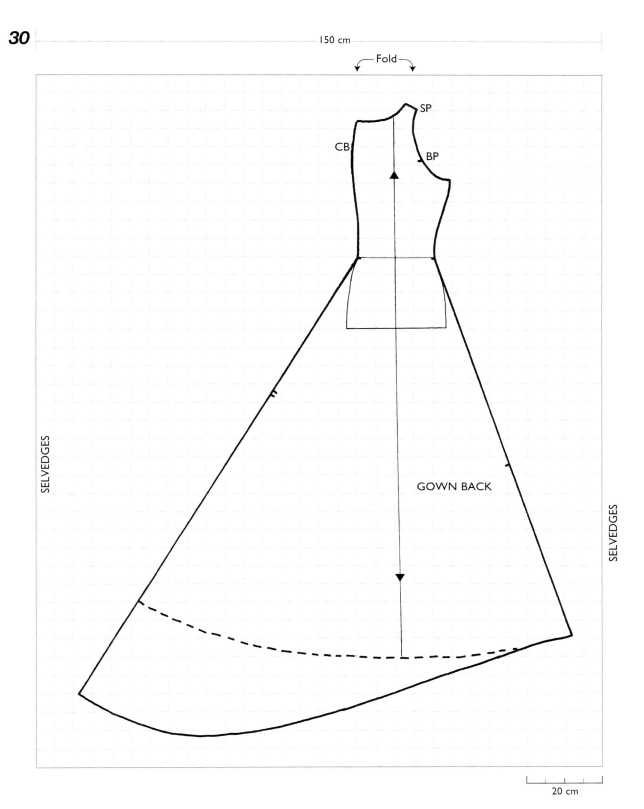

20 cm

Back – Extend the bodice construction line using the waist-to-hem measurement. Mark off the hem width on either side of the construction line: 45 cm towards the side seam line, and 70 cm towards CB, where the bulk of the hem will fall. Extend the CB line by 30 cm to form a train. Draw the CB and side seam lines from the hem to join the bodice at waist level, or on the hip curve.

Make sure the flare on the side seam lines of both Back and Front is the same, here 45 cm.

Plate 16. Woman in overkirtle, c.1440, Flemish

Background figure from the painting, wearing a brown overkirtle lined with grey, turned up over a red kirtle. Black shoes, bare arms (for working) with smock sleeves rolled up, and white kerchief.

St Luke drawing the Virgin (detail) by Rogier van der Weyden,
Groeninge Museum, Bruges

Outer working garments

smock

hose

kirtle

overkirtle

kerchief

apron

Outer working garments

Overkirtles

'Overkirtle' is used here as a convenient term to describe the common outer working garment for women throughout the 15th century (Fig 1). Women are rarely shown in a kirtle alone: the overkirtle would normally be worn over it.

The style varied in detail but the basic form was the same: a bodice slightly shaped to the waist, and skirts flared from the hips; a round neckline large enough to pull over the head, and sleeves set in plain. The sleeves could be short, though more often long, and wide enough to roll above the elbows, leaving the sleeves of the kirtle or smock visible.

Overkirtle skirts could be ground length, but were generally hitched up for work, revealing the kirtle beneath and sometimes a lining. The belt was usually worn round the kirtle rather than the overkirtle.

Some overkirtles became tighter and more fitted from the middle of the century, matching a similar trend in the kirtle. The most likely arrangement for fastening was a discreet laced opening in the back or side seam at the waist.

As a working dress it would be worn with a linen head-dress (*Linen head-dresses*, Figs 1-4) or plain hood (*Cloth head-dresses*, Figs 2, 3). Often a kerchief or wimple was used to fill the neckline.

1. c.1440, Flemish, Pl 16

Background figure from the painting, wearing a brown overkirtle lined with grey, turned up over a red kirtle. Black shoes, bare arms (for working) with smock sleeves rolled up, and white kerchief. (Detail from *St Luke drawing the Virgin* by Rogier van der Weyden, Groeninge Museum, Bruges).

Materials

A woollen cloth of light or medium weight is best, in a muted colour. For lining use woollen cloth or linen. White or undyed fabric is suitable. The garment could also be lined or edged with an inexpensive fur such as rabbit.

Women

1

Loose-fitting overkirtle

2

Men's outer working garments

Various forms of outer garment were worn by working men in the 15th century (Pl 18). They included a persistent form of the surcote; a short form of the gown, possibly known as a frock; and a closer-fitting buttoned coat.

A common feature of these garments was their length, reaching between mid-thigh and knee. This made them practical for wear over a long doublet and separate hose, as depicted for workmen over most of the century.

Use a hard-wearing woollen cloth or cheaper broadcloth in a muted colour. The quality of the garments and their cloth would have varied a good deal, even for those issued as livery; they were not necessarily lined. Use lightweight cloth, linen or canvas if you wish to line your garment.

Cloth buttons are suitable for fastening (*Methods*, Figs 19-21). The buttons were spaced well apart, sometimes in pairs and sometimes just five from neck to waist. To position five buttons fold the edge into quarters.

Surcote for working wear

Untailored garments probably continued well into the 15th century, especially for poorer workers. To make this see *Surcotes*, Fig 4, possibly shortening the skirts.

Frock (or tunic)

Many outdoor workers wore a garment which seems related in cut to the gown, though not more than knee length. It typically had long plain sleeves, a buttoned opening at the neck, and was worn pulled in by a belt. It can be made as a shortened version of *Gowns*, Fig 4. As it is a simple garment, both Front and Back might be cut in one on the fold.

Coat (or jerkin)

Commoner than the frock for indoor workers, this is open down the front and buttoned. The cut is comparable with the cotehardie, though later versions often show a waist seam, sometimes with the skirts pleated on at the waist. To make these see *Cotehardies*, Fig 4, but plan it with more ease all round the Block and long plain sleeves.

Men

1. 1423, French
Carpenter (building Noah's ark) in a full surcote or frock, pleated under the belt, and a hood with its liripipe wound round the head. He has hose and ankle boots. Note the hammer tucked through his purse. (Bedford Hours, British Library, MS Add 18850, f.15b).

2. 1465, French/Burgundian
Peasant in belted frock or surcote with sleeves rolled up to show buttoned doublet sleeves. His hose are baggy and probably separate. Hood with liripipe wound round the head and working boots. (Burgundian tapestry, Burrell Collection, Glasgow).

Overkirtle

2

2. Overkirtle, 15th century

A loose-fitting overkirtle. The skirts are ground length, tucked up and revealing the kirtle, which is short-sleeved. The overkirtle has elbow length sleeves and the smock sleeves are rolled up.

3. Bodice and sleeve for Fig 2

a. Bodice Trace the personal Block to hip level. Check the waist size by asking a friend to measure the smallest looped tape that will slip over your head and shoulders, as if putting on a dress. ⟶

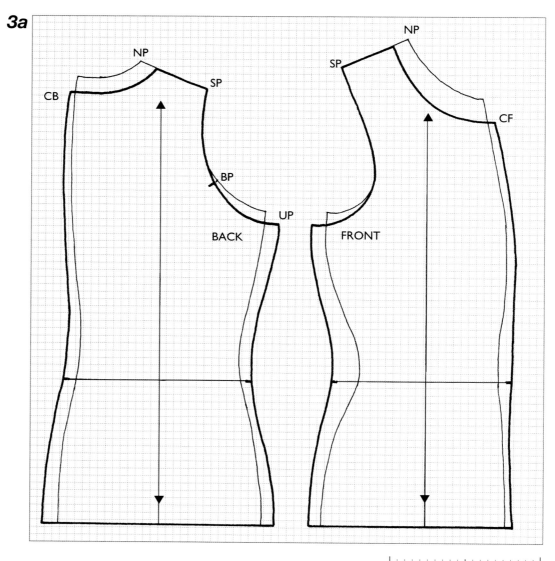

3a

20 cm

Lower the armhole by 1-3 cm. Widen the sides by 1-3 cm, and widen CB and CF by 1 cm, reducing the shaping down the CF. Ensure the back and front waist combined equal at least half the looped tape measurement. Rule a vertical construction line through the waist centre on Front and Back.

Enlarge the back and front neckline to a size which will slip on over the head, about 60 cm all round: here the neckline has been lowered by 2 cm at CB and NP, and 3 cm at CF. To plan the skirts see Fig 4.

b. Sleeve Measure the new armhole. Trace the sleeve Block and enlarge the sleeve head to match, here by a total of 3.5 cm, see *Blocks,* Fig 25. The sleeve shown is elbow length, 35 cm down the Back seam and 40 cm wide at *A-A*. Complete the pattern, marking SP, SG and seam allowances.

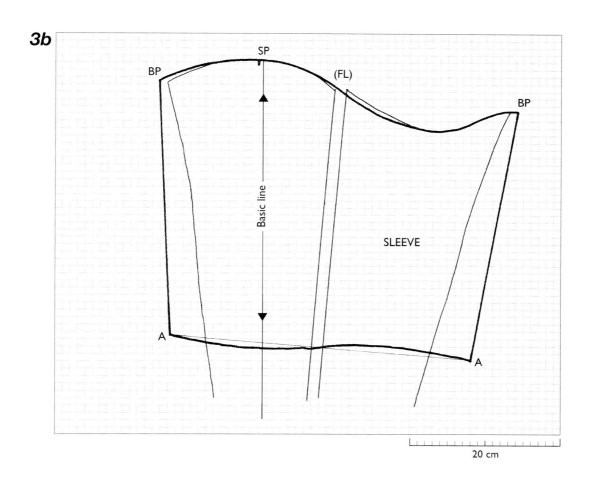

3b

20 cm

171

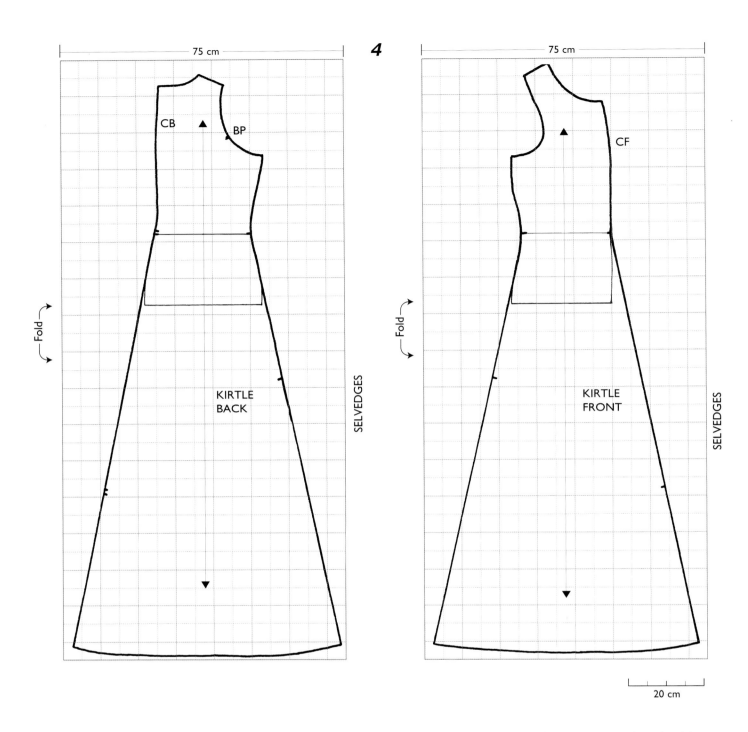

4. Full pattern and layout for Fig 2

The patterns are shown on 150 cm wide cloth folded lengthways. Front and Back hems are each 72 cm, giving a total hem of 288 cm. The method is given in *Blocks,* Fig 27.

Extend the construction line on the adjusted Front and Back (Fig 3) from the waist to hem level using the Waist to floor measurement, here 115 cm. Here both Back and Front are planned with the hem width centered on the construction line. Extra width could be added at CB for a fuller skirt.

Check the side seam lines are equal and add balance points. The construction lines are on SG. Add seam allowances. Cut out the completed patterns, ready for laying on the cloth.

For small sizes, you can cut both sleeves from the spare fabric on the left. For larger sizes, open out the fabric after cutting the Front, and cut one sleeve from the spare. Cut the other sleeve similarly from the spare of the Back.

Cloaks

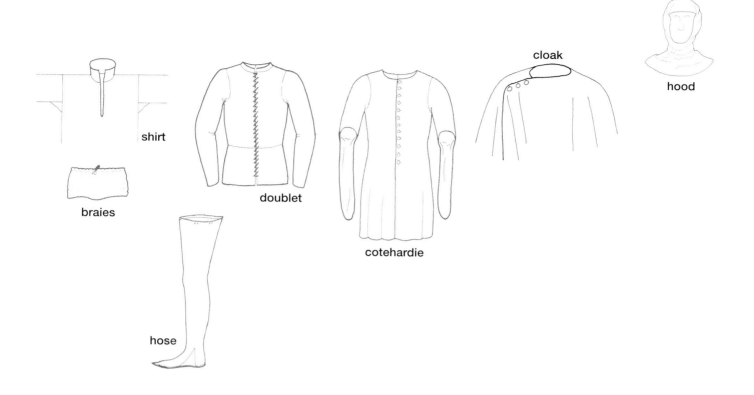

shirt

braies

doublet

hose

cotehardie

cloak

hood

smock

hose

kirtle

surcote

cloak

173

Cloaks

Cloaks and mantles

The distinction between the two appears to be one of status. Mantles seem to have been largely worn for display, while cloaks were worn for protection, though not often illustrated.

The cloak was the commonest form of protection, used by all classes throughout the medieval period. By 1200 it was generally cut as a circle, but its size depended on the wearer's wealth or rank. A half-circle (Fig 3) was quite adequate for protection from the weather, but those in Figs 1 & 2 are ceremonial and therefore larger: common travellers' cloaks are rarely illustrated.

Neck finishes of cloaks can be difficult to make out in illustrations, and in some the neckline is simply hollowed out to fit round the shoulders (Fig 2). Where the hood is shown round the neck (Fig 1; *Gowns,* Fig 1) it is impossible to tell if this is separate, or part of the cloak. Some neck finishes and fastenings are shown in Fig 4.

Materials

Use a densely-woven wool cloth or Melton for protection from the wind and rain. For a ceremonial garment use lighter, finer cloth.

All were normally lined: use loosely-woven wool for warmth. For a grand mantle use fur or silk, which will look impressive.

Planning and cutting

Measure the required length for the cloak from the back neck. This measurement is the only one needed, and it can be adjusted to fit the cloth. For outdoor wear, make sure it is well clear of the ground. A good firm cloth needs no hem allowance as the curved edge can be left raw.

Lay out the unfolded cloth – the floor may be better than a table for this. Using tape measure and pins, mark the shape on the cloth. Chalk a final outline before cutting. Cut the lining like the outer layer.

Fig 3 shows a half-circle cloak, with a pieced hem for a cloak wider than the cloth. Fig 4 shows various neck styles.

Use the same planning method for larger cloaks.

For a three-quarter circle cloak plan a half-circle, as for Fig 3, and add two gores at the front, starting from the neck cut-out. Sew the gores with their bias edges to the selvedges of the cloak.

For a full circle cloak, cut two half-circles with a join at the centre back. If your material has firm woven selvedges these can be oversewn together to make the back seam (*Methods,* Fig 1). Make the radius of the neck cut-out about 10 cm.

Letters indicate joining points.
For abbreviations and symbols see p. 10.

1. 1370-80, English

Cloak fastened on the right shoulder. The bulk round the neck is probably a hood. Possibly a mourner's cloak, which was ample, ankle length and always hooded. Cut from at least a three-quarter circle. (Mourner, tomb of Edward III, Westminster Abbey, London)

2. 1455, English

Ceremonial mantle worn by ladies from the late 13th century on. Corners on the front neck edges support the two brooch-like bosses, whose shanks are pushed through eyelets and the elaborate cord is threaded through the shanks. (Brass to Isabel Manfield, spinster, Taplow church, Buckinghamshire).

174

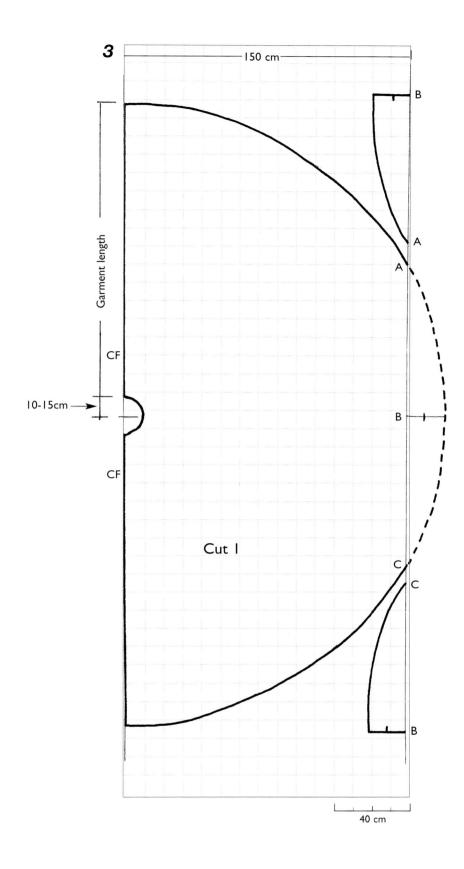

3. Basic half-circle cloak – pattern and layout

Lay out the cloth in a single layer, here shown on 150 cm wide cloth. Along one selvedge measure the Garment length, plus 10-15 cm for the neck, and mark the centre of the neck. From here measure out radially to mark the neck and hem curves, first with pins and then with chalk.

If the cloak length is greater than the width of the cloth, the back can be pieced as shown. Mark and cut the main part, then use the off-cuts to make the piecings, joining them selvedge to selvedge.

Making up

Make up any piecings on the outer fabric and lining. Lay the two layers with wrong sides together, starting from the CF edges, pinning and tacking them round the neck. Turn in the edges on the CF and oversew or stab-stitch them together (*Methods*, Pl 1). Finish the neck in the chosen manner (Fig 4).

On the curved outer edge you can leave the lining loose. Woollen lining can be left raw, and trimmed shorter than the outer fabric. Silk or other light fabrics will need hemming. The lining may 'drop' below the outer edge as the garment stretches in wear, so trim if necessary.

4a

b

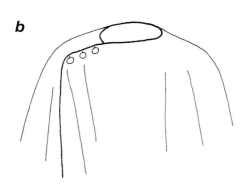

c

4. Cloak necklines and fastenings

a. **Fastening for a ceremonial mantle.** You will need two metal bosses, like large shanked metal buttons, and heavy silk cord and tassels such as an old-fashioned dressing-gown cord, or a fancy curtain tie-back. Push the shanks of the bosses through eyelets made in the garment (*Methods,* Fig 16), put split rings or wire loops through the bosses and thread the cord through them.

b. **This men's style, from c.1350,** is suitable for three-quarter circle cloaks or larger. You will need three large buttons, self fabric or metal. These are fastened on the wearer's right shoulder (*Methods,* Figs 19-21).

c. **Simple neck finish** using the ends for fastening. Use a straight strip of cloth (spare selvedge is excellent), stitch it round the inside neck edge and leave the ends hanging as ties. The cloak neckline is often hidden by the cape of the hood.

Children

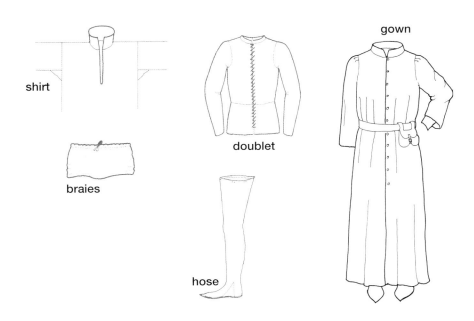

shirt

braies

doublet

hose

gown

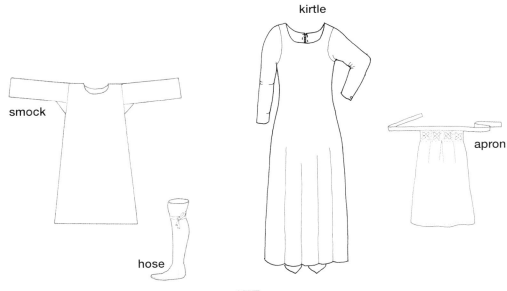

smock

hose

kirtle

apron

Children

Images of children from the period are scarce. Those available are mainly from wealthy families and tend to show dress of similar materials but simpler styles than the dress of their elders. Other children's clothes would have been mended and remade, and commonly handed down. Teenage children would often have lived away from home as servants or apprentices, with their clothing supplied by the employer.

This chapter includes examples from different stages of childhood.

Maternity wear

Many common garments were loose enough to need little adaptation for pregnancy, for example an unshaped cote or a flared gown. Even the fitted kirtle could be hitched up, or worn with the lacing loosened, while the overkirtle might have both side seams opened out with lacing (Fig 3), and the seams resewn later. The sleeveless surcote might also have served as a convenient outer garment during pregnancy, and would have hidden any loosened lacing of the garment beneath.

Babies

The medieval baby wore a shirt and a tail-clout (nappy), and was wrapped in a linen 'bed'. A linen coif (Fig 6) like those in *Men's hats*, Fig 5 might be worn. A tail-clout was a folded square of linen, often in diaper weave – a fancy weave with greater absorbency. Babies' shirts were open down the front to make them easier to put on. An example is shown in Fig 4.

The linen 'bed' (Fig 5), which was held in place with swaddling bands, covered the body and sometimes the head. Everything close to the baby would have been of washable white or unbleached linen, with a woollen shawl or blanket on top in cold weather.

1. 1404, English
Young boy in ankle length buttoned gown, fitted, with a high collar and bag sleeves like an adult gown. Worn without a belt and with ankle shoes. (Brass to Sir Reginald Braybrook, Cobham church, Kent).

2. c.1475, Flemish
Young girl at prayer in V-fronted gown of dark cloth, laced over a red stomacher or kirtle. The body is close-fitting to the hips and she wears no belt (The hemline is not visible in the original). The neckline is filled in with a fine kerchief. Fashionable tight sleeves with mitten cuffs. Her hair is loose, drawn back under a black frontlet, probably velvet, decorated with a jewel. (Detail from *The Donne Triptych,* Hans Memling, National Gallery, London).

1

2

Overkirtle for pregnancy
3

Infant's summer outfit
6a

Plate 17. Passover scene, c.1320, northern Spain

The head of household, in long cote and cloak, oversees the distribution of Passover foods to children, who wear simple round-necked cotes and dark hose and shoes. At the back a woman wearing a draped kerchief holds a baby, wrapped and with a coif.

Golden Haggadah, British Library MS Add. 27210, f.15 (detail)

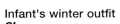

Infant's winter outfit
6b

Boy's gown
7

Girls' kirtle and gown
10

179

3. Overkirtle for pregnancy, 15th century

The overkirtle (*Overkirtles,* Fig 2) could be modified for the late stages of pregnancy by opening up both side seams for lacing. The inner kirtle might be front-laced, so any gap in it would be covered.

4. Baby's shirt – pattern

Shirts for very young babies are square-cut like all linens. With its open Front, it is simplest to cut the body in one piece, as shown. Plan the body to reach down to the thighs, and wide enough to overlap round the chest. This example is 30 cm long by 60 cm wide round the chest. Stitch the shoulders to make the body, make up the sleeves, and set them into the armhole slits (*Methods,* Fig 7). Underarm gussets may not be necessary if the sleeves are made wide.

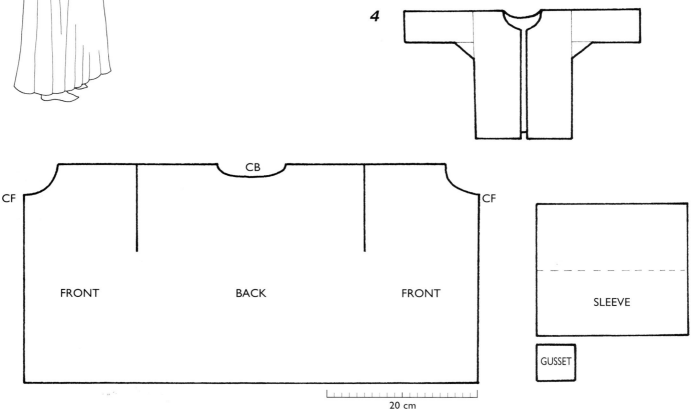

CB

CF

FRONT   BACK   FRONT

CF

SLEEVE

GUSSET

20 cm

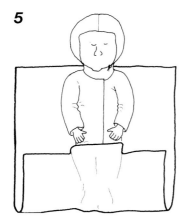

5. Baby's 'bed'

This baby is dressed in a shirt (Fig 4), coif and tail-clout, before being wrapped in the 'bed', a large piece of plain linen. The bed would be secured by a band wound from shoulders to feet and back again, its ends tied or pinned.

180

Infants

The dress of this age group, from a few months to about three years, would have comprised a simple outfit of shirt or smock under an ankle-length cote, with bare feet and legs in summer and short gartered hose or felt bootees for cold weather. Boys and girls often wore a coif. For added warmth they might wear a surcote, or later a buttoned gown, and a hat or hood (Fig 6).

There was little change in style over the period, the clothes being made to the simplest of shapes.

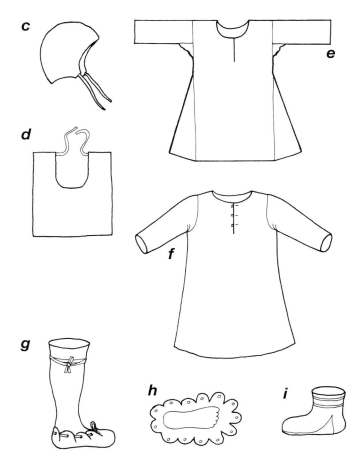

6a

b

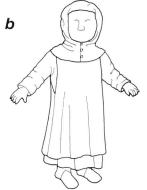

6. Clothes for larger babies and infants

a. Summer outfit of shirt or smock and cote, with coif.

b. Winter outfit of sleeveless surcote and cote (over body linen, unseen), buttoned hood and bootees.

c. Coif, a smaller version of *Hats,* Fig 5.

d. Bib, as found at all periods.

e. Simple cote, see *Cotes,* Fig 3.

f. Cote, made to a shaped pattern.

g. Short gartered hose for boys or girls, shown with a crude shoe.

h. Pattern for g. It is drawn up with a thong through the eyelet holes.

i. Bootee of thick cloth or felt, cut like *Hose,* Fig 4. A leather sole could be added.

Boys

Most boys continued to wear full-length clothes to the age of 6 or more. Those attending school or college might remain in a long cote or gown to adulthood (Figs 1, 7). Boys starting a trade might be provided with adult clothing: a short cote in the earlier centuries, later a doublet under a cotehardie, frock or gown. Joined hose would only be for smart wear by wealthier young men.

Girls

Girls continued to wear full-length garments, moving into women's dress as they grew up. Girls in work would be in adult dress from about the age of 12 (Fig 10 *left*). From adolescence to marriage, girls of higher status were more likely to wear distinctive fashions such as the gown in Figs 2 & 10 *right*.

Girls generally wore their hair loose or dressed in plaits, but wealthier girls can be seen wearing part of a fashionable head-dress over flowing hair (Fig 2).

Accessories – toys and games

Scant information on toys has come down to us, but they were probably few and precious. Rattles, carved wooden animals and figures, and wooden or cloth dolls, may well have been made to keep children amused.

Active games such as leap-frog, hoodman-blind, and piggy-back wrestling have been illustrated. Other games such as kails (ninepins or skittles), marbles, and five-stones were probably played as well.

7

7. Boy's gown, 15th century

Schoolboy's gown first seen in the late 14th century and persisting in a few schools into modern times. The cut is like the plain adult gown (*Gowns,* Fig 4), but reaching only to calf or ankle, with perhaps 1.5-2 m round the hem, depending on size. It can be made with or without a collar, and with plain or bag sleeves (*Gowns,* Fig 11). The gown might be worn over a long doublet and separate hose, either belted or left loose.

> **To plan boys' and girls' garments use a personal bodice Block matching the wearer's age and figure. Make a simple Block for a child (*Blocks,* Fig 24) or an adult one for an adolescent. The patterns shown here fit chest size 70 cm (28 in) and height 134 cm (53 in) for the boy, and chest 78 cm (31 in) and height 152 cm (60 in) for the girl.**
>
> **The fine lines show the original Block outline. Heavy broken lines indicate alternative outlines. For abbreviations and symbols see p. 10.**
>
> **Check that the side seams of the skirts are the same length and at the same angle to the construction line on Back and Front. Add seam allowances and balance points.**

8

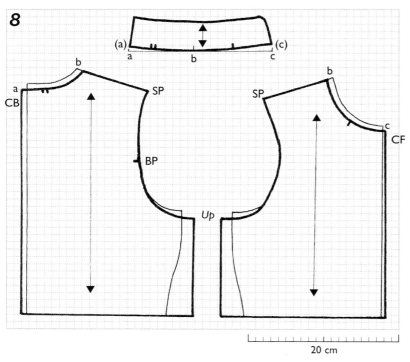

20 cm

8

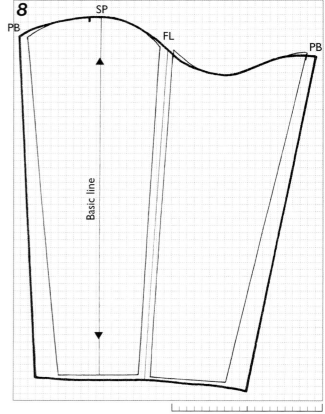

20 cm

8. Bodice and sleeve for Fig 7

Trace the Block to waist only, then enlarge it (see *Gowns,* Fig 5), keeping the enlargement in proportion, but leaving plenty of room for movement – and growth.

This example shows a Block for a 70 cm chest. Rule new CF and CB lines, here 0.5 cm outside the Block. Move out and lower UP, here 1.5 cm out and 1 cm down. Rule vertical side seams and redraw the armholes to match.

Collar – Plan the round 2-piece collar shown in *Gowns,* Fig 5a. Lower the neckline by 0.5-1 cm. Here the neckline *a-c* is 19 cm and *a-b* is 8.5 cm. Where *a-c* is less than 20 cm, as here, raise *(a)* by

0.5 cm and *(c)* by 1 cm. Collar height here is 4 cm. For making up see *Methods,* Fig 14a. You could leave the neckline plain instead.

Sleeve – Use the sleeve Block, enlarging it to match the armhole as described in *Blocks,* Fig 25, and widening it a little at the wrist. Alternatively plan a bag sleeve, or one with pleats at the shoulder (*Gowns,* Figs 11, 21).

9. Full pattern and layout for Fig 7

For this small size the Back and Front are shown on cloth 150 cm wide, folded lengthways. Extra length is needed for the sleeves.

To plan the skirts and make the pattern see *Gowns,* p 139. Gown length here is 106 cm (ankle length); side seam length is 86 cm. Hem width is 46 cm for Back and Front, giving a hem of 184 cm. For small simple gowns such as this the Back may be cut in one on a fold, rather than in two pieces; use the round necked collar in *Gowns,* Fig 5.

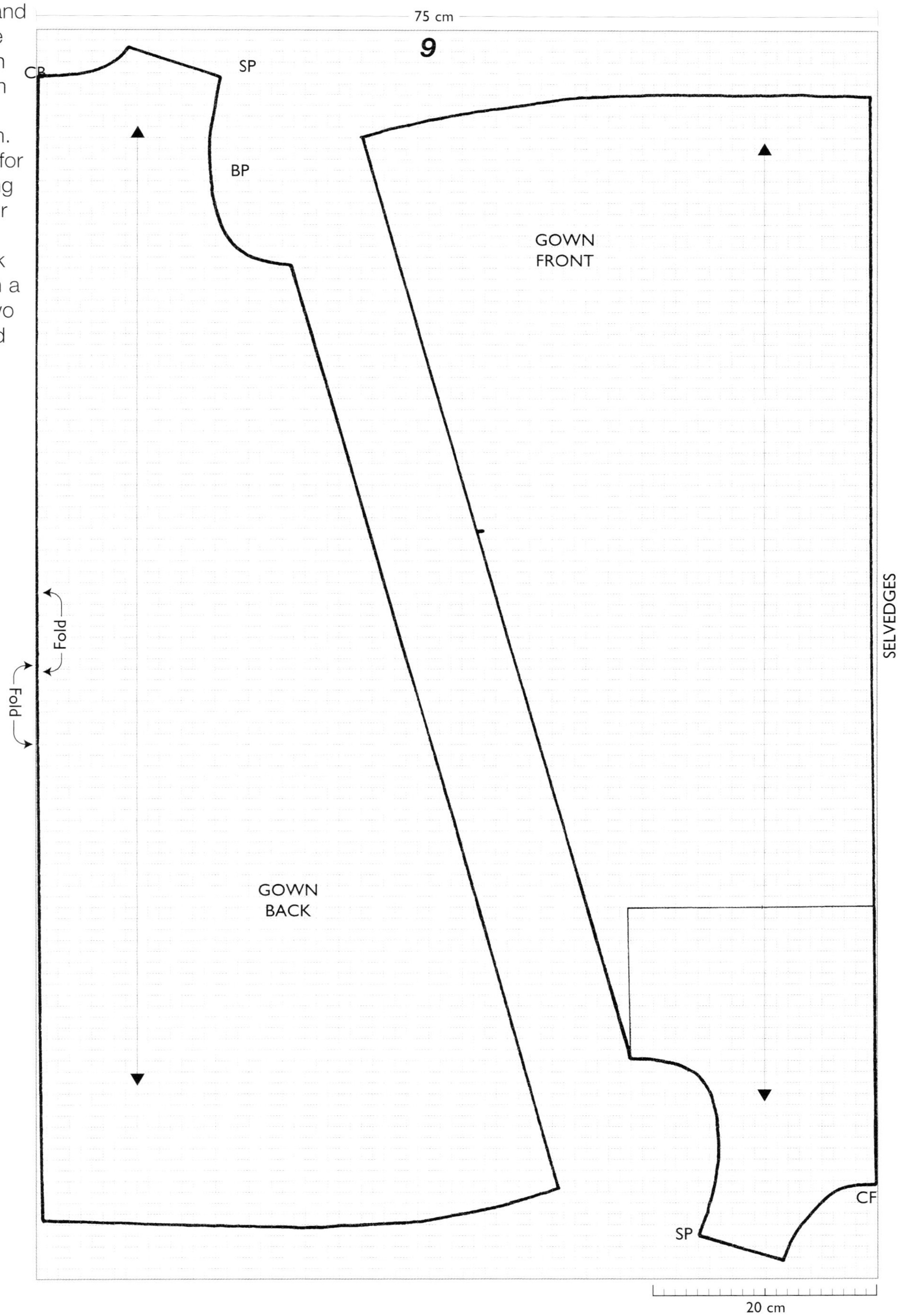

75 cm

9

CB

SP

BP

GOWN FRONT

Fold

Fold

GOWN BACK

SELVEDGES

SP

CF

20 cm

10

10. Girls' kirtle and gown, 15th century

Left Kirtle, normally full-length. For an undeveloped figure the front can be cut on a fold with slight shaping in the side seams, as here. The lacing is at the back.

Right V-fronted gown seen on wealthier girls, later 15th century. It shows similarities to the adult gown: the skirts flare from the hips and the sleeves are tight-fitting with cuffs. The style is ideal for the growing 13- to 15-year-old. It may be worn over a side-laced kirtle (*Kirtles,* Fig 10) or a stomacher (*Methods,* Fig 15) stiffened with canvas, or over both.

The bodice pattern for both is in Fig 11.

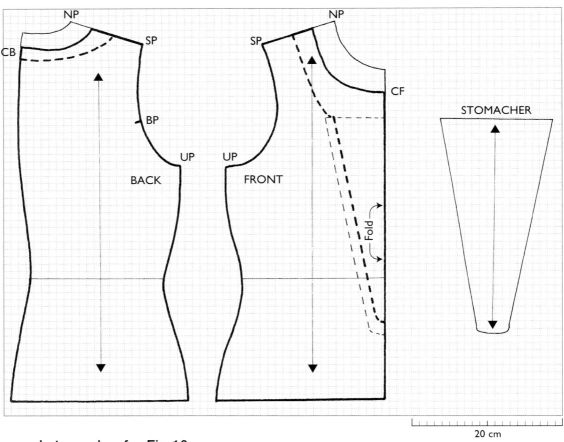

11. Bodice and stomacher for Fig 10

Younger girls – Use the child's Block (*Blocks,* Fig 24) for planning both styles.

Adolescent girls – Use the adult Block for planning both styles. For the kirtle use the outline shown, also *Kirtles,* Fig 3. For the V-fronted gown use the outline shown here, and Fig 12. Plan the Front with CF on a fold from the waist down. Transfer any hip shaping to the side seams.

Kirtle, Fig 10 left – Shown by the solid outline, with the Block neckline slightly lowered. Plan the skirts (*Kirtles,* Fig 4) using the girl's Waist to floor length, and a modest hem size, from 1.5 m up to 2.5 m, depending on size. Being cut on the fold, the front

skirt cannot be very wide. Use the sleeve Block to make a plain long sleeve.

V-fronted gown, Fig 10 right – Plan a lower neck, and a front opening reaching below the waist (heavy broken outline). Here the neck is lowered by 6 cm. Don't make the top of the V too wide: here it is 6.5 cm from CF. Use Fig 12 as a guide to planning the skirts.

Plan the stomacher (lighter broken line) with 2-3 cm underlap beyond the opening. Trace this off twice along CF to make the complete pattern.

Use the sleeve Block to plan a plain sleeve, or the sleeve in *Gowns,* Figs 31.

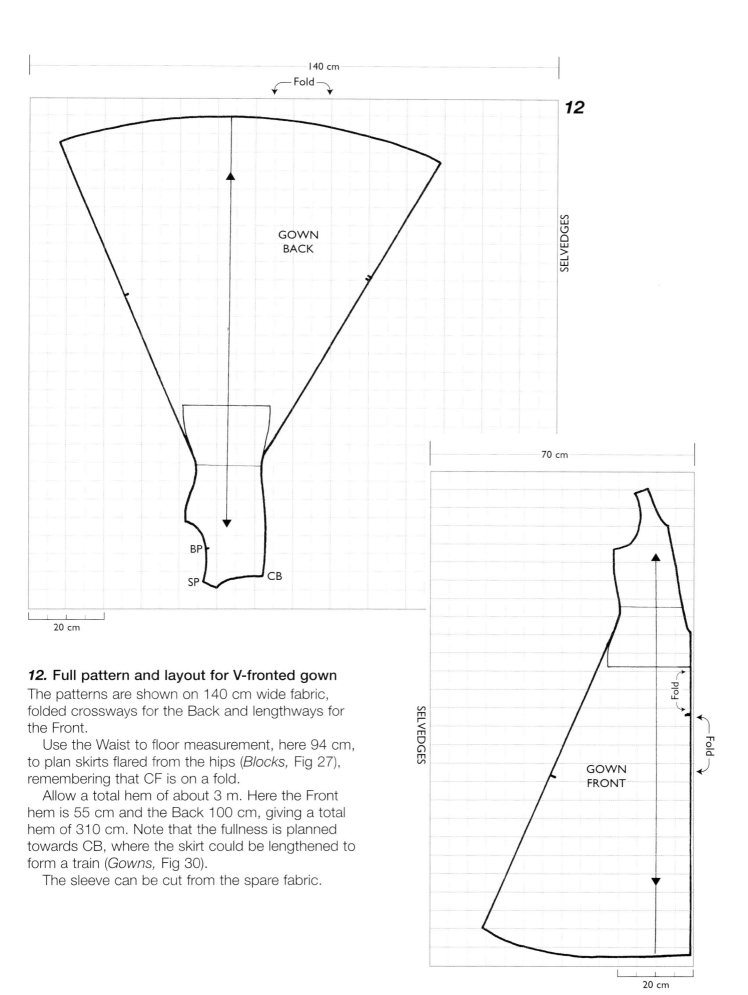

140 cm

Fold

12

GOWN
BACK

SELVEDGES

20 cm

BP

SP   CB

70 cm

Fold

SELVEDGES

Fold

GOWN
FRONT

20 cm

12. Full pattern and layout for V-fronted gown

The patterns are shown on 140 cm wide fabric, folded crossways for the Back and lengthways for the Front.

Use the Waist to floor measurement, here 94 cm, to plan skirts flared from the hips (*Blocks,* Fig 27), remembering that CF is on a fold.

Allow a total hem of about 3 m. Here the Front hem is 55 cm and the Back 100 cm, giving a total hem of 310 cm. Note that the fullness is planned towards CB, where the skirt could be lengthened to form a train (*Gowns,* Fig 30).

The sleeve can be cut from the spare fabric.

185

Head-wear

Plate 18. Building the Tower of Babel, 1423, French

The supervisory group in the left foreground are wearing the dress typically used to denote foreign or ancient peoples. Most of the workmen wear loose frocks or early cotes pouched over belts. The man mixing mortar, left, wears an open buttoned coat: the man working the windlass, right, has dagged sleeves revealing the sleeves of his doublet. Only one, the stonemason, centre front left, has removed his outer garment, and is working in his doublet. The doublet is made with separate wristbands and collar, front buttoned, and meets his hose at thigh level. The points securing his separate hose are clearly visible. The man immediately to the left of the tower has his hose rolled down below his knees, and the unfortunate individual falling from the scaffolding reveals short hose with front points and well-fitted braies. All wear hose, and short boots mostly flaring out at the top. Only three men appear to wear hoods, though there is an assortment of wrapped 'turban' forms of hood or chaperons. The man in the doublet wears a large bag-hat and there are various shapes of felt hat; only one is bare-headed.

Bedford Hours, British Library MS Add. 18850, f.7v

Head-wear

This chapter covers a variety of head-wear for men and women, listed generally by type, though not all examples fall readily into categories. A head-dress should of course match both the period and style of the rest of the outfit (*Preparation,* p. 13).

Men's hats and caps

This section covers most kinds of hat, including some sewn cloth types. Other cloth hats, including the chaperon, are included with hoods in the next section.

In the 13th century men often went bareheaded, or wore a close-fitting linen coif (Fig 5; *Braies,* Fig 1). Hats (and hoods) were functional rather than fashionable (Pl 5). For most of the 14th century the hood was predominant, though a felt hat (Fig 1a) might be worn over it to keep the rain off. About the second quarter of the 15th century the hat became an item of fashion (Figs 1-3). By the third quarter hats were replacing the hood, and were usually tall and often brimless (Pls 9, 11). By the 1470s soft cloth hats such as the square cap (Fig 6) were coming into use. By this time the hat might be attached to a long scarf-like tippet and hung over the shoulder like the chaperon.

Knitted caps (Fig 3) were in use from the 14th century and possibly earlier.

Women rarely wore hats, and when they did it was for protection against the weather.

Hats are often associated with particular activities, for example the pilgrim's wide-brimmed felt hat with its scallop shell badge, and the peaked hat seen on huntsmen (Fig 1c). The linen coif was retained mainly by lawyers after going out of general use.

By the 15th century you would be expected to remove your hat to a superior, or on entering a church. Smart men might put their hats under one knee when praying, to protect their hose.

Materials and patterns

Most of the hats described are specialist products, but some can be made or modified at home. Re-enactment or theatrical suppliers carry most shapes of felt hat. Many modern hats, whether felt, straw or fur, are suitable if modern trimmings are removed and replaced with appropriate cords or braids. Charity shops are good places to look for hats.

Patterns for coifs and cloth hats are shown in Figs 5 & 6. They can be made from oddments of material, but careful measurement and fitting is important.

Men's hats and caps

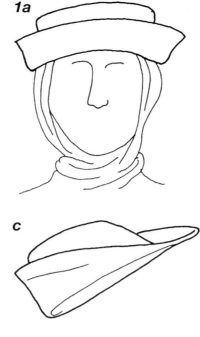

1a

1. Felt hats

***a.* Plain hat** worn over a hood, 13th and 14th centuries.

***b.* Fashionable tall form** from the mid 15th century. These were sometimes attached to a scarf and hung over the shoulder.

***c.* Up-and-down brimmed shape,** 14th and 15th centuries, often worn by huntsmen.

b

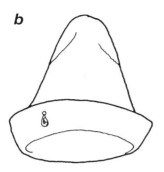

c

2. Fur hats

Long-haired fur hats worn by men during the 15th century were made in the shapes seen for felt.

***a.* Shaggy fur hat.**

***b.* Round hat** combining a felt crown and fur brim. Many of these fur styles would have to be made by a specialist, but some, like *b*, can be made up by combining materials, or by modifying a modern hat.

2a

b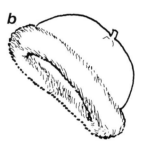

d

b

3a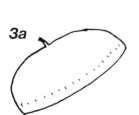

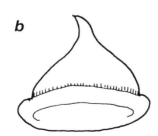

c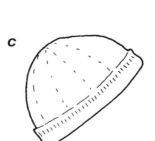

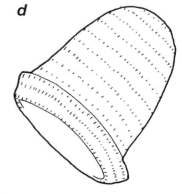

3. Knitted caps

These were in use by the mid 15th century, but are hard to identify in illustrations.

***a.* 13th century 'beret'.** This would be a suitable shape for knitting.

***b.* & *c.* Plain round caps**

***d.* Fashionable tall hat, c.1460**

Cap-knitting is done 'in the round' on four or more needles, starting from the centre and adjusting the stitches to shape the cap. A wide variety of shapes can be made. Remember to allow extra for shrinkage when you 'full' the cap. This involves soaking it in warm water and pounding it to felt the fibres together.

189

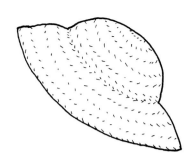

4

4. Straw hats

Straw hats were worn by workers as protection from the sun. They appear to have been made of plaited straw stitched into shape, a technique still used today. A plain broad-brimmed shape is suitable.

5. Coif and pattern

a. **The coif** was close-fitting, and made in linen with a seam over the crown and strings under the chin (*Hose,* Fig 1). In the 13th century it was widely worn, often under a hat or hood. It gradually fell out of use and by the 15th century is seen mainly on babies and toddlers, and on professional and older men.

b. **Pattern** shown on a rectangle of fabric, folded in half. The coif is made in two halves with a seam from front to back, and unlined.

Scale up the pattern and fit it on the wearer or start with a toile. For a toile start with a rectangle of light fabric, about 30 x 60 cm. Fold it in half crossways and place the fold over the head. Outline the curved seam line with pins, from forehead to nape, fitting it closely to the head. Mark the corner position just below the ears and trim the face and neck edges to shape.

From the toile make a paper pattern, as shown. Cut this twice from white or unbleached linen. Make up with run-and-fell seams and double hems. You can bind round the face and neck edges with narrow strips of the same linen, extending the binding strip to form the chin strings, or hem all round and sew the strings onto the corners (*Methods,* Figs 2, 6, 9).

5a

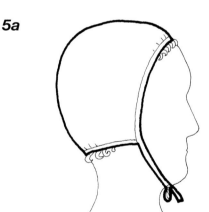

b

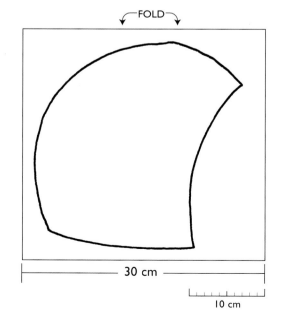

FOLD

— 30 cm —

10 cm

6a

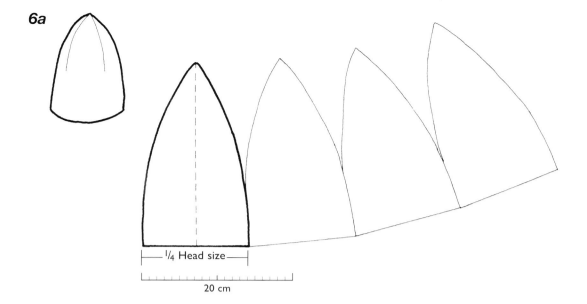

├── ¹/₄ Head size ──┤

├─────── 20 cm ───────┤

b

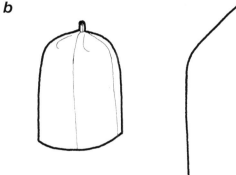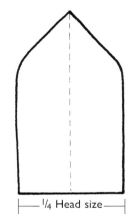

├── ¹/₄ Head size ──┤

6. Cloth hats, from c.1450
a. Conical 'acorn' hat, shown made in one piece
b. Squared off hat, shown made in separate panels
c. Shallow square cap, plain version and version with turned up brim. It is made from four separate panels. The crown of each panel must be a right angle, so the top is flat and the edges square.

For an unlined hat use heavy felt or firm cloth. For a lined hat use two layers of lighter weight cloth (*Methods,* p. 51; Pl 1).

Plan the pattern for all styles as a quarter of the finished hat, with the base line a quarter of the Head size. The base to point height is 20-25 cm for tall styles; less for the flatter square cap, *c*. Patterns for *a* and *b* can be planned as a repeat of the basic shape and cut in one piece, as shown in *a*.

For felt or firm cloth cut with minimal seam allowances, and oversew or stab-stitch the edges.

Any of these caps may have a little stalk at the crown, made of a 2-3 cm square of cloth rolled tightly on itself. Hem down the outer edge and stitch one end of the stalk firmly at the centre.

c

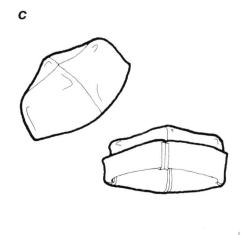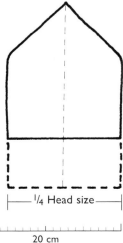

├── ¹/₄ Head size ──┤

├─────── 20 cm ───────┤

Men's hoods

This section covers the hood, and its derivatives – the bag-hat and the chaperon.

By 1200 the basic hood was already seen on shepherds and other outdoor workers. It was a pull-on, caped garment with a slightly extended peak at the back of the head (Figs 1a, c). By 1300 many men wore one (Pl 5) and for most of the 14th century a hood was a common part of a man's outfit. It was often worn as a cape, with the head section thrown back and pulled up as needed (Fig 1b). The cape of a fashionable hood might have a dagged edge, with the peak extended into a long tail, the liripipe (*Cotehardies,* Figs 1, 2). Tight-fitting hoods had a short buttoned opening under the chin.

Around 1400 new ways of wearing the hood were found (Fig 1d), and it began to be worn as a hat (Fig 4). Other new styles emerged, including the bag-hat (Fig 5), see *Gowns,* Fig 2; Pl 18. A prominent example of the transformation was the chaperon (Fig 6; Pls 12, 19), which appeared about the 1420s. This is also seen carried, slung over the shoulder by the liripipe, sometimes by a man already wearing a hat.

By the mid 15th century the hood is seen only occasionally, on shepherds or travellers. About this time the chaperon too went out of fashion and hats became usual, with a few bag-hats persisting towards the end of the century.

How you wear a hood is as important as its shape, so it is useful to practise, especially with the wrapped types.

Materials

Like other outer clothing, hoods were most often made of woollen cloth. Sheepskin (with the fur outside to shed the rain) would have been worn for outdoor work. Lining is optional but will add warmth and can provide contrast when the face edge is rolled back round the head. Smarter hoods were lined with fine fur. Some hoods have small cloth buttons (*Methods,* Fig 19-21), but many hoods have no fastenings.

Men's hoods

1a
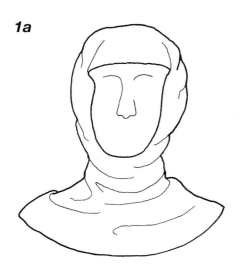

b
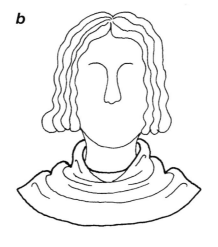

c
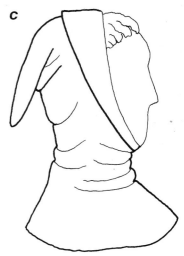

d
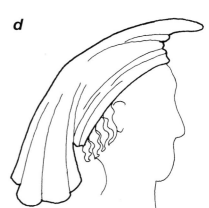

1. Basic hood, 13th and 14th century
a. This simple shape was already in use by 1200 and became common by 1300.
b. The same style was worn on the shoulders through much of the 14th century and pulled up as needed.
c. The hood can be tensioned round the chin by pulling the face edge back over the head.
d. Hood worn like a hat, 14th century.

2. Pattern for Fig 1

This pattern is for a loose hood which will pull on without a front opening and can be worn as shown in Fig 1.

Draw a square with sides equal to half the Slip on measurement, or use 30 cm square. Plan the cape (gorget), short liripipe and face opening as shown. Here the cape is 30 cm deep at the shoulder, the liripipe about 20 cm long, and the extended face edge from 3-6 cm wide. Alternatively, the pattern can be scaled up and adjusted to the wearer.

Cut the hood in one piece with a fold along the top, or in two pieces.

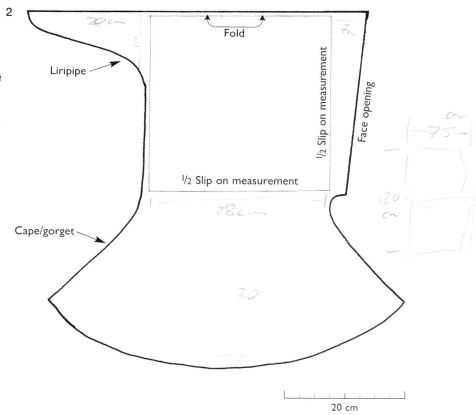

3. Hood with front opening – pattern

This open hood is buttoned under the chin, and side gores are used to widen the small cape.

Plan the pattern from a square as for Fig 2, or scale up the drawing and adjust it to the wearer. Insert the quarter circle gore at A. Cut the liripipe as a separate strip, make it into a tube and stitch it to the point of the hood.

For buttons and buttonholes see *Methods, Figs 19-21.*

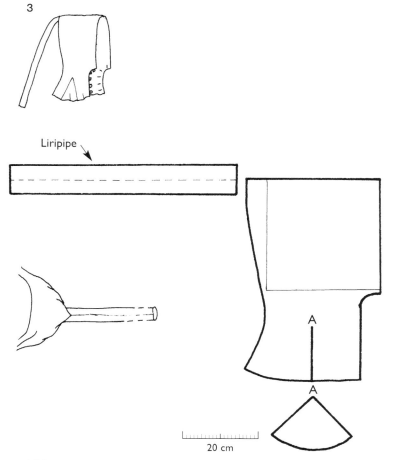

193

4a

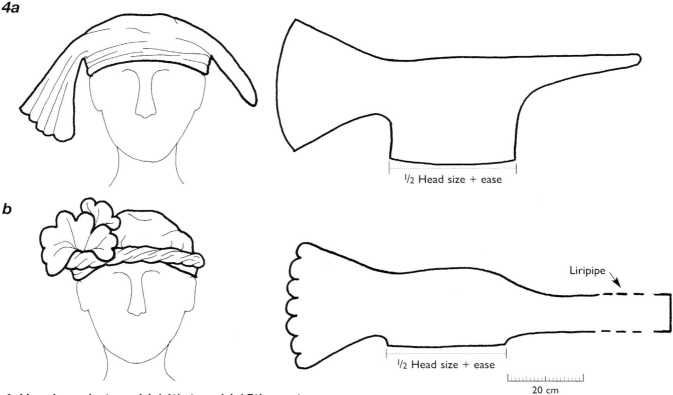

1/2 Head size + ease

Liripipe

1/2 Head size + ease

20 cm

4. Hoods as hats, mid 14th to mid 15th century

From about 1350 many hoods were made to be worn as hats, which allowed the shape to evolve in different ways.

The examples also offer a basis for experiment. You can make the face edge deeper, for rolling up, or enlarge the head section and extend the liripipe for a 'turban' effect.

a. **An early style.** The original hood shape has been turned and flattened to reduce the bulk on the crown of the head. Extra depth on what was the face opening is rolled up on the forehead.

b. **A later style.** Instead of rolling up the face edge, the liripipe is extended up to a metre or more, and wrapped round the head. Here the dagged cape is pulled up and held in place by the liripipe, but some wearers leave it hanging down.

They are made as two halves sewn together. Scale up the patterns to match your measurements and try them in spare fabric, or experiment with your own design.

Any lining need not extend into the liripipe. For dagging see *Methods,* Fig 24; Pl 4.

5

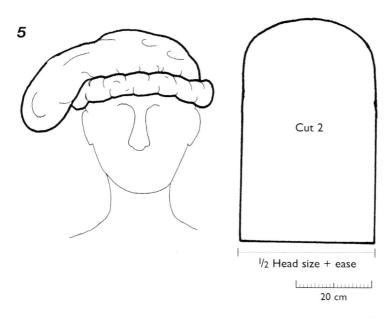

Cut 2

1/2 Head size + ease

20 cm

5. Bag-hat, late 14th to later 15th century

Although possibly derived from the hood, this is really a one- or two-piece cloth hat, usually worn with the edge rolled up to form a brim (Pl 18).

This tall bag is cut in two pieces, with depth for the rolled up brim. Add about 5 cm ease to half Head size to allow for the bulk of the roll: the measurement on the pattern represents the *outside* of the roll.

Scale up the patterns to match your measurements and try them in spare fabric, or experiment with your own design.

194

Plate 19. Chaperon, mid 15th century

The classic chaperon, seen here in black broadcloth, is made up of three parts (Fig 7) – the liripipe and shoulder cape (gorget), which are sewn to a padded roll. The roll sometimes appears quite solid and may have been felted. The chaperon is often seen slung over the shoulder where it would stay in place with a long enough liripipe.

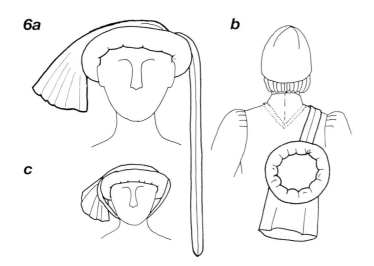

6. Chaperon, mid 15th century, Pls 12, 19

a. The final development of the hood into a hat. The classic chaperon is made up from three parts (Fig 7). The liripipe and gorget (the earlier shoulder cape) are made separately and sewn to a padded roll (roundlet), originally the rolled-back face opening. The roll sometimes appears quite solid and may have been felted.

b. Back view. The chaperon is often seen slung over the shoulder. It would stay in place by itself if the liripipe was long enough.

c. The liripipe used to secure the chaperon.

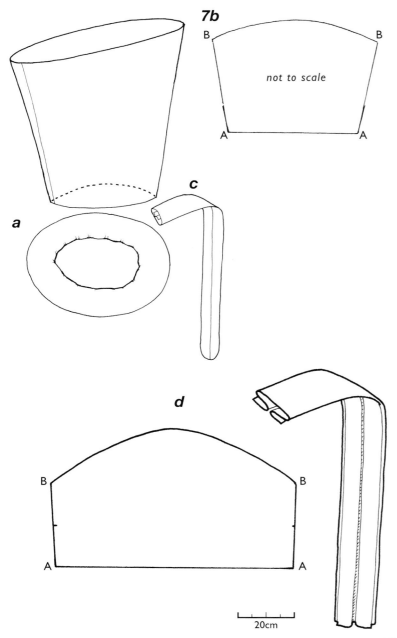

not to scale

20cm

7. Cutting and making up Fig 6

a. Padded roll Cut a strip of cloth 15-25 cm longer than the head size. This length is the outside measurement of the roll: the inside will fit the wearer's head. The width should be at least 20 cm; or up to 40 cm for an outsize version. Sew the strip lengthways into a tube and stuff it with polyester wadding, cotton wool or a roll of soft felt or cloth. Turn in the ends of the tube and oversew the ends firmly together to complete the ring.

b. Gorget Pattern outline and made up form. Plan and cut a flared piece of cloth, following the shape of the diagram. The narrower edge, AA, must match the inner dimension of the roll. The outer (here top) edge, is usually cut on a curve, BB, as shown, to hang level in wear.

The gorget may be lined or dagged (Pl 4). Join the sides, AB, to form a tube, matching the balance marks. Stitch the narrower edge of the tube round the inside of the padded roll.

c. Liripipe Make this as a tube, from a strip 10-25 cm wide and at least a metre long. It may be made long enough to trail on the ground. Stitch the end firmly to the inside of the padded roll.

d. Gorget pattern & liripipe for black chaperon, Pls 12, 19. The gorget is 84 cm at the base and a maximum of 50 cm high. For dagging, which can be done before or after making up, see *Methods*, Fig 24.

The liripipe is a single strip of fabric, 120 cm long and 25 cm wide. Firmly steam-press it lengthways into a box-pleat before attaching it inside the padded roll.

196

Women's linen head-dresses

This section includes the kerchief, wimple, fillet and tailed cap.

Kerchiefs, Pls 6, 10

Throughout the period most women wore nothing grander on their heads than rectangles of linen, which were covered with a woollen veil or hood in colder weather (*Surcotes*, Fig 1). The Church required women to keep the hair covered, but kerchiefs also changed with fashion, and their quality and complexity reflected the status of the wearer. Being well turned out showed a woman could afford the necessary quantity of kerchiefs and the services of a laundress.

The simplest versions were in one piece, wrapped and tucked, or tied, to keep them in place (Figs 1, 2). In more elaborate versions one or more pieces might be pinned to a fillet tied round the head (Fig 3).

Towards the end of the 15th century a made-up cap could sometimes be seen, its two tails wrapped round the head (Fig 6; *Kirtles*, Fig 1).

Materials and making up

The weight and fineness of the linen used for head-wear reflected the status of the wearer and how it would drape and wrap. A peasant woman would probably have used unbleached linen for a normal kerchief, but have bleached for best. Fine quality linen is required for satisfactory pleating of a wimple.

As the head covering is probably the most conspicuous part of your outfit you should use linen finer than that of your smock or apron. Approximate dimensions are given in the captions. Experiment with spare material to find the right size for the style you want. Most kerchiefs would have used lengths from narrow looms with the selvedges for two edges, but today they will be cut from wider pieces and the raw edges finished with narrow hems.

Women's linen head-dresses

1a

b
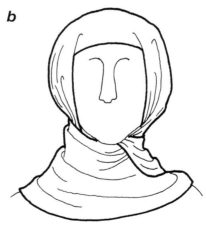

1. Wrapped kerchief, 1200 onwards

The basic way of wearing a single kerchief, as seen on working women throughout most of the period. It is rectangular, at least 45 cm by 100 cm, but can be larger provided its length is at least twice the width. The drawing is based on a kerchief 60 cm by 120 cm.

a. **Stage 1.** Drape one end over the head, tucking in the folds which form above the forehead.
b. **Stage 2.** Bring the long end under the chin, pass it round the back of the neck and tuck in the end at the front. Take care to secure both ends and it will stay in place without pins.

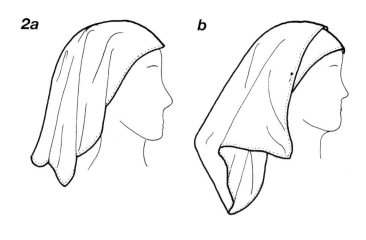

2. Knotted kerchief, 14th century on (Pls 6, 10)

As more women left the throat bare this style became commoner. It can be combined with a separate wimple (Fig 4b). The kerchief must be about 70 cm wide to tie round the head, and may be square or rectangular.

a. **This kerchief is 70 cm square.** Knot two adjacent corners at the back of the head and allow the rest to fall back over the knot.

b. **This kerchief is a rectangle,** 70 cm by 120 cm. Knot the corners of a short end at the back of the head. Allow the rest to fall back over the knot then bring the end back up over the head, ensuring the back of the neck is still covered, and pin at the sides.

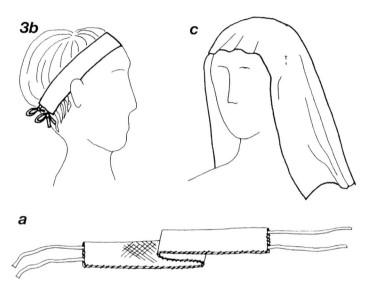

3. Fillet

A fillet is probably present in many head-dresses, even if it can't be seen. It can be an ornamental band, but here it is a functional one. It provides a foundation for outer layers. If you wear a fringe, use a fillet to hold it back under other head-wear. At its simplest the fillet can be a strip of linen tied round the head, but a made-up one is stronger.

a. **The fillet.** Cut a strip on the bias (for a better grip) about 10 cm wide and fold it lengthways. The band should not quite meet round the head. Turn in the edges and oversew all round, stitching two tape ties at each end.

b. **Fillet in place.**

c. **This draped kerchief** would be pinned to a fillet to keep it in place.

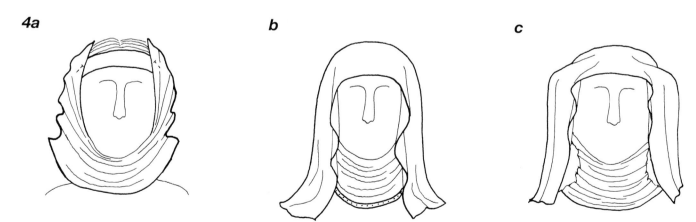

4. Kerchief with basic wimple, 1200 onwards

a. **Wimple.** Use a rectangle of linen at least 36 cm by 60 cm. Draw one long edge under the chin and up over the ears: it can be pinned to a fillet as shown, or to itself on the crown of the head. Draw the other ends round the neck and pin them at the back. Tuck the lower edge into the neck of the dress.

b. **The wimple in place** with a kerchief worn over it, also pinned to the fillet (not visible).

c. **Later style.** From about 1300 to 1360 the wimple can be seen drawn out and pinned to the fashionable side buns, with the kerchief draped over them.

198

Wimples

The wimple was a covering for the throat worn by most women in the 13th century. It could be part of the kerchief (Fig 1b), or the wimple might be a separate piece and more stylish in its effect (Figs 4, 5). During the 14th century it gradually went out of general use, being seen mainly on elderly women, widows and nuns.

The first separate wimple was simply a rectangle of linen draped under the chin and pinned round the head and neck (Fig 4). From about 1300 it was sometimes pleated or 'pinched', accordion fashion. Later in the century it might be hollowed out under the chin for a closer fit (Fig 5).

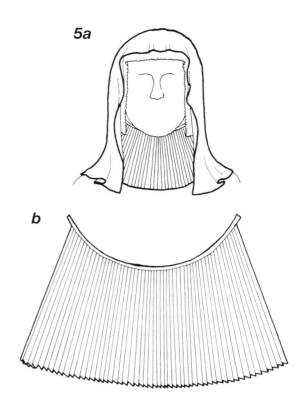

5a

b

5. Kerchief with shaped and pinched wimple, 15th century

a. Assembled head-dress. A small, fine kerchief is pinned to a fillet. A pinched wimple is added, curved to the neck and set into a band. A plain black cloth veil is worn on top.

b. The wimple. Cut a rectangle of fine linen 80-100 cm long and 30 cm deep, and a band of the same linen about 35 cm long and 3-4 cm wide. Fold the band lengthways and turn in the raw edges. Hem the ends and lower edge of the rectangle.

Form small, regular pleats, up to 1 cm wide, following the straight grain, damping the linen if necessary. Tack through the top of the pleats in the shape of the neck curve, dipping to about 5 cm at the centre. Cut out above the tacking, and enclose the edge in the prepared band. The ends of the band are secured to the fillet in wear.

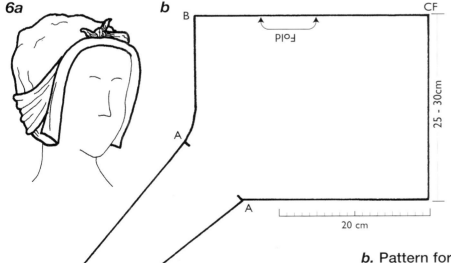

6a

b

6. Tailed cap, second half of 15th century

The kerchief was the commonest form of head-dress, but in the late 15th century made-up caps had begun to replace it.

a. This two tailed example, cut in one piece with a fold along the top, is related to the kerchief. The tails are crossed behind and knotted above the forehead.

b. Pattern for a. Allow 25-30 cm for the CF edge, giving a total face edge of 50-60 cm. Measure about the same length from the bottom of the face edge to the start of the tail, A, depending how much turn-back is wanted round the face. Make the tail about 75 cm long. Cut the pattern on the fold. Sew each tail into a tube from the tip to the balance marks, AA, then join the back of the cap up to the fold, AB. Hem the face and neck edges.

Women's cloth head-dresses and hoods

This section includes the plain veil and hoods worn over the kerchief (Figs 1, 2), round hoods – the less formal wear of fashionable women (Fig 3), and some late 15th century styles (Fig 4).

Throughout the period many women wore a thick veil of dark cloth over the kerchief out of doors. The veil was roughly semi-circular with the straight edge framing the face (Fig 1; *Surcotes*, Fig 1). It is still worn today by some nuns.

In the 14th and 15th centuries working women wore hoods as protection against the weather. They were open at the front (Fig 2; *Kirtles*, Fig 1). Women did not wear closed hoods or chaperons, and their hoods were not normally decorated with dagging.

A looser, fuller form, here called a 'round' hood, could be seen about the mid 15th century (Fig 3), worn by women of higher status. Towards the end of the century more elaborate versions appeared (Fig 4; *Gowns*, Fig 23). These replaced the spectacular head-dresses of the mid 15th century (see *Fashionable head-dresses*), and culminated in the early Tudor gable hood.

All these hoods were pinned on over a linen head-dress comprising a fillet, kerchief and perhaps a wimple. The hair, always long, was worn in a bun at the crown of the head, which supported the hood shape.

Materials

All these styles of veil and hood would be made of woollen cloth, thick enough for warmth but not too heavy. Some of the later fashionable forms (Fig 4) might be of velvet and could include fur.

The open hood might be made in brighter colours, but the cloth veil was typically black, dark grey or blue. The round hood and its later forms were usually black.

The front edge of some styles can be stiffened with a strip of canvas interlining, and the outer material doubled over it. All styles can be unlined or lined, possibly in white or a contrasting colour of silk (*Methods*, p. 50, 51; Pl 1).

Women's cloth head-dresses and hoods

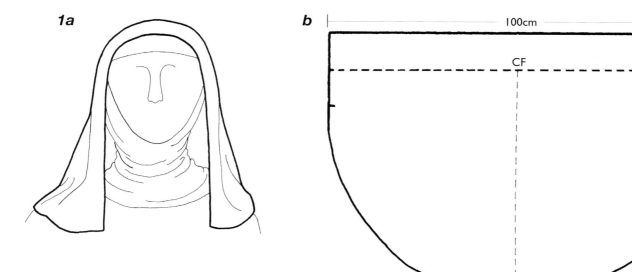

1. Cloth veil, 1200 onwards

a. Plain style. Seen on widows and older women, it is made in dark cloth. The inner linen kerchief and separate wimple are visible beneath; the veil is secured to these to keep it in place.

b. Pattern. The veil could be a simple rectangle, but most have a curved outer edge as shown. Plan the straight face edge 80-100 cm across, and the back as a deep half-circle to give plenty of length (fine broken line). Here it is 60 cm deep. The face edge is extended by 10 cm and folded under, to the balance marks, to form a firmer band.

2. Open hoods, mid 14th century onwards

A practical garment, worn by women of lower status over a linen head-dress, and seen in different forms.

a. **Early form,** like the 14th-century men's hood, but open down the front. The face edge is 40 cm from top to bottom, giving a very small cape. Scale up the pattern and cut in two halves. A firm cloth will hold up the tip.

2a

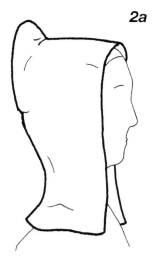
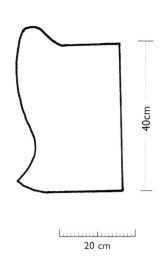

40cm

20 cm

b. **Later style,** common in northern Europe in the mid 15th century, with a turned-back brim, extended liripipe and close-fitting back neck. It was usually worn open but often had a row of buttons and buttonholes under the chin. Scale up the pattern and cut in one piece on the fold.

For more details of planning hood patterns see *Men's hoods,* Figs 2, 3.

2b

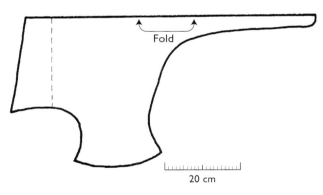

Fold

20 cm

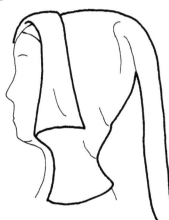

201

3a

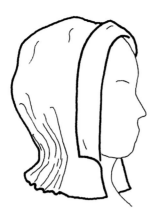

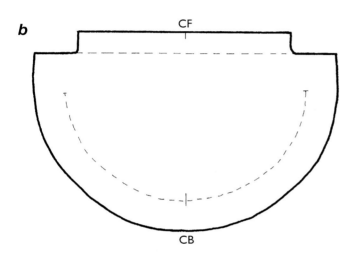

b

CF

CB

c

d

3. Round hoods, mid 15th century onwards

These forms, derived from the open hood and cloth veil, would be worn over a fillet (sometimes with a loop, see *Fashionable head-dresses,* Fig 12) and small kerchief, by townswomen, senior servants and ladies in their homes. They were usually black. It is unclear whether they were lined, but you could line them with silk or linen (*Methods,* p. 51; Pl 1). Firm cloth can be left with raw edges, but finer types should be hemmed if unlined.

a. **Hood.** Half-circle shape with the front edge extended to form a brim. It is pleated into the neck at the back and would be gathered and stitched to a stay band on the inside, as in *c.*

b. **Pattern for a.** Broken lines show the fold line for the brim and the position for gathering and stitching to the stay band round the neck.

c. **Inside detail,** showing the stay band, a strip of cloth to secure the pleats. First pin it in place, then adjust the length to fit comfortably round the neck before stitching.

d. **Another style,** related to Fig 2b. The wide liripipe is folded forward on the crown up to the turned back front edge. At the nape the lower edge is pleated onto a short stay band.

e. **Pattern for d.** Scale up the pattern and cut it in one piece on a fold. To make up, stitch the CB seam and underside of the liripipe, then flatten the liripipe and stitch across the end. The loop on the forehead is attached to the fillet beneath, see *Fashionable head-dresses,* Fig 12.

e

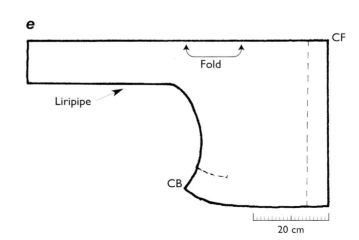

CF

Fold

Liripipe

CB

20 cm

4. Black head-dresses, late 15th century

a. Frontlet, cap and veil combination worn by English ladies in the late 15th century (*Gowns, Fig 23*).

b. The pattern pieces: crown of cap, side of cap, veil and frontlet.

Scale up the pattern pieces and adjust to the wearer's measurements. Check the length of the cap side against the wearer's head size, or make up a toile to check the fit. The cap and frontlet must be interlined with canvas; the cap and veil can be lined with silk or linen (*Methods, Fig 13*).

Cap – Interline both pieces. Join the side piece ends (BC) to form a loop, and ease in the crown. Make up the lining, if required, but don't insert it yet.

Veil – Hem the long curved edge, or line the veil with silk. Stitch it to the back of the cap from G to E, via C (!), matching C on cap and veil.

Frontlet – Cut this double, with the long edge on a fold. Interline one half with firm canvas. With right sides together stitch across the ends of the folded strip. Turn out and stitch the two long edges to enclose the straight edges of the veil and the front of the cap (DEFGH). Put in the cap lining, or use a length of tape or binding to enclose the raw edges round the back of the cap (ECG).

continued overleaf

4a

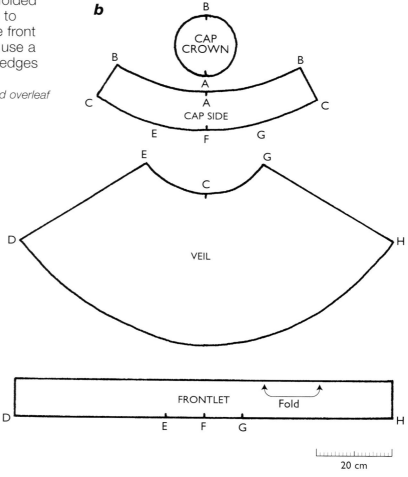

b

CAP CROWN

CAP SIDE

VEIL

FRONTLET

Fold

20 cm

203

4c

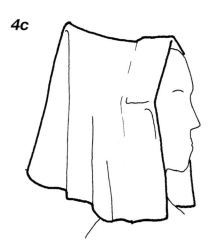

continued from p. 203

c. **'Gable' head-dress,** late 15th century.
This is cut like the half-circle cloth veil (Fig 1), but wired and stiffened to form a rigid structure. It is pinned in place over a fillet and a small kerchief or linen cap, and could be lined.

d. **Pattern.** Scale up and cut the pattern, plus any lining. Bend a length of 2 mm copper wire to the T-shape shown by the heavy line, and stitch it inside the head-dress. Fold the straight front edge of the head-dress under, along the broken line. Stitch it, enclosing two panels (shaded) of heavy buckram or cardboard, 6 cm by 13 cm. Hem the curved back edge, if the head-dress is unlined. Bend the wire to form the 'gable' shape at the front and the ridge over the crown. The cloth will fall in pleats at the back.

4d

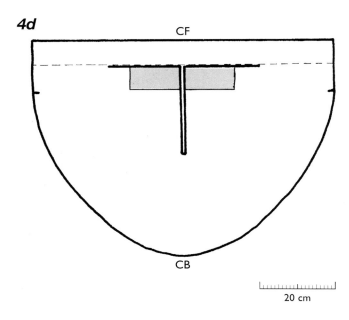

CF

CB

20 cm

Women's fashionable head-dresses

This section includes several elements of head-wear which were combined or developed over the period, sometimes producing spectacular results.

Hair played a significant part, both decoratively and as a support. Women plaited their hair and used the plaits for display (Fig 2). From the late 13th century until the mid 14th, plaits were worn coiled at the sides to widen the outline of the face. Hair nets (Fig 3) became fashionable in the mid 13th century, either worn alone or under the linen barbette and fillet (Fig 4), which is the characteristic fashion head-dress of the century, with the fillet in a decorative role (Pl 5).

The frilled and stacked veil (Fig 5) was a fashionable development of a simple veil. Veils were also worn over structured head-dresses such as templers, horns and hennins (Pl 11).

Templers (Fig 9), which evolved from the side pockets of the caul (Fig 6), were succeeded by separate horns (Fig 11), which for a large part of the 15th century was the main style for women of the English gentry. The shape changed gradually from a broad to a tall outline, while the associated veil became shorter. The very large head-dresses of the 15th century (Fig 13) do not seem to have been widespread in England. The tall hennin and its truncated 'flowerpot' form (Fig 15) were fashions of France and Burgundy, though the shorter 'butterfly' head-dress (Fig 16) was an English fashion.

Fine transparent veils were a feature of elaborate head-dresses. The veil would be draped over a large horned head-dress or henin, and sometimes extended 'banner' style over a wire structure, as in Fig 15.

In selecting a head-dress, bear in mind that in practice several different styles, including earlier ones, might be in use at the same time, depending on the rank and age of the wearer (Pl 11). In the 1470s, for example, an older woman might still be wearing horns (Fig 11) while her daughters wore the 'butterfly' head-dress (Fig 16).

Without the support of plaits, some head-dresses may be difficult to wear. Modern women with short hair will need to use false plaits (known in the 14th century) or be selective in their choice of head-dress. Modern colours, fringes and hairstyles will need to be hidden.

Materials

For this type of head-dress silks and gold braid are in order and offer the chance to be a little flamboyant.

Wide pair of 'horns' worn with a veil.
Brass to Alice Boleyn, Salle church, Norfolk, 1440

Fillets – Use bright-coloured ribbon or fine flat braid, or a fine tablet-woven band, for the visible fillets of the 14th and early 15th centuries. For hidden, supporting fillets, use dark-coloured velvet, which grips the hair and helps to support the larger stiffened shapes attached to them.

Cauls, templers, horns and hennins – Use fine buckram or very firm interlining for stiffened shapes, velvet ribbon for binding edges so they grip well, and discreet tapes for supporting the components. Use real silk taffeta, satin or patterned silk for covering.

A lining is part of the construction, though not seen in wear. Use a lightweight cotton, linen or silk.

Decorate with pearl beads and sparkly paillettes or sequins; these would have been punched from metal, but modern plastic versions will serve in most contexts.

Work lattice patterns in fine gold or silver braid, or narrow silk ribbon. Use fine brass pins, sold as 'wedding dress' or lace-making pins, to hold the parts together.

Veils – Use fine linen or cotton lawn for the earlier horned head-dresses. Silk organza, which is light and crisp, is needed for the later transparent veils. Veils were normally rectangular, and some were very long and narrow.

Making up

Fine and accurate sewing is required for head-dresses to look their best, as well as some creative flair for the shapes and arrangement of trimmings. Be realistic about your ability before attempting anything too ambitious. You will probably need help to fit and arrange the more elaborate ones.

Women's fashionable head-dresses

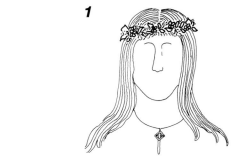

1

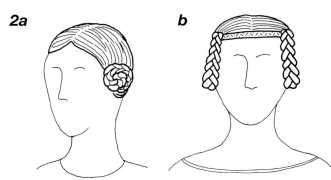

2a   **b**

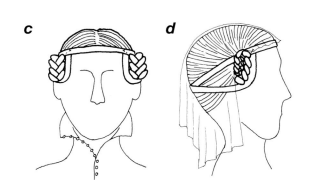

c   **d**

1. Chaplets

These can be seen on well-dressed young women (and men) of the 13th century, though less often in the 14th. Girls and young brides might wear their hair flowing, often with a chaplet of flowers or a fillet of fancy ribbon.

A chaplet can be a plait of fresh flowers and leaves, silk flowers, or a length of silk braid or embroidered band tied round the head. Flowers should be appropriate for the season.

2. Plaits, 14th and early 15th century

a. **Coiled plaits,** often worn with a wimple and kerchief. Arranged to widen the outline of the head-dress (see *Linen head-dresses,* Fig 4c).

Plait the hair from just above the ears, coiling and pinning it at the sides.

b. **Vertical plaits,** worn by richer women from about 1340. They were supported by a fillet, or possibly a circlet, and sometimes partly hidden by a linen head-dress.

Start the plaits above the temples, looping them in front of the ears and securing the ends behind the loops. Pin them through the ribbon. If the plaits are long they can be crossed at the back of the head as well.

c. & d. **Shorter vertical plaits,** from about 1400. They would be worn with a small veil attached to a fillet and arranged to fall behind the plaits (*Gowns,* Fig 3). The veil is shown here in faint outline, but should be of opaque linen.

Start the plaits above the temples, as for b, but pin them into tight buns. The fillet must be long enough to cross at the back and be brought forward round the plaits. Tuck the ends under and pin them at the front.

3a

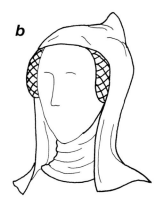

b

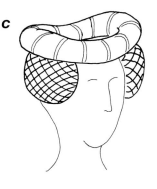

c

3. Hair nets, mid 13th to mid 15th century

Combinations like *a* & *b* can be seen in the first half of the 14th century.

a. Hair net with veil and narrow fillet over it.
b. Hair net with wimple and hood.
c. **Hair net with padded roll,** first half of 15th century. See also Fig 14.

Medieval hair nets were made of silk mesh edged with narrow tape or braid. The net was drawn under the hair and secured by pinning through folds in the braid.

Hair nets can be found in old-fashioned hairdressers, and saddlers or catering suppliers. Avoid heavy nets of crocheted wool or chenille.

4. Barbette and fillet, 13th and early 14th century, Pl 5

a. The barbette was a bandage-like strip or shaped piece of linen, narrow under the chin and wider at the crown where it was pinned together. The fillet was the 'coronet' of linen worn over it: this might be damped and finger-pinched to give the characteristic crimped look. They were often worn over a hair net, or over plaits rolled or looped, and pinned.

Make the barbette about 60-70 cm long and at least 4 cm wide after hemming. For a shaped barbette make the middle part narrower where it passes under the chin.

b. Fillet. Make this from two pieces. For the binding (the lower edge), cut a narrow band of linen 4-5 cm wide and long enough to fit snugly round the head, plus seam allowances. Sew the ends together to form a loop.

For the main (upper) part, cut a second band, this time on the bias, 10-12 cm wide and up to 5 cm longer than the first. Sew the ends together to form a loop, then fold it double. Run a gathering thread through the two raw edges and draw them up slightly, to fit the binding strip.

Turn in the raw edges on the binding strip and fold it round the gathered edge of the fillet. Hem down on both sides, or stitch through all layers, to secure. Turn the narrow binding to the inside, and use it to pin the fillet to the barbette.

4a

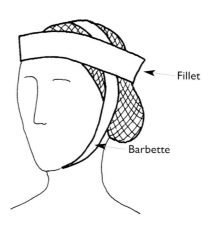

b

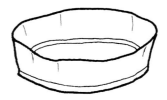

5. Frilled veil, second half of 14th century

Often called the 'nebula' head-dress, this used a weaving technique now no longer practised. A length of linen about 50 cm wide was woven with the selvedges longer than the main fabric to form frills. The veil so formed was folded into several layers, so a stack of frilled edges framed the face. It would be secured to a fillet.

a. Frills. When worn with a low-necked garment like the cotehardie they could reach to the shoulders.

b. Pattern for modern version. Gather a narrow strip of cotton tape, or a folded strip of fine lawn, into frills and stitch it to the edge of a plain piece of linen. The linen should be about 50 cm wide and 2 to 3 m long; the frilled material should be at least half as long again.

5a

b

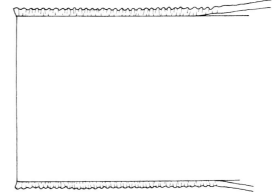

6

6. Caul, late 14th to early 15th century

A made-up cap, consisting of an inner linen layer covered in silk and decorated with a lattice of fine braid. The lattice work was often held down at intersections with a pearl or other small ornament. The edge was bordered and decorated, especially across the forehead. It can be worn alone, or with a padded roll; a veil may be worn draped at the back, except with very high collars.

7a

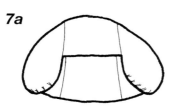

7. Pattern for Fig 6

a. The made up cap. The centre section runs from forehead to nape with two side pieces. The sides are enlarged at the front and pleated onto a tape to give firm pockets which fit over the plaits.

b. Pattern. Scale up the pattern and try out a toile for fit. Mark the edges as a guide for setting the pleats which will form the pockets at the front.

Cut out the pieces in a firm linen or calico for the inner layer, and in a good plain-coloured silk for the covering fabric.

Make up each layer separately. Start with the inner layer. Join the sides to the centre section along AB of the linen or calico. Turn in the raw edges on the wrong side and stitch them to a tape all round, forming pleats where marked. Repeat for the outer, silk covering. Match the two layers; tack if you wish. Turn in the edges of the silk covering and stitch them to the edges of the inner layer (Pl 1), forming pleats to fit.

Decorate with the lattice work in Fig 8.

b

Nape

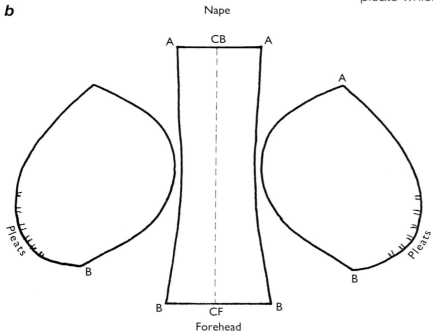

20 cm

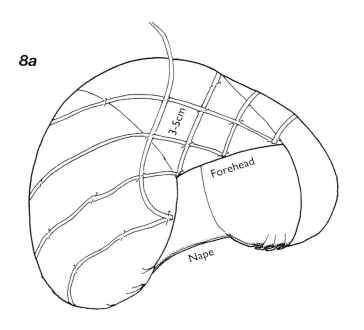

8a

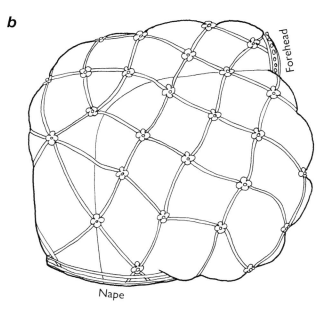

b

8. Lattice work for Fig 6

Fitting a regular pattern to a curved object requires patience. Use narrow ribbon or flat braid and pin all the strands in place before stitching them down.

a. **Stage 1.** Start at CF and curve the two ends of the first strand down each side. Add strands on each side alternately, 3-5 cm apart and equally spaced, and pin at each intersection.

b. **Stage 2.** Continue the pattern of squares to the crown and almost to the seams at the back, where several ends will meet. Finish some at the intersections, keeping the design as symmetrical as possible, but expect less regular shapes down the back. It can always be covered with a veil!

Stitch down all strands in turn, marking each intersection with a sequin and bead. Add a row or two of braid round the edge and extra decoration across the forehead, emphasising the angles at the sides of the face. If the wearer has plaits to tuck into the sides, the caul will probably stay on by itself; if not, pin it to a fillet.

9a

LEFT TEMPLER

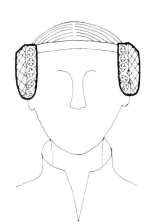

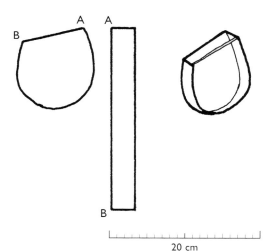

20 cm

9. Templers, early 15th century

Templers were decorated cup structures worn on the temples. They were intended to widen the head outline and to support a veil. The hair was worn inside and helped keep them in place.

a. **Earlier templers,** covering only part of the ear. They are pinned to a fillet and shown without the veil for clarity.

Patterns (for a and b) – Both show left templers, so reverse the pattern for the right ones. Scale up the pattern and try out the shapes in card before cutting any material. Cut and make up the final shape in light buckram, a fine lining and an outer layer of silk (*Methods,* Fig 13). Ensure you cut and make right and left halves. Decorate the templers and front band (*b* only) with a lattice pattern (Fig 8) in metallic thread, but finer and closer (about 2 cm apart) than for the caul.

Both *a* and *b* have a tape (shaded) linking the open top corners. The tape holds the shape and provides an edge to pin through to the fillet.

continued overleaf

209

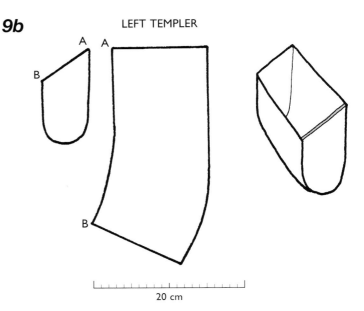

9b LEFT TEMPLER

20 cm

9b. Fashionably wide bucket style templers, worn with caul, veil and padded roll (Fig 14).

For pattern planning and making up see 9a on p. 209.

This larger version may be pinned to a caul with cut-outs to draw the plaits through (Fig 10).

10a

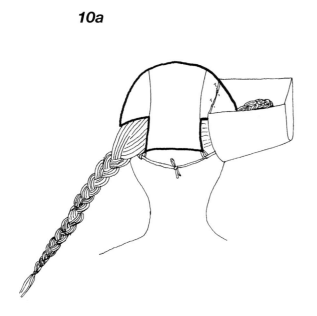

b Nape

CB

Forehead

20 cm

10. Cut-away caul, early 15th century

a. A close-fitting cap (back view). It provides support for large templers (Fig 9b) or separate horns (Fig 11), which are pinned to it. It allows the plaits to be drawn out at the sides. The area over the forehead can be decorated with a lattice pattern. It is held in place by tapes which are threaded through loops at the nape and tied.

b. Pattern. Scale up the pattern and try out a toile for fit. Cut out the pieces in linen, and in silk for the outer layer. Join the sides to the centre section along AB. Make up the silk covering to match, turn in the raw edges, and stitch or bind all round before adding the loops and ties (*Methods,* Figs 9, 13).

Pin the templers or horns to the cap and drape the veil to conceal the structure.

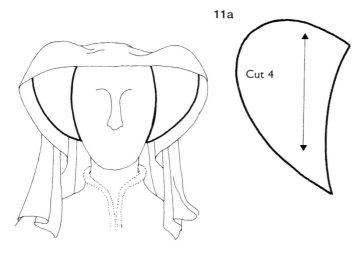

11a

11. **Separate horns, 15th century**
a. **Broader style,** c.1430
b. **Late style,** c.1470.

Cut 4

Scale up one of these patterns, or plan your own, and try it out in stiff paper first. The shape of the inner edge, which fits over the head, is as important as the curve of the outer edge. The horns should be stiff enough to retain their shape, even if the wearer doesn't have plaits.

Cut out the pattern (x4) in buckram. Cover them with the outer material and line them, remembering to make left and right shapes (*Methods,* Fig 13). Add any decoration. Sew each back and front together round the outer edge and bind the open edges with velvet ribbon (*Methods,* Fig 9).

To wear the horns, tie a velvet fillet (Fig 12) round the head and pin any plaits to it where they can support and fill out the horns. Open out the horns over the plaits, pinning the edges to the fillet. Drape a fine linen veil over the horns, draw it back between them and pin it discreetly in place.

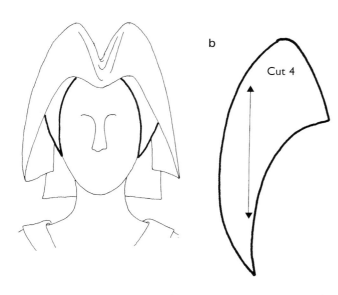

b

Cut 4

20 cm

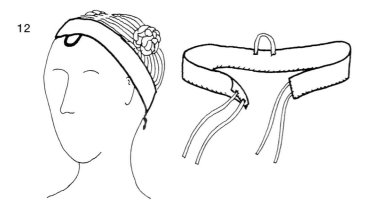

12

12. **Black loop and velvet fillet, mid 15th century on**

A black loop at the centre forehead appears on many head-dresses at this time. It was probably attached to a velvet fillet worn beneath the other parts of the head-dress. It could have been there to pull the fillet into place if it started to slip, or may have been an ornament to set off the fashionable high forehead.

This fillet is similar to Fig 3 in *Linen head-dresses,* but made of black velvet cut on the bias, with a loop of velvet or ribbon sewn to the centre.

211

13. Large horns, mid 15th century

Each horn is made from a shorter inside section and a longer outside section, joined along a seam running from forehead to nape.

Each section of the horn is made in three layers and finished separately. The main layer (buckram) is in the middle, with a lining and a fine outer material. This outer material could be patterned or embroidered, or decorated with lattice work (Fig 8).

Try out some shapes in stiff paper before finalising your pattern. The left and right horns are the same. Cut out the four sections in buckram. Cover each section in the outer material (silk), adding any embroidery or lattice work at this stage and line them (*Methods,* Fig 13).

Sew the finished inside and outside sections of each horn together round their outer edges, AB. Bind the open edges with velvet ribbon and oversew the horns together for a few centimetres over the crown. For frequent use the structure can be reinforced by stitching soft wire into the seams and round the open edges.

The head-dress is worn over a velvet fillet, perhaps with a loop (Fig 12). If the wearer has plaits they should be pinned above the ears to help wedge the structure in place. To complete the head-dress add either a padded roll, sewn in place and following the shape of the horns (Fig 14), or a fine silk veil draped over and between them (*Gowns,* Fig 22).

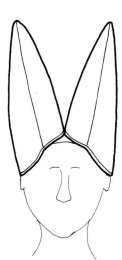
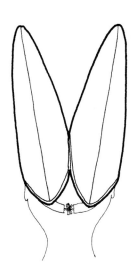

a. Earlier style. The horn is made up of sections of equal width and similar outline. The outside section curves down over the ears: the inside section curves up to rest over the crown. The higher the inside curve, the more upright the horn will sit on the head.

13a

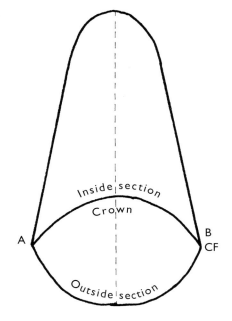

b. Later style. By the mid 15th century the horns were made to fit closer together by cutting the inside section narrower than the outside. Altering the width of the sections will change the outline of the head-dress.

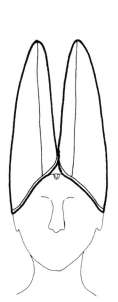

13b

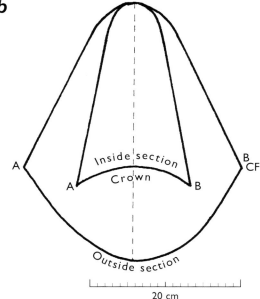

20 cm

14. Padded roll, early to later 15th century

The roll was a decorative addition to a head-dress. It was pinned on top of a net, caul or templers, or was part of a made-up horned head-dress. It was not worn alone.

a. **A heavily decorated roll,** from the early 15th century, which emphasises the width of the head-dress.

b. **A long roll** sewn to the outside edges of a large horned head-dress (Pl 11).

To make the roll cut a strip of silk, 15-30 cm wide by the required length (at least 60 cm, and up to 2 m). Make it longer than you think you need – it can easily be shortened! Decorate with embroidery, bands of braid, beads or sequins. If the decoration is heavy you will need to sew up the roll from the right side, otherwise stitch the long edges together on the wrong side, turn it right way out and stuff it with polyester wadding or cotton wool before joining the ends. It needs to be firm enough to hold its shape, but flexible enough to fit round curves.

For use on a horned head-dress, allow enough length for all the curves. Attach the roll to the horns along the seam lines by oversewing.

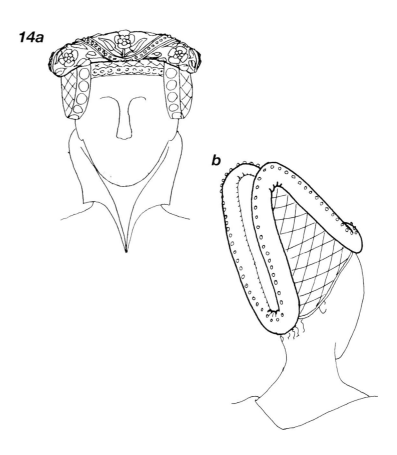

14a

b

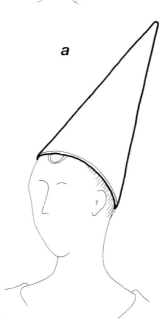

15

a

b

15. Hennins and wired veil, second half of 15th century

a. **The hennin** – a courtly fashion

b. **The 'flowerpot' style** (truncated henin) – more widely worn, sometimes with a veil draped over it.

Both *a* & *b* were worn over a velvet fillet, usually with a loop (Fig 12), with the hair in a single bun on the crown of the head. The hennin was usually worn with a transparent veil: this was rectangular, wider than the height of the hennin and 2 m or more in length. It was draped across the cone, extending beyond the top and falling down on either side (*Gowns,* Fig 22). Occasionally the veil was raised on wires (*d*).

The 'flowerpot' style, and sometimes the hennin, was combined with a frontlet, a doubled band of black velvet draped over the base of the cone to frame the face. The frontlet is 5-15 cm wide and 80-100 cm long.

continued overleaf

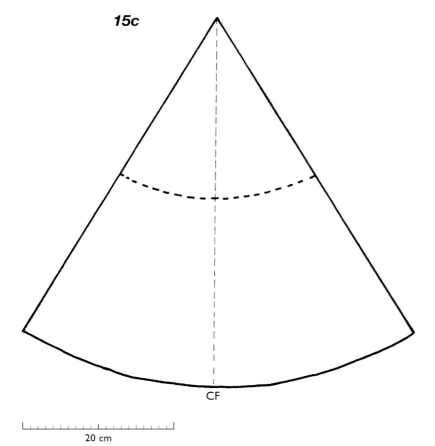

15c

CF

20 cm

15c. **The pattern** is made up to form a cone, with the join at the back. The base of the cone, which must fit snugly round the head, equals the Head size. The hennin shown is 50 cm high. The 'flowerpot' style is left open on top and the pattern here is cut off 20-25 cm below the tip along the heavier broken line.

Cut the pattern in buckram, cover it with your chosen silk, line it and make it up (*Methods,* Fig 13). Bind the lower edge with velvet ribbon for a better grip (*Methods,* Fig 9).

d. **Wired veil, 'banner' style.** The veil here is 60 cm by 2 m but could be much longer, on a hennin 50 cm high. Pin the veil to the cap at CF and draw it up over the two wires to fall on each side.

To make the frame use 2 mm electrical copper wire, florist's wire or jeweller's brass. Bend it to shape and stitch it to the cap at the peak.

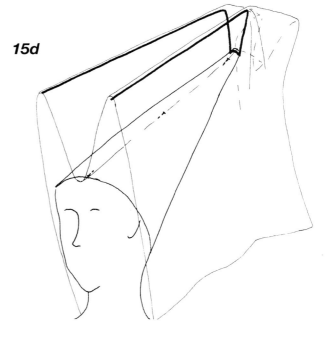

15d

214

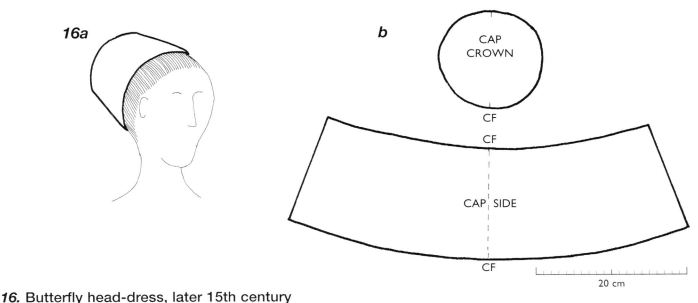

16a

b

CAP CROWN

CF
CF

CAP | SIDE

CF

20 cm

16. Butterfly head-dress, later 15th century

a. Cap for 'butterfly' head-dress, an English fashion. The name reflects the wired veil arrangement usually worn with it (*Gowns,* Fig 22). The hair must be drawn tightly back and pinned at the back of the head, to keep the cap as horizontal as possible.

b. This pattern is made up into a cone section: the lower edge fits round the back of the head and the upper edge is topped with a round crown. The length of the upper edge is equivalent to the circumference of the crown (*Blocks,* p. 39).

Scale up the pattern and try it out in stiff paper before cutting it in buckram. Cover it with silk and make up the cap (*Methods,* Fig 13). Bind the open edge with velvet ribbon for a better grip (*Methods,* Fig 9). Secure it with hair grips.

c. Wire frame. The wire extends forward about 10 cm at the forehead, as well as 15-20 cm behind the cap. To make a frame use 2 mm electrical copper wire, florist's wire or jeweller's brass. Bend it to shape and stitch it to the cap at several points with couching stitches. Put a small kink in the wire at the front stitching point to prevent the frame slipping.

d. Wired veil. The veil is 60 cm by 100 cm. Pin or stitch the middle of one long edge of the veil to the front tip of the wire and draw it back sharply, with most of the width hanging between the wires at the back. This head-dress is worn almost horizontally.

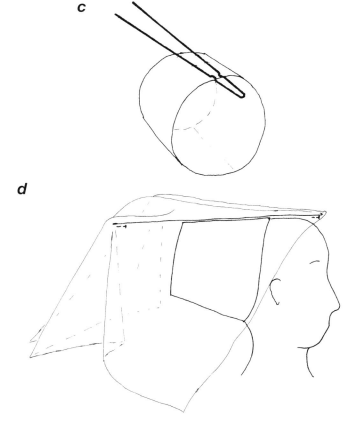

c

d

Accessories

One or two well-chosen accessories will complete your outfit and make it look right. Some can be made at home, but others are best bought from specialist suppliers.

Belts, purses and pouches, Figs 1, 2

A belt (or girdle – the terms are interchangeable) was part of almost every outfit. It was mainly functional, but could also be a feature of a style. It was not always visible – it was often worn round an inner layer of clothing, or the outer garment might be pouched over it. It is worth studying the historic illustrations of a particular period to see how the belt was worn and what it supported.

Working men normally wore a belt and used it for tucking in gloves or tools (*Men's outer working garments*, Fig 1) and for hitching up the skirts of the cote. During the 14th century the belt was often worn fashionably at hip level. Noblemen might wear a 'knightly girdle' of metal plaques mounted on leather or canvas. Men's gowns were usually belted at the natural waist (*Gowns*, Fig 3).

Men often wore a visible pouch or purse at the front or side (*Cotehardies*, Fig 2), and possibly a knife.

---

1. Men's belts, purses and pouches

a. Belts were generally 2 to 5 cm wide. They were made with buckles and strap ends, and often worn knotted as shown.

b. 14th century pouches. *Top* Closed, with a tie. *Bottom* With a buckle, and a more pronounced 'kidney' shape; shown open. The front is a separate piece of leather attached to the back and flap. The pouch had two loops to fit it on the belt, with a dagger sometimes stuck in the gap.

c. Simple moneybag to be carried inside the pouch, stitched on the wrong side from a folded piece of leather.

d. 15th century purses with elaborate metal frames, as worn by merchants and gentlemen. *Top* Round shape, used for most of the century. *Bottom* Rectangular shape on bar mount, from about 1460. For clarity, these two are shown without the drawstring closures or hinged lids seen on some examples.

The purse itself is a square velvet bag folded at the base, stitched up the sides and gathered onto the frame. Some examples have three tassels across the base.

1a
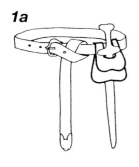

b
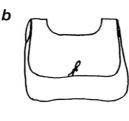

c
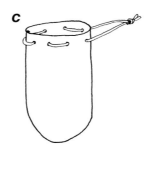

d
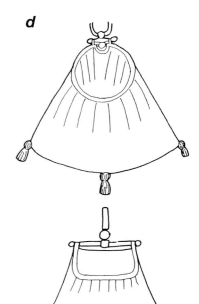

Women's belts are less often seen on contemporary illustrations. They were more likely to be worn beneath the outer garment, hiding a suspended purse (*Kirtles*, Fig 1), or were hidden by skirts raised for walking and pouched over them. With the arrival of the gown in the late 14th century the belt became a feature of women's fashion. Nothing was hung from this belt: the lady either had somebody to carry her purse, or wore another belt under her gown.

Materials and fittings

Most belt straps were of leather, or tablet-woven linen, worsted or silk. Belts for everyday wear were generally narrow, 2-5 cm wide at the most. A modern plain leather belt is suitable, but good reproductions are also available. Tablet-woven bands need to be finished with a tag end and a buckle plate to enclose the ends and prevent them fraying. Some ladies' wide belts of the 15th century may have used embroidered material on a stiff backing.

Replicas of belt buckles, tag ends and decorative mounts from archaeological digs are available from traders. Metal tag ends were used on leather as well as textile belts. Buckles were often made with a hinged buckle plate to enclose the strap end. As well as the end fittings, studs and metal plaques were often riveted along the length of the strap for decoration.

2. Women's belts and purses

Most women wore narrow belts similar to those worn by men; those shown here are examples of the more elaborate styles worn by wealthier women.

a. **Wide belt, second half of 15th century.** The strap could be tablet-woven silk, or embroidered material mounted on a stiff backing, and long enough to reach the ground. The buckle is often worn out of sight at the back, showing the decorated strap at the front, and is made with a hinged plate enclosing the end of the strap.

b. **Slim belt,** seen on some fitted gowns after 1475. The leather strap ends in fine chains, one with a hook and one with a pendant.

c. **Popular early Tudor belt.** The fittings are large and heavy, and the strap is threaded across the buckle; the belt is often decorated with a repeating design.

d. **Simple drawstring purse,** common throughout the period. It is lined for strength and has three tassels across the base. The purse hangs at about knee level from a belt; the drawstrings and hanging cord can be ordinary rayon cord or a round braid.

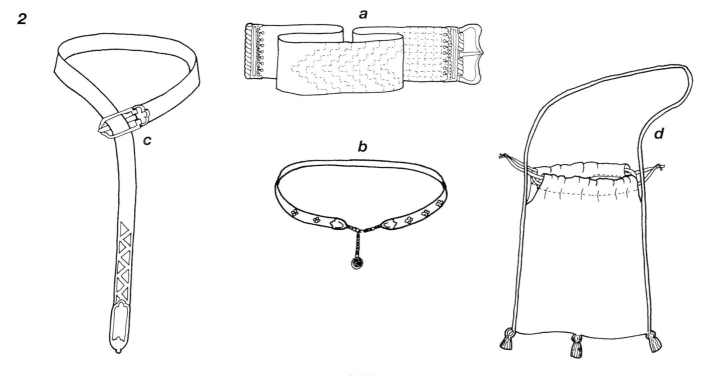

2

Gloves and mittens

Men and women of importance wore (or carried) gloves for outdoor occasions. Fine gloves were a sign of wealth and rank, while heavy-duty gloves or mittens were for outdoor workers.

Modern glove patterns are supplied by some leather merchants, but require a high standard of cutting and sewing. With ready made gloves look for a light natural colour rather than brown, or get them dyed to match your outfit.

Working mittens are not difficult to make (Fig 3). Use hide or sheepskin in a natural colour.

3. Mittens

Mittens were worn for warmth and protection throughout the period. They were made of hide, or of sheepskin with the fur inside. These materials are cut without seam allowances and joined by oversewing.

***a.* Measuring.** Draw an outline round the hand laid flat, then measure round the palm as shown to find the conventional glove size.

***b.* Basic mitten pattern.** Using the outline drawing of your hand, draw a large, simple pattern as shown, checking that it is larger than the palm measurement, above. Back and front outline are identical either side of the broken fold line; the thumb hole is off-centre. This figure shows the left-hand pattern: turn it over to cut the right hand.

The thumb part itself is symmetrical along its fold line. Its curved base (B-B) must fit the curve of the thumb hole exactly, excluding the triangular extension which runs into the thumb seam at A. Always set the thumb in first. First stitch the thumb seam from the tip to A, then set the thumb into its hole, working round A-B-B-A. Ease it in if it is slightly larger than the hole, and stitch the mitten closed from the top of the fold round to the wrist.

***c.* Split mitten pattern.** Adapt the basic pattern *(b)* as shown, following the shape of the hand. Cut a straight gusset, 1-2 cm wide, tapered at the ends to finish before the finger tips. Set in the thumb as in *b*. Stitch the gusset to the back of the mitten, from C to each finger tip. Stitch the mitten closed from the top of the fold round to the wrist, including the gusset.

3a

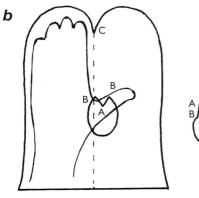

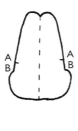

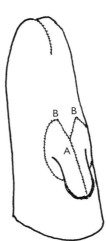

b

c

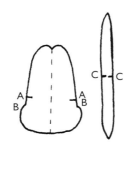

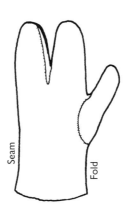

20 cm

Aprons

Aprons were worn to protect the outer clothing from dirt and damage, and their form depended on the task (Fig 4). A blacksmith wore a leather apron with a bib, while a mason or carpenter wore a short, wide cloth apron. A cook might tie a length of linen round his waist to wipe his hands on.

Women's aprons (Fig 5) were often pleated into a waistband.

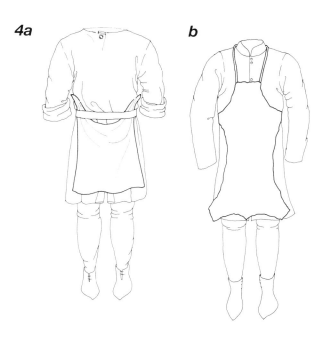

4. Men's aprons

These were strictly functional.

a. Cook. The apron would be a piece of linen, hemmed for washing and tucked into the belt. A larger piece could be used, wrapped round the body and tied at the back.

b. Smith's apron, made from a small hide with neck and waist strings sewn on. Similar one-piece bibbed aprons were made of fabric, and waist aprons set plain into a band were also worn.

5. Women's aprons

Women also wore protective aprons, but they tended to be more decorative. These are both rectangles of linen, about 75 cm wide and up to 100 cm long, hemmed round the edges. The waist bands are folded double with all raw edges turned in, and oversewn to enclose the top edge (*Methods,* Fig 9).

The decorated band, seen in the 14th century, might be worked through the pleats to keep them in place, or it might be a separate piece.

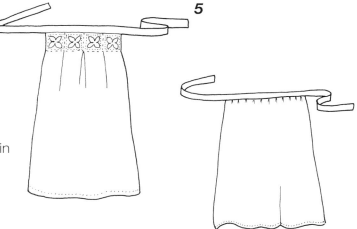

Jewellery

This ranged from items richly worked with gems and enamel, to brooches and finger rings in pewter or bronze. Replica brooches and pilgrim badges are available from traders. Earrings and body piercings should not be visible.

Men of status wore gold or silver neck chains, often incorporating heraldic or livery badges (*Gowns,* Fig 16); more modest versions were worn by persons of lesser rank. In the 15th century women's necks became an area of display – for necklaces of beads and goldsmith's work (*Gowns,* Fig 23a). Modern beads and second hand jewellery can be used to make replicas, but choose 'gems' which are rounded or pebble-like; faceted gems were a later development.

Rosaries were sometimes carried in the 15th century (*Gowns,* Fig 17). These were often a strand rather than a loop, with 20 to 50 small beads separated into tens by larger beads (decades): the beads could be wood, glass, or coral and silver, according to status.

Hand luggage

Hand luggage (Fig 6) forms part of an historical character. Every individual would need to carry his possessions. For the wealthy, boxes and coffers would be loaded onto a cart or packhorse. Others might sling their bundle or blanket-roll on their back, or carry a basket at the hip, or on the head (*Surcotes,* Fig 1). Baskets of all shapes and sizes were used and any modern basket made of natural willow or rush will look acceptable.

Pilgrims and friars might carry a scrip, like a small satchel, and shepherds a distinctive netting or canvas belt bag. Many people travelled very light, however, with just a knife on the belt.

6. Hand luggage

***a.* Coffers for valuables.**

***b.* Bundles.** Tie the pairs of opposite corners to enclose the contents completely. A small bundle would be carried on a stick; a larger one would be slung over the shoulder.

***c.* *Left* Pilgrim's or friar's canvas scrip** (wallet or satchel).

***Right* Shepherd's bag.**

***d.* Flat rush skep,** about 50 cm in diameter, also made in canvas. It might be filled with tools and carried with the two handles together.

***e.* Baskets.** The small basket can be used to show off your period possessions. The larger basket with its fresh linen covering can be useful for hiding your modern necessities.

Glossary

Since many garments probably had more than one name, and names have changed or altered in meaning over the centuries, historic terms in this glossary reflect the interpretations used in the book.

Acorn cap – Men's tall cloth or felt cap (*Men's hats and caps*, Fig 6)

Aglet – Metal tag attached to the ends of points and lacing cords (*Methods*, Fig 18).

Bag-hat – Men's simple cloth hat developed from the hood (*Men's hoods*, Fig 5).

Bag sleeve – Large gown sleeve with tight wrist, also 'poky' or 'bagpipe' sleeve (*Gowns*, Fig 11).

Barbette – Band of linen, straight or shaped, passed under the chin and secured over the crown. Worn by women with a hair net or fillet (*Fashionable head-dresses*, Fig 4).

Bias – Line at 45 degrees to the **warp** and **weft** of the material.

Block – Personal pattern fitting an individual. Used to develop working patterns for fitted garments for that individual.

Bodice, body – Part of a garment or pattern fitting the body from neck to waist.

Braies – Men's linen drawers (*Braies*, Figs 1, 2, 4).

Breech – Upper portion of joined hose, fitting round the lower body.

Breech clout – Piece of linen wrapped as underwear, forerunner of **braies**.

Breech girdle – Cord or strip of fabric or tape holding up the **braies**.

Broadcloth – High quality woollen fabric distinguished by its dense, even surface; see *Materials*.

Brocade – Woven fabric, usually silk, with a raised pattern in added threads.

Burlet – See **chaperon**.

Butterfly head-dress – Elaborate head-wear based on a cap with wired veil (*Fashionable head-dresses*, Fig 16).

Caul – Woman's silk cap covered with a network of braid (*Fashionable head-dresses*, Fig 6).

Chaperon – Men's hat which evolved from the hood (Pl 19; *Men's hoods*, Fig 6), also called **burlet**.

Clout – Cloth; baby's diaper or man's basic underwear.

Coat – Outer working garment for men, sometimes called **jerkin**, see *Men's outer working garments*.

Codpiece – Bag-shaped attachment covering and supporting the genitals on joined hose (*Hose*, Fig 11).

Coif – Close-fitting cap, usually of linen, worn by men, babies and infants (*Men's hats and caps*, Fig 5).

Dagging – Decorative edging of garments (*Methods*, Fig 24).

Damask – Weave producing a figured design on a fabric of single colour.

Ease – Allowance in a garment over the actual body size for movement or fitting, e.g. the extra length of a **sleeve head** over the armhole it is set into.

Felt – Fabric made by pressing matted wool or other fibres together. Commonly used for hats; sometimes for footwear and other garments.

Fillet – Band of linen or velvet worn round the head to support women's head-dress, or as decoration (*Linen head-dresses*, Fig 3; *Fashionable head-dresses*, Figs 4, 12).

Fitchet – Vertical slit in an outer garment giving access to purse or girdle.

Fitting line – Position of the stitching or finished edge on a pattern or garment piece: the cutting line lies outside it with the seam allowance in between.

'Flowerpot' style – Truncated hennin head-dress, a Burgundian fashion (*Fashionable head-dresses*, Fig 15b).

Frilled veil – See *Fashionable head-dresses*, Fig 5.

Frock – Here a loose outer working garment (*Men's outer working garments*, Figs 1&2).

Frontlet – Band of stiffened fabric, usually black velvet, part of a woman's head-dress (*Cloth head-dresses and hoods*, Fig 4a; *Fashionable head-dresses*, Fig 15b).

Fustian – Napped fabric of cotton or cotton and linen, used particularly for doublets.

Garter – Band of braid or fabric used by men and women to support separate hose, and as leg decoration.

Goffered veil – **Frilled veil** (*Fashionable head-dresses*, Fig 5).

Gore – Triangular piece of fabric inserted to widen or shape a garment (Cotes, Fig 4).

Gorget – See *Men's hoods*, Fig 6.
Grain – Direction of the warp threads on a woven fabric.
Gusset – Small piece of fabric, usually square or triangular, inserted to enlarge part of a garment, here a sleeve (*Cotes*, Fig 8).

Hennin – Conical head-dress fashionable at the French and Burgundian courts, (*Fashionable head-dresses*, Fig 15).
Horned head-dress – Head-dress based on a pair of stiffened shapes (*Fashionable head-dresses*, Figs 11, 13).
Houppelande – Fashionable gown for men and women, often high necked and fitted down to bust level, then flowing out below into rich folds; with open sleeves (*Gowns*, Fig 12).

Jerkin – See **coat**.

Kerchief – Plain piece of linen used in dress, here as a head covering (*Linen head-dresses*, Figs 1&2).

Liripipe – Long tail of a hood or **chaperon** (*Men's hoods*, Fig 6).

Mantle – Ceremonial form of cloak worn by men and women (*Cloaks*, Fig 2).
Mitten cuffs – Cuffs on tight, buttoned sleeves, extending to the knuckles, seen mainly on women's garments (Pl 2).
Modelling – The process of making a pattern by fitting fabric round the wearer's body.

Nebula head-dress – Frilled veil (*Fashionable head-dresses*, Fig 5).

Open sleeve – Normally a gown sleeve, flared out to the cuff and sometimes reaching to the ground.
Overkirtle – Here describes the outer garment seen on women at work, see *Outer working garments*.

Paltok – Fashionable doublet (*Doublets*, Fig 3).
Parti-coloured – Garment divided vertically in two colours, fashionable in the 14th century.
Piecing – Making up a pattern piece by joining smaller bits of fabric for economy.
Points – Ties used to fasten men's clothing, holding hose to doublet. Made of leather, tape, ribbon or cord finished with **aglets** (*Methods*, Fig 18).

Roundlet – See *Men's hoods*, Fig 6.

Selvedge – Edge of a woven fabric, finished so that it doesn't unravel.
Shift – See **smock**.

Shirt – Man's undergarment, usually linen (*Body linens*, Fig 2).
Sleeve head – Top edge of the sleeve, fitting over the shoulder and sewn to the armhole.
Smock – Woman's undergarment, usually linen (*Body linens*, Fig 3).
Stomacher – Triangular piece of fabric, usually on a backing, worn by men and women to fill in a wide neck or front opening. Could be in rich material, or embroidered.

Tablet weaving – Ancient technique for making ribbons, belts and trimmings.
Tail-clout – Linen square, often of diaper weave; nappy.
Templers – Stiffened head-dress components worn in pairs (*Fashionable head-dresses*, Fig 9).
Tippet – Extension of the sleeve hanging from the elbow, or streamer hanging from the upper arm of a shortened sleeve (*Cotehardies*, Figs 1&2).
Toile – Pattern in sturdy fabric used for **modelling** or trying out a pattern.
Tunic – Alternative name for the **cote** or **frock** or other loose garment.
Twill – Weave structure showing characteristic diagonal lines on its surface.

Vamp – Upper part of a shoe or hose foot.
Veil – Head covering of fine linen or other fabric usually draping the head and shoulders, or in dark-coloured cloth worn for warmth over a kerchief (*Cloth head-dresses and hoods*, Fig 1). Also part of a fashionable head-dress (*Fashionable head-dresses*, Fig 5).

Warp – The lengthways threads of a woven fabric.
Weft – The crossways threads of a woven fabric.
Wimple – Part of a woman's head-dress covering the neck up to the chin, sides of the face, and hair (*Linen head-dresses*, Figs 4&5).
Wheel piece – Small gore added to widen a skirt at the hem.
Worsted – Fabric of combed wool yarn with a smooth lustrous finish.

Suggested reading

Some of the older titles may go out of print, but libraries, specialist costume and secondhand booksellers often have copies.

Medieval costume

Buck, A and Cunnington, P, *Children's Costume in England*, A&C Black, 1965

Cunnington, CW & P, *Handbook of English Medieval Costume*, Faber, 1952

Cunnington, P and Lucas, C, *Occupational Costume in England*, A&C Black, 1967

Cunnington, CW & P, *The History of Underclothes, 1951*; Dover Publications, 1995

Houston, M, *Medieval Costume in England and France, 1939*; Dover Publications, 1996

Kelly, F and Schwabe, R, *A Short History of Costume and Armour, 1066-1800, 1931*; David & Charles, 1972

Newton, SM, *Fashion in the Age of the Black Prince*, Boydell and Brewer, 1999

Piponnier, F, and Mane, P, *Dress in the Middle Ages*, Yale University Press, 1997

Scott, M, *Visual History of Costume: Fourteenth and Fifteenth Centuries*, Batsford, 1986

Scott, M, *History of Dress series: Late Gothic Europe 1400-1500*, Mills & Boon, 1980

Techniques and stitching

Christie, A, *Samplers and Stitches*, Batsford, 1986

Clabburn, P, *The Needleworker's Dictionary*, Morrow, New York, 1976

Collingwood, P, *The Techniques of Tablet Weaving*, Faber, 1982

Rutt, R, *A History of Handknitting*, Batsford, 1987

Smith, A, *Needlework for Student Teachers*, Pitman, 1984

Staniland, K, *Medieval Craftsmen: Embroiderers*, British Museum Publications, 1991

Wild, J, *Textiles in Archaeology*, Shire Archaeology, 1988

Medieval garments and archaeology

Geijer, A *et al*, *Drottning Margaretas gyllene kjortel (The Golden Gown of Queen Margareta in Uppsala Cathedral)*, Almqvist & Wiksell, Stockholm, 1994

Medieval Finds from Excavations in London, Boydell & Brewer
    Vol 2, Grew, F *et al*, *Shoes and Pattens*, 2001
    Vol 3, Egan, G and Pritchard, F, *Dress Accessories*, 2002
    Vol 4, Crowfoot, E *et al*, *Textiles and Clothing c.1150-c.1450*, 2001

Rogers, W, *Textile Production at 16-22 Coppergate*, York Archaeological Trust, 1997

Suppliers and information

Some materials and accessories will need to be obtained from specialist suppliers. This list includes some of them, as well as other useful sources of information.

United Kingdom

Fabrics and haberdashery

MacCulloch and Wallis Ltd
25-26 Dering Street, London W1R 0BH
www.macculloch-wallis.co.uk
Shop with mail order catalogue and wide range of haberdashery, tools, fabrics, including large sheets or rolls of pattern drafting paper.

Whaleys (Bradford) Ltd
Harris Court, Great Horton, Bradford, West Yorkshire BD7 4EQ
www.whaleys-bradford.ltd.uk
Shop and mail order for fabrics, mainly in white for dyeing, including wools, linens and silks.

Books on costume

Caliver Books
818 London Road, Leigh-on-Sea, Essex SS9 3NH
01702-473986
www.caliverbooks.com

R D Franks Ltd
Market Place, Gt Titchfield Street, London W1W 8HY
020-7636 1244
www.rdfranks.co.uk

Paul Meekins
34 Townsend Road, Tiddington,
Stratford-upon-Avon, Warwicks CV37 7DE
01789-295086
http://members.tripod.co.uk/pmbooks/index.htm

Felicity J Warnes
82 Merryhills Drive, Enfield Middlesex EN2 7PD
020-8367 1661
www.fjwarnes.u-net.com

Publications
Call to Arms
1 Lyng Lane, North Lopham, Norfolk IP22 2HR
www.calltoarms.com
Comprehensive directory, updated annually, of re-enactment societies and traders.

The Garter
Frances Tucker, 228 Sydenham Road, Croydon, Surrey CR0 2EB
Directory of costume makers and suppliers of all kinds, updated periodically.

Organisations
The Costume Society
www.costumesociety.org.uk

The Medieval Dress & Textile Society(MEDATS)
www.medats.cwc.net

United States and Canada
Organizations
Costume Society of America
55 Edgewater Drive, PO Box 73, Earlville, MD 21919
800-CSA-9447
www.costumesocietyamerica.com

The Society for Creative Anachronism, Inc. (SCA)
PO Box 360789, Milpitas, CA 95063-0789
408-263-9305
www.sca.org

Websites
The Labyrinth, sponsored by Georgetown University. Resources for medieval study.
www.labyrinth.georgetown.edu

The Sheridan Libraries of the John Hopkins University. Medieval study.
http://milton.mse.jhu.edu/research/history/medieval.html

The Costume Gallery
www.costumegallery.com
Historic costume study and links

La Couturière Parisienne Costume and Fashion
http://marquise.de/index.html
Historic costume study and links

Suppliers
Burnley and Trowbridge Co.
108 Druid Drive, Williamsburg, VA 23195
757-253-1644
www.burnleyandtrowbridge.com
Linens, wools, linsey woolsey, fustian, notions, patterns and books related to costuming.

Wooded Hamlet
4044 Cosey Town Road, Greencastle, PA 17225
717-597-1782
www.woodedhamlet.com
Silk, linen, wool tapes and trims

La Fleur de Lyse
1649 rue Labonté, Chambly, Québec J3L 5M6
450-447-8289
www3.sympatico.ca/gousse-matte/fdl/fdl.htm
Historically accurate patterns

Unicorn Books & Crafts Inc
1338 Ross Street, Petaluma, CA 94954
707-762-3362
Books

Lacis
2982 Adeline Street, Berkeley, CA 94703
510-843-7290
www.lacis.com
Books, patterns, trims and notions

Chivalry Sports
8677 East Golf Links Road, Tucson, AZ 85730
520-546-8223

The Costume Page
Costume resources online
http://users.aol.com/nebula5/costume.html

The Whole Costumer's Catalogue
CBTB Press
Box 207 Main Street, Beallsville, PA 15313-0207
412-632-3242
Sourcebook for historic costuming

Smoke and Fire News
PO Box 166, Grand Rapids, OH 43522
1-800-766-5334
www.smoke-fire.com

Publications
Renaissance Entertainment Corporation
www.renfair.com

Costume Research Journal
(United States Institute of Theatre Technology)
Dept of Communication & Theatre Arts
Western Carolina University, Cullowhee, NC 28723
and at
Dept of Theatre Arts, Furman University
Greenville, SC 29613

Costumers Quaterly
c/o Maura Rebholz, editor
14450 Pickwick Lane, Garden Grove, CA 92644
Newsletter of the International Costumer's Guild

Smoke and Fire News
PO Box 166, Grand Rapids, OH 43522
1-800-766-5334
Newspaper listing reenactments across the USA